The American Legionnaires

The American Legionnaires

Accounts of Two Notable Soldiers of the
French Foreign Legion During the First
World War

ILLUSTRATED

"L. M. 8046"
David Wooster King

Letters and Diary of Alan Seeger
Alan Seeger

LEONAUR

The American Legionnaires
Accounts of Two Notable Soldiers of the French Foreign Legion
During the First World War
ILLUSTRATED
"L. M. 8046"
by David Wooster King
Letters and Diary of Alan Seeger
by Alan Seeger

FIRST EDITION

First published under the titles
"L. M. 8046"
and
Letters and Diary of Alan Seeger

Leonaur is an imprint of Oakpast Ltd

ISBN: 978-1-78282-616-3 (hardcover)
ISBN: 978-1-78282-617-0 (softcover)

http://www.leonaur.com

Publisher's Notes

The views expressed in this book are not necessarily
those of the publisher.

Contents

"L. M. 8046"

The title "L. M. 80 W refers to the author's identification tag.

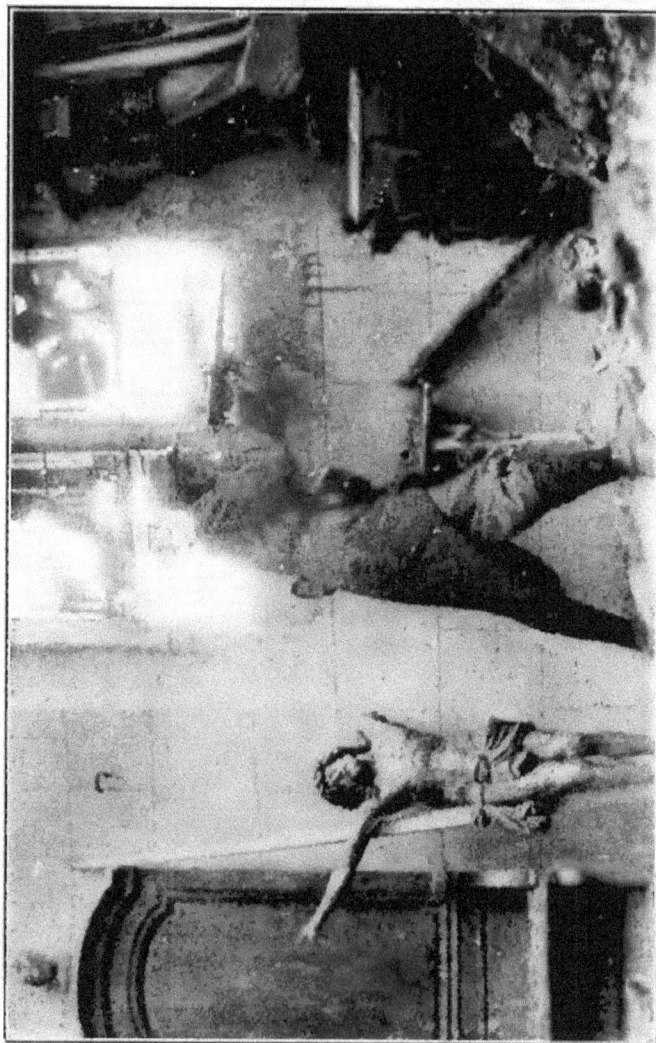

Sniping from the church, Craonnelle.

Contents

TO THE GAMEST MAN I KNOW,—THE LEMON

Foreword

It was in the year to tell you the truth I don't exactly remember the year but it was in that strange era before the war when all the problems of the human race had been settled for good and all when the millennium was merely a question of time it was in that vague prehistoric period of our middle-aged selves before the year of grace 1914 that I paid my last visit to Cambridge.

I don't remember exactly why I should have returned to the banks of the Charles River, but in those days (if my memory serves me right) there were a few well-intentioned people who thought that I ought to teach history and they made discreet arrangements with certain college authorities (for whom I had a wholesome respect) to let me give a few lectures on my own chosen subjects and show what I could do and to see what could be done with me.

And it was, I think, during one of those futile expeditions into a hostile territory that Lin Neale, most faithful of friends, told me that he knew some sort of an infant in the Harvard freshman class and that whenever I got tired of being on my good behaviour (which happened with astonishing and most regrettable celerity) I ought to call on this child and refresh my sagging spirits.

And I remember that I climbed many stairs of a dormitory somewhere near or on the Gold Coast and that I met a pleasant youngster (thirty-five talking to twenty-one) and that we tumbled at once into an incredibly rapid and vulgar jargon of French and American that we went to strange culinary establishments (it was before the days of the hygienic cafeterias, when ham-and-eggs was ham-and-eggs and not a combination of calories and hormones) and that whenever the conversation lagged we listened to the wails of those Hawaiian guitars which were then conquering the country by storm.

Whereupon I departed (having been weighed and found wanting) and floundered for years through the dismal swamps of failure and disappointment and then someone in a distant land shot an inconsequential Hapsburg *grandee* and this fine pretty world came to an end and some of us were blown to shreds and the others were flown to the four corners of the compass and the curtain descended upon the final act of our youth.

How and when and where and under what circumstances I met young King again I really could not tell. I have a hazy recollection that his brother one day swore loudly and eloquently and said, "Look what that damn-fool kid has done now" and showed me a cable which read:

"The joke is on you. I enlisted and am in the Foreign Legion."

Then silence until it was all over and seventeen million people (white, brown, red and intermediary shades) lay dead and buried and the rest of us returned from our different tasks to pick up the odds and ends of existence and try and shape ourselves some sort of tolerable future amidst the ruins of our glories and our hopes.

When I saw King again he sported the remnants of a uniform, he coughed distressingly, he hobbled slightly, and was no longer a creature of flesh and blood but one composed of the usual ingredients plus a considerable quantity of platinum and silver. Furthermore, he grinned as if he had just lived through a very ghastly joke and talked a French dialect which was as utterly beyond my reach as if it had been a combination of Hindustani and Finnish.

By and by a few English phrases filtered through his torrent of words and then I began to understand that he had not only served in the Foreign Legion but had, actually survived the experience and was willing and even eager to let me know what he had seen and done and thought.

But this was no easy task for he resembled a man who has spent himself in a race. He had reached his goal but he was too much out of breath, too miserably exhausted to do anything but gasp and beat the air and say "oof."

And so, we looked at each other, smiled sheepishly and let it go at that. Until after nine years of restless wandering, of endless trekking from place to place, he caught up with whatever was left of the procession and did a wise thing.

He rid his memory of its ghastly burden and wrote a book.

I am glad that he did and I am even more glad that he did it the way he did it because we are sorely in need of just such honest scraps of downright and fearless documentation.

To tell you the truth, I detest war. In the first place, I am dreadfully scared whenever people begin to fire off guns and throw bombs. In the second place, I have spent my life among the events of the past and I can see no earthly good in almost any war except that it affords a Roman Holiday to the more sadistically inclined among our females and gives a large number of our male neighbours a chance to escape from the uncomfortable bondage of modern civilization and for once in their career do the things they would like to do if they had been given their choice.

At the same time, I fully realise the futility of fighting the idea of "war" by mere oratory and moral precept.

The brass bands are all on the other side and what chance has a shabby prophet against a lieutenant-colonel in full dress uniform?

But books, my friends, those little books writ by the poor devils who did the dirty work, they are a different matter.

They had a hard time coming into their own. Who wanted to read what the common soldiers had to say when the Honourable Statesmen had just condescended to explain their blunders and to favour us with their alibis?

For a long time, the answer was "no one."

But a change is coming over us.

The incredible is happening.

The cannon-fodder of yester-war is just becoming articulate. The Unknown Soldier is endeavouring to explain why he lies beneath a heavy slab of granite instead of disporting himself with his kids among the blood-red poppies which looked so lovely in the dear poems about the Flemish slaughter-house.

This book of David King's is not a sermon.

It does not preach and it carries no moral.

It says in fact:

Here, my good friends who made me into a beautiful hero, is what happened to me while I was gaining that title. Take it or leave it and be damned to you or have a drink with me or do whatever you please, but for Heaven's sake don't kiss me for I am splashed with the blood of my dead comrades and I am dirty with the grime of a million miles of road.

It says all this without any rancour, without any show of ill-feeling, patiently and a little pityingly for those who remained at home and sold ribbons for war medals and saved prune-stones for gas-masks.

May the Lord in his mercy deprive them temporarily of a sense of shame. Amen.

Hendrik Willem Van Loon

Westport, Conn., May 11

CHAPTER ONE

War Fever

"Take off those socks!"

My turn. No chance of deception, as flat feet were a grave defect in the early days of the war, when men were still plentiful.

Name. Age. Nationality. Stethoscope. Open your mouth. Weight. Height. . . . A few prods and I was in. "*Bon pour le service.*"

Not very convincing, that scribble on a bit of paper with some sort of government stamp on one corner. The little clerk in uniform seemed satisfied, however, and scribbled away like mad after every question. The cigarette, stuck to the left side of his lower lip seemed a permanent part of him, but as I looked, it suddenly appeared on the right side, though both hands were busily engaged with the papers. It shifted again, and this time I discovered, with awe and admiration, that he could roll it from one side of his face to the other.

I produced another cigarette which the scribe filed for future reference behind his left ear, and asked him a few questions.

"What regiment will they assign me to?"

"Can you ride?"

"Yes."

"Probably the Dragoons or Hussars then."

Good news. That meant active service and no danger of being stuck guarding railroad bridges miles from the front.

"Here you are. 9:10 a. m. tomorrow. Rouen. Gare St. Lazare. And report at the barracks of the 135th when you get there."

A hurried breakfast with two Hollanders I had picked up the day before, then by fighting, kicking, struggling, and the aid of a sergeant major, we gained the privilege of standing in a compartment with sixteen others.

At Rouen, we arrived at the barracks just in time to see the regiment, the 135th, march out to entrain. Fascinating scene—company after company filing out of the barracks-building into the square; adjutants and sergeant majors running from section to section checking up equipment and emergency rations, officers standing around the colonel receiving final instructions, and the feeling of excited orderly confusion run riot through twenty-five hundred men tuned up to war pitch. A sudden sharp order and the confusion ceased. The lines stiffened into solid blocks of red and blue. Another order, drums began to roll. The blocks broke up into columns and swayed out of the barrack gates. The brazen blare of bugles swelled the rumble of the drums as they moved down the street, the glorious music rising and falling till only the distant rhythm of the drums could be heard. Last the clink of equipments and the steady soft swishing of hundreds of feet in step.

We found the volunteers quartered in what had been a school for young ladies. An Arab in *Spahis* uniform stopped us at the gate, till we produced our orders from the recruiting office. We passed into the court and into the army.

The place was crowded but I found a bale of compressed fodder and camped down on it, fully convinced that I was already experiencing the hardships of war. I fell asleep listening to a couple of King's hard bargains discussing the possibility of drawing two uniforms each and selling one.

Five o'clock the next morning and everything stir and confusion. "*Deux hommes de bonne volontée!*" My imagination ran wild. Perhaps the Germans were advancing on Rouen! It might mean lighting the fuse to blow up the bridge, or a forlorn hope, and seeing myself the last man in a desperate rear-guard action, I sprang forward to volunteer. Another American followed and the sergeant led us off.

Disillusionment was ours. He handed us each a mop and bucket, and planted us before a row of filthy latrines. "Report to me when you've cleaned them all." We had learned our first lesson: when sergeants are wandering around collecting men, pick up anything in sight and look busy.

The city was teeming with a marvellous, heterogeneous collection: wounded from the British Army, stragglers from the Belgian Army, refugees, French reservists, British Army Service Corps units—all wandering around the streets aimlessly, some terribly depressed, others hilarious and singing, and a good portion of them drunk.

We sat down in a *cafe* by the river, but before our drinks came someone had started a row. There were no windows or doors in front,

just one huge corrugated iron shutter, so when the trouble began the proprietor simply pulled down the shutter. Naturally, feeling that they were shut off from the police, the trouble-makers redoubled their efforts. Then the *patron* made his second blunder: he put out the lights. Something whizzed past my ear and exploded with the noise of a shell. A woman screamed like a horse, evidently cut by glass from the siphon which someone had hurled, and hell broke out in the dark.

Five minutes later the police were hammering on the iron front and prying it open with crowbars. There was a moment's silence until they had lifted it high enough for a man to pass under, and then came the inevitable rush for freedom. Glasses, tables, chairs and police went down under the onslaught, and in thirty seconds the *café* had emptied itself into the street.

At reveille, next morning, we were told to prepare to leave in an hour's time, and two hours later we were awaiting entrainment at the station.

By this time there were four companies of new recruits. Drawn up on the station platform, they presented a mixed spectacle as far as equipment went. The first company had drawn *bougerons*, (coarse linen blouses and trousers used for work in the French Army) and *képis* (caps). The second had *képis*, but the only thing uniform about the third and fourth companies was the regulation French Army blanket, carried in a roll over one shoulder, and the army *quart* (tin cup) tied with string to the end of the blanket roll.

Fifty-six into forty—even without the eight horses—makes the only possible position, a half squatting one, until some climb out on the roof. Four days of this in the middle of August.

At the beginning of the trip, large tins of Bully Beef were issued, containing enough meat for one man for four days. The weather was hot, so we were told to form groups of four and open one tin a day amongst us. The Russian volunteers, however, were somewhat suspicious of one another, and each one cherished and opened his own tin the first day. All went well till the beginning of the third day when most of them came down with ptomaine; and by the morning of the fourth, they were being taken out of the wagons dead. This, and the constant rights to fill our water bottles at the various stations, served to keep up interest in military life.

We arrived after sundown on the fourth day. The companies fell in on the station platform and moved off smartly, in columns of four through the streets of Toulouse toward the barracks of the 183rd Infantry. We felt a certain amount of pride as we marched out, for each nationality of volunteers had its own country's flag in the group. Surely the good citizens of Toulouse would appreciate our *beau geste*, and realize we were there of our own volition! To our amazement and chagrin, the column was greeted with hoots and boos, and presently apples, rotten eggs, and even dead cats. I was totally bewildered till I began to pick out some of the invectives hurled at us.

"*Ah, les brigands! Salles Boches! En v'la des prisonniers!*" Brigands, Huns. Some prisoners!

I realised then they mistook us for German prisoners. It was impossible for the officers and non-coms to make that howling mob understand the real situation, so we ploughed through our baptism of fire to the security of the barracks square. Here we were allotted to rooms, and, luxury of luxuries, beds again.

In spite of four days in a truck, I tossed and pitched all night and woke in the morning convinced of a high fever. One look at the bites and marks on my chest, however, calmed this suspicion, but aroused another. I picked up the end of the barrack cot, and letting it down again with a bump, could actually hear them as they plopped on the floor and scuttled for cover. The old timers knew what to do. After coffee, a crusade started, and every bed was scorched by improvised torches and then painted with kerosene. The straw in the *sacs* à *viande* (coarse canvas bags filled with straw used as mattresses) was burned, and the bags themselves boiled.

There were thirty-two men in the room. In the bed on my right was an American of French origin, one Phelizot, who had spent most of his life professional elephant hunter, round Lake Tchad. To my left a Belgian butcher with a mania for ripening little cheeses under his mattress. This, and a fixed idea on his part that it was dangerous to open the windows at night, leagued Phelizot and me together in a struggle for fresh air. Three times during the night I woke half suffocated and opened the window. Finally, we rose together, and advancing on the sleeping Belgian, each hurled one of his boots through the panes of the fast-closed window. Then we slept, in spite of the coughs sneezes and curses of our cheese-cuddling neighbour.

Barrack life began; but no one knew to what regiment the volunteers had been assigned. The training was carried on by old reserve officers, and one or two corporals and sergeants from the Foreign Legion.

Drawing uniforms and equipment was comic. We were marched

off by sections (sixty men) to the magazine. Here harried *sous-officiers* passed us out weird garments: uniforms, belts, buckles, shoes and caps, and we felt like Christmas trees as we staggered out.

Back in the barrack room things began to take some sort of order. The *capote* (great coat) had to be folded and placed first on the shelf above the beds, then the *vareuses* (shell jackets) and so on, until the pile was some three feet high. The belts, cartridge pouches and bayonets hung on hooks below, and any private belongings had to be hidden in the bed or behind the pile of uniforms.

That day a detail was marched into the arsenal to bring back rifles, which were stacked in the arm racks at the end of the room. Route march training began. Every day the distance was increased and the loads were heavier. By the end of a fortnight the recruits were able to do at least twenty miles a day with full African Army equipment of a hundred pounds.

Headed by a drum-and-bugle band, a battalion of bearded *légionaires* marched into the barracks square, stacked arms, and were divided amongst the three battalions of volunteers. By nightfall they had sold the eager recruits all their spare equipment, and two days later they had it all back again.

There are certain hard and fast rules in the Legion. To take money or valuables is stealing. To sneak equipment or any government issue from your own section or squad is neither etiquette nor healthy. otherwise, you can shift for yourself. (This is called System D.—*Debrouillez-vous*.)

Having bought the same blouses twice from two different *légionaires*, Phelizot and I planned a comeback. Regulations required a *légionaire* to wear all his decorations on full dress parade and this rule was carefully checked. Our method was simple. These medals were for sale not to be worn, but as souvenirs; also, they were easy to hang on to, so that by buying and holding them one could sell at exorbitant rates before dress parade, thereby breaking even.

★★★★★★

The French Army is sufficiently fed but only just. The *bleus* (recruits) are always hungry; you even see recruits scraping the squad soup kettles to get a little extra. As time goes on, their appetites fall off and the old timers eat about half the rations served out to them, saving the rest for future reference.

The first meal—four in the morning—is a cup of black coffee, sweetened, if the cook and the quarter-master corporal have not been

On Parade

able to swap sugar for wine, otherwise not. No bread is issued in the morning. At eleven, comes the heavy meal of the day: soup with bread and meat in it, one cup of coffee and one cup of wine; at five, more meat made into a *goulash* with potatoes, beans, lentils or rice, and another cup of coffee and wine. This fare is occasionally varied, especially in the field where sections can draw and cook their own rations. The bread—one loaf per day—is coarse peasant bread, and heavily seasoned with saltpetre, for obvious reasons, stamped with the date of baking. Theoretically, you can refuse it after the tenth day, but refusal merely means self-denial.

In time of peace, you have tin plates, knives, forks and spoons, but war-time equipment is simpler: a *gamelle* (tin-plated bowl with a tight cover, that is strapped at the top of the pack) , a tin cup, called a quart, alleged to hold a quarter of a litre, and a fork and spoon.

The food is all heaped into your *gamelle*, and coffee poured into your cup when you have finished your wine. *Pinard* (red army wine) is brought in, in a canvas bucket and ladled out with the corporal's cup, into each individual cup. By placing his thumb well down into his cup, in giving out wine to the half section, (thirty men) he can come out ahead, to the amount displaced by thirty thumbs. There is always a yell, and always the same excuse given: the canvas bucket leaks— although the buckets are usually so thickly covered with grease and grime that they could hold live steam under thirty: pounds pressure. The only way to prevent this cheating is to watch the deal. At the front, during the winter months, a quarter of a cup of rum is issued at daybreak, but no one dare take liberties with this.

The emergency rations were as follows: two cans of preserved meat known as *singe* (monkey), twenty biscuits and a small bag of sugar and coffee. The latter was carefully checked at all inspections— "unauthorised use of reserve rations: eight days prison." This did not deter us from making coffee on the sly, as inspections took place in double rank and it was easy to cheat. All full sacks of coffee and sugar were lent to men in the front rank, and as the officer inspected and passed on, they were flipped back to the rear rank, to be inspected a second time as their turn came.

Biscuits were as hard as rock, unless you knew the trick. No amount of soaking affected them, but put them in the oven or near the fire, and you could almost eat them. As for tobacco—considered as firewood it wasn't bad. Every ten days the government issued a package per man, called *Scafarlati des Troupes*. It was mostly the stalks of tobacco plants, and you had to spread it on a handkerchief, pick out the longer pieces, and chop them up before you could possibly roll it into a cigarette. Hardly worth the trouble as it was poisonous stuff, anyway.

The barrack rooms became orderly, even quiet at night: The Legion cure for snoring is crude but effective. When they are sure the offender is asleep, two men picked for the job gently varnish his lips and close them. On waking, his mouth is firmly sealed, and the first unwary yawn tears strips of skin and flesh from both lips. Once or twice is enough. The victim takes his own precautions not to snore, even if he has to bind up his jaw with a handkerchief.

As recruits we drew the magnificent sum of one *sou* a day. It did not spell luxury, so it was possible, if you had the cash, to hire old *légionaires* to do anything from cleaning your rifle to replacing you on guard duty if you wanted to go in town. But this scale of pay did not apply to men in their second and third enlistments. There were privates of fifteen and seventeen years' standing, who, thanks to the bonus for reenlistment and high pay for previous service, were drawing two and three *francs* a day.

Non-commissioned officers were forbidden to borrow money from their subordinates, but most of them did, especially the corporals. It was not bad policy to lend, even if you never expected to see the money back. They rarely borrowed twice from the same man, and it certainly greased the wheels. Strictly speaking sergeants could not drink with soldiers. Occasionally they would graciously drink off a proffered glass in passing a table, but to sit down at that table was beneath their dignity. Regulations are all very well, but what's the use of stripes if you can't profit by 'em?

Dry-nursed by the old *légionaires* we began to shape up. Within three weeks, stiffened by three hundred *anciens* per battalion and the *cadre* of regular officers and non-coms, we were ready for service.

We were a job lot, for the most part Russian, Swiss, Belgian and English, though almost every neutral nation was represented. Some were there for the adventure, others from a sense of obligation to France, or because they could not get back to their own countries to join up, and quite a number because the war had thrown them out of a job. The old *légionaires* were made of quite different stuff and were in it for reasons ranging from manslaughter to unrequited love. It struck me as strange, at first, that there were even Germans and Turks among the *anciens*.

Vetman, the corporal of our squad, had been a Prussian guardsman in his day, but some dispute with a superior had forced him to desert and take refuge in the Legion. Where else could he go? Born and bred to soldiering, it was the only life he knew or cared about, "*Che foutrais être un bombier à Baris*" (His way of pronouncing "I would like to be a Paris fireman"—This was his highest ambition. Tall, scraggy, and ungainly, except on parade ground, he was the typical soldier, and his lank form was tireless. Though a strict disciplinarian he had unlimited patience with stupid recruits. It was true he had been in the German Army, but after seventeen years' service in Africa the French considered him a *légionaire*, and their confidence was justified. He was killed six months later defending an exposed outpost.

Thérisien, a Breton, was my ideal of a *sous-officier*. He had been a lieutenant in the navy. A fit of temper, a hasty blow, and cashiered! He buried himself in the Legion. With his ability and previous rank he soon rose to the grade of *aspirant* (cadet officer). Another hasty blow, and back to the ranks again. Now he was sergeant once more. He could do what he liked with us, and his lectures on field tactics were worthy of a colonel. These were the best types but not the most amusing.

Conti, an Italian, offered to show me the ropes and valet me. He was a likable sort of rogue, but things had an unfortunate habit of disappearing. When my tooth brush went, I put him through a third degree.

"Conti, what did you do in civilian life?"

"Me? I pinched bikes."

"Do you mean to say you were a bicycle thief?"

"Sure, that was my profession and my father's before me." Such talent was beyond my means.

Most of us Americans were in the same section, 57 varieties. My closest friends Phil, the elephant hunter, Denny Dowd, a lawyer from New York, Fritz—, an engineer, Stuart—, an artist, and Alan—, our dreamy, but martial, poet.

★★★★★★

Note: The reference here and later is to Alan Seeger, the poet who wrote the *Rendez-vous With Death,* shortly before being killed in action, and is the subject of the second book in this edition.

★★★★★★

Going into town was not so simple as it sounds. Every man had to pass the inspection of the sergeant-of-the-guard at the gate. Brass buttons must shine, boots, if not polished, be neatly greased; the broad blue woollen belt of the Legion must be wound around without a crease, and, as it was nine feet long, this was quite an accomplishment. If the sergeant happened to be in bad humour a man might be told to go back two or three times to make good minute defects. Coming back was easier, as all returned together. But even so, the lynx-eyed sergeant was on the watch for any men he considered sufficiently drunk to shove into the *boïte* (prison).

Re this, it was an amazing sight to see some of the old timers. They would reel up the street roaring obscene songs, at the tops of their lungs. Twenty yards before they came to the gate the songs ceased, shoulders went back, and they would march through the gate, saluting smartly like automatons. Out of sight of the guard the singing would break out anew, as they zig-zagged across the yard and lurched up the stairway to their barrack room.

I wangled my way into a *peleton de sous-off.* (school for non-coms), and soon regretted it. There were no privileges, and lots of extra work, and chances of promotion in the immediate future were slim.

CHAPTER TWO

Moving Up and Shaking Down

Alarums *and excursions!* The Powers-that-Be had decided to send off one battalion at once. Five hundred old *légionaires* and five hundred volunteers picked from those with previous military experience. I wracked my brain and finally remembered the Columbia Institute Military Academy in New York. I was only seven at that time, but the words *école militaire* work wonders in France; and that night I was in the *premier bataillon de marche*, likely to be sent to the front any day.

Nothing happened for three days, but we put on an extra amount of swank which we mistook for *esprit de corps*. Late one afternoon, town leave was refused, and we were assembled in the barracks square for kit inspection. Next morning, headed by the drum-and-bugle band, flowers in the muzzles of our rifles, we were cheered through the town to the station.

"*40-8's*" once more, but this time what a difference! Forty men, and forty men only, to a truck. Two climbed in, and the rifles and sacks of the other thirty-eight were passed up to them, and stacked at both ends of the car. The rest of us piled in; corporals stood in the doors to prevent anyone leaving, and the train pulled out. At the first big station the cars spewed forth food-seeking *légionaires* like a disturbed ant hill; and we got our first inkling of what the rest of the world thought of the Legion.

We headed for the buffet to buy provisions, but the door was slammed in our faces by an enormously fat *chef de gare*, who then rushed down the platform shouting at the top of his lungs, "*Fermez toutes les portes! Voici la Légion!*" Scouting around, we found a canteen in a tent behind the station, and after a struggle we bought sausages and white bread and returned to our car, hurt and indignant at the attitude of the authorities.

The train pulled out of the station, and the *anciens* pulled out their loot. From under blankets, like rabbits from a hat, came a prodigious supply of food and drink—

More beer, in little kegs,
Many dozen hard boiled eggs,
And goodies to a fabulous amount.

No deception—quite simple. Merely a matter of slitting the back of the tent, and helping themselves, while we—innocent decoys—engaged the enemy over the counter. Maybe that *chef de gare* wasn't so far wrong after all! We thought this was worthy of commemoration in song, so, to the tune of the *Boys in Blue are Marching:*

We are the famous Legion
That they talk so much about.
People lock up everything
Whenever we're about.

We're noted for our pillaging,
The nifty way we steal.
We'd pinch a baby carriage,
And the infant, for a meal!

As we go marching,
And the band begins to play—Gor'blimee!
You can hear the people shouting,
Lock all the doors, shut up the shop,
     the Legion's here today.

At the Camp de Mailly we saw the effects of shell fire for the first time. The iron shutters of the station were riddled with shrapnel and some of the buildings demolished. Decidedly, we were getting nearer the war. The next day we were sent out to round up some *Uhlans* hiding in the woods. They had been cut off during the retreat, and had managed to exist on their iron rations, raw vegetables and anything else they could steal, hoping to lie hidden till the German Army should advance once more, and free them. They were a sullen crowd, gaunt and ragged, but we admired their pluck.

It was at the Camp de Mailly, that *Monsieur Toto et Cie.* made his first public appearance. He probably came from the Arabs in the Legion—the *Koran* extends a closed game season to cooties. It was the irony of fate that our poet should be the first to complain of the roughness of army underwear. For several days, Alan scratched body and soul in forced aloofness, but there was no avoiding them. From

A month later

that time, like the poor, they were always with us. How Alan must have suffered! He took them as seriously as he did everything else. I never saw him laugh. He was always scribbling and occasionally showed me the results. At the time, I didn't realise he meant his *Rendez-vous With Death*, in earnest. He could fight as well as write though, but that comes later. . . .

Then the march to the front began; thirty-five kilometres a day, with full equipment. The first night our squad was in luck; no sore feet, and billeted in a real house. The old lady who owned it was horrified at the idea of our sleeping on bare boards, and produced four enormous eiderdowns.

The next day brought out the real discipline of the Legion. There is no issue of socks in the French Army, and the *bleus* began to suffer. You can either put your boots on bare-footed, or use little squares of cheap muslin, (*chausettes russes*). Placing your foot in the middle of it, you wrap the muslin carefully around the foot and ankle and slide into the shoe. This sounds simple, but it takes months of practice to do, without having the cloth shift and the feet blister. Those of us who could afford socks had chosen them badly and Stuart and I were suffering acutely. Our shoes felt as if they were filled with painful marmalade, and we fell out by the side of the road to investigate. Sure enough—they were blistered and bleeding. We decided we were fit cases for the ambulance. This illusion, however, was rudely shattered by a bull voice coming from the top of a horse.

"*Que faites vous là?*"

Heroically, we stood up, saluted our colonel and exhibited the pitiful spectacle of our feet.

"*Nos pattes sont en marmalade,, mon colonel. Nous ne pouvons plus marcher.*" ("Our dogs are cut to ribbons, colonel. We're all in.")

Revolver, in hand, he roared, "*Marches quand même!*" And we did, rejoining our section at the double.

The night was spent in the arcades of a monastery; where Vetman took us in hand and showed us what to do for our feet.

★★★★★★

The Legion cures blisters by passing a greased thread through them, cutting the ends off each side—this acts as a drain. They then smear the whole inflamed part with tallow, also the outside of the sock, to prevent chafing. This done, they put their boots on again— painful, but easier than doing it next morning when feet have had a chance to swell.

31

★★★★★★

Stuart and I had it out, in the morning.

"Look here, Cocky—I'll carry a razor if you'll pack the blades."

"All right—and one mirror will do for both of us. What's more, I don't see the use of keeping a hair brush."

"What about this packet of Bromo paper—can't we split it?"

"Oh, all right—be fussy! But the sooner you ask your friends to write you on thin, soft paper the better!"

"How in Hell can I?"

"Kid 'em along: tell 'em you like to carry their letters with you, to read over—"

A two-day march had taught us that possessions are a curse—Other bright volunteers had reached the same conclusion, and the shower of safety razors, mirrors, combs, extra soap, shirts, and underclothes was eagerly seized upon by the old timers.

The third day we hit the little town of Verzy near Epernay. This was on the front. The town itself was on raised ground, and the edge of it, looking over the green vineyards, was like a quay by the sea. About three miles from the town were front line trenches, and we all crowded into the streets to see the shells bursting till an enemy plane went over, and we were driven back into quarters, like chickens when a hawk hovers near. Rumours began to fly again: we were going into line that night—we were to attack—*etc. ad nauseam.*

In the meantime, we were confined to billets during the day. Our company was quartered in some long sheds used by the grape gatherers during the vintage, and we slept on concrete platforms, which sloped toward the middle of the room, divided by low partitions like stalls in a modern stable. The *anciens* found wine, and the night was made hideous by song, drunken laughter, and squabbles. African troops had been there before us, and we were given a warm welcome by the Algerian Cooties' Rotary Club.

Here we waited for orders to join some army corps, but the various generals seemed to think the Legion might corrupt the morals or discipline of their troops. Anyway, there was no ugly rush to take us over.

One morning motor trucks appeared out of nowhere, and all that day Battalion C rolled along the roads to Fismes. We arrived just at nightfall and our section being the section of the day, went on ahead to act as *campement* (billeting party) for the rest.

The battalion was to be quartered at a little village called Cuiry les

WAITING FOR ORDERS TO ATTACK

Chaudards, but in the dark we must have passed beside it, and struck the first line. In those days, there were no trenches or barbed wire. The first intimation we had of our mistake was a salvo of 77's from the enemy's batteries. The shells were high and burst some hundred yards behind us. The old *légionaires*, and the men who had seen service before, flopped on their stomachs. The rest of us stood dumb-founded, for a moment, and then, in our ignorance, began to laugh at the nervousness of the veterans. The main thing proved, however, was that the section was off its course, so we retraced our steps and eventually found the village, with the battalion already installed and the major furious.

The night was restless. Violent fusillades broke out in the line in front of us, and each time, our *sous-officiers*, accustomed to the suddenness of Moroccan warfare, had us stand to arms.

Our squad was quartered in the attic of a one-storey house, and hostile relations with the owners were established immediately. In the first place, they bitterly resented our efforts to clean up the quagmire and dunghill in the farmyard. Nor were matters smoothed over by the fact that a bed-ridden grandmother had been drenched during the night by a *légionaire* too drunk or too lazy to find his way down the ladder into the farmyard. Also, we found out later, this family and three others were in communication with the enemy, and naturally, thirty men snooping around cramped their style.

Cuiry les Chaudards was a small farming village, which in summer was entirely surrounded by fields of crops, and in winter by mud. It boasted some forty surly inhabitants, of whom, one or two of the more enterprising had opened little shops in their houses. They were driving an amazing trade in sweet biscuits, infamous tin-canned jam, and *vin mousseux*. The *caporal ordinaire* (quarter-master corporal) took a wagon to Fismes every day, and could be bribed to buy extras there. Such were the luxuries of life. The labours consisted of drills, manoeuvres, digging a second line of trenches, carrying logs for struts and shores, and cleaning up the village.

I was flat—*fauché*—broke! At Cuiry les Chaudards they mistook my American gold pieces for gold bricks. It hurt to plunk my last few *francs* into soap, but the laundry business seemed the only industrial opening for a bright young man, so I went into partnership with a Norwegian architect. Down by the river, the day's work was divided:

"All right, Henri, my turn to wash—Where's the soap?"

"I put it in your haversack."

34

Scrub—scrub—

"Here—rinse these, and spread 'em on that log—No—not the rock. Picot's got his stuff too near it—he'd pinch ours."

"Dave, where is the *adjudant's* shirt?"

"I gave it to you to dry. For God's sake—didn't you watch it? There goes Conti! Catch him, and tell him you want it back."

Five minutes later Henri returned with the shirt—Conti had made a slight mistake in picking up his wash! And so it went on—business throve—if you watched while you washed.

★★★★★★

"Faites les sacs—Tout le monde en bas! Les sous-offs au capitaine—et grouillez—vous!" ("Make your packs—everybody turn out! Sergeants call. Make it snappy!")

A brief consultation with the major, the captains joined their companies, and we moved off through the night, in column of twos. We soon left the metaled roads for a lane through the woods, and there struck one of the real horrors of war—mud. Liquid mud—full of treacherous roots. Mud like chewing gum—squelching—sucking our boots off. Mud with a stench obscene and putrid—Black mud—black night. Somebody down. Up again, cursing foully . . . We were in Indian file now, picking our way by the sky-line of the trees . . . . Hours and hours we floundered through the pit black night. Then suddenly we were through the woods.

Shadows rose out of the ground—whispered hurried directions and warnings, disappeared into the night. We slipped into the rifle pits.

With the dawn came reaction. The peaceful landscape hardly seemed to justify last night's caution, and five *bleus* wandered off in the sunshine to see where the war was.

They saw nothing . . . . .

Three of them probably never even heard the shell. You see, we wore red trousers in those days—they were beautiful targets. We paid high for the thoughtlessness of the five as the sector came in for an hour's heavy shelling.

There was no barbed wire as yet, so at nightfall covering patrols were sent out into No Man's Land, I went out with one commanded by an American soldier of fortune, veteran of Spanish-American-Philippine, and Mexican campaigns—he was a good soldier, but slightly erratic and impatient. The long, cold vigil on the ground exasperated him—we were all pretty jumpy. About midnight the moon began to show through the clouds and my heart skipped a beat. "Christ—here

My partner in the laundry business

they come!" Stealing silently up the slope in skirmish order were ten or twelve shadowy forms. A warning hiss from Sergeant Morlae, and we retired to our lines to report.

"Everyone up—Load—Commence firing!"

Denny and I held our fire, waiting to see something to shoot at, congratulating ourselves on our coolness. This, however, called down the wrath of the top sergeant, who told us in no gentle manner to fire level with the ground till we could pick our shots. The enemy replied. A gale of bullets whistled overhead, and we could see the flashes of rifles towards the left of the line. This went on for half an hour; then firing stopped, and an old Legion sergeant volunteered to go out and reconnoitre.

Half an hour later he came back convulsed with mirth. The enemy we had seen proved to be twelve cows grazing between the lines, of which nine had paid the full penalty. The firing came from another battalion of the Legion that had come up and occupied the edge of the woods in front of us, forming one side of a V with our own lines. Naturally, these trenches were dubbed les *Tranchées des Vaches*.

The officers believed in having the field kitchens as near the front line as possible; consequently, a magnificent emplacement was dug for the *hash guns*. A German plane circled overhead, and half an hour later Fritz, having mistaken the kitchen for a battery, proceeded to demolish it, just as grub was ready. More casualties and no soup. The kitchens were moved back and soup details became a nightmare. Stumbling through the woods, sliding and falling in the mud, with two kettles full of hot, greasy stew or a bucket of coffee to fill one's cup of bliss. How we loved our enemies!

Ajudant Pellotti was a Corsican; there were a lot of them in the Legion. He was a thick set, coarse little swine with homosexual tendencies, and had been bothering the life out of a big, mild sort of fellow called Marco. When Marco ignored the sly pats and pinches Pellotti made his life Hell, in a hundred and one ways, as a *sous-officier* can and still keep within regulations.

★★★★★★

The grade of *Ajudant* is the equivalent of Battalion Sergeant Major in our army. What we call an Adjutant the French call *Capitaine adjoint*. (Captain attached to the Colonel) usually the senior Captain, in line for his majority.

★★★★★★

The night of the relief we were in high spirits, in spite of the march

E. Morlae.

before us. Marco had a good, trained voice, and was giving vent to his feelings in song. Suddenly the men behind him were pushed aside as Pellotti bustled forward. Whipping out his revolver, he shoved it into Marco's ribs.

"*Sacre cabotin de bordel*—singing again! Stop that bloody row or I'll blow your liver through your backbone! Shut up!"

Marco shut up: the threats and abuse went on. Nothing was said, but somewhere behind Pellotti there were three ominous clicks, the noise of breech bolts being snapped closed as three cartridges went home. Pellotti fairly hurled himself to the front of the line. It was too easy for somebody to stumble and have a rifle go off by accident in that dark, muddy labyrinth. The hint was enough.

Men will forgive much in a brave and efficient *sous-officier*. Pellotti was neither. Once during rifle inspection, a victim of his persecutions, maddened by *cafard*, threw up his rifle and fired at him point-blank. Unfortunately, he missed the *ajudant* and killed a corporal standing nearby.

★★★★★★

Cafard comes from the word meaning "black beetle." In army jargons it means blues or melancholia. The African Army troops are very subject to this periodically, due probably to the heat and bad wine. In the more acute cases the victims are convinced that their brains are being eaten by black beetles.

★★★★★★

A night came, however, when Pellotti took out a reconnoitring patrol. He advanced a certain distance into No Man's Land, and ordered them to proceed while he waited for them. Half an hour later he crawled back, dying, with three French bullets in him. The rest of his patrol had lost their bearings and mistaken him for a German outpost. At least, that was their story, and they stuck to it.

Chapter Three

In for Keeps

In the early part of the war troops were scarce, and reliefs were few, and far between. I have done as much as twenty-eight days at a stretch in the first line. Often our rest was merely a few days in the second line dugouts. The word "rest" was euphemistic. By the end of ten days digging trenches, building dugouts, cutting and carrying enormous logs of wood and barbed wire, we were quite ready to go up into line again.

During one of these rest cures, Denny and I came down with dysentery, and were too weak to crawl when the battalion moved up. Nobody seemed to care. The sergeant mumbled something about reporting to the doctor, and we were left alone in a little hut in the woods. Two days later we managed to drag ourselves to our infirmary to beg some opium pills, but found, to our horror, the medical staff of another battalion. There was no way to get medicine or food, nor was there anyone to vouch for us. We suddenly realised that if anyone in authority should question us they would consider us deserters——so we beat a hasty retreat. We lived like hunted animals; stealing what we could from the kitchens after dark, and hiding whenever we saw an officer or a sergeant. The third day a cyclist from our own battalion turned up, and we went up into line with him that night.

It was only November, 1914, but we realised that trench warfare had come to stay. In two months, the rifle pits of the Marne had spread into a complicated system of trenches, dugouts, machine gun emplacements. Finally, a vast web of barbed wire was spun along the whole front.

Our new sector was called Oulch on the map, Piccadilly Circus by the English volunteers, and the *fer* à *cheval* (horseshoe) by the Legion. We found ourselves in a sort of quarry with well-made dugouts built

AMERICANS IN THE FOREIGN LEGION

Showing type of hand-grenades

into the chalk above it. There was no further need of covering patrols at night, thanks to the barbed wire, but the sector was much more heavily bombarded than the last, so we remained under cover when not on duty.

The machine gun section was, naturally, installed in the strongest dugout—machine guns cost money. We saw what an H-E 105" could do when a lucky shot passed through the loophole and burst clean inside. Our squad rushed in to help the survivors—there were none—so we set to work to clear up the mess. I was struck by the practical coolness of an old *légionaire* who was transferring a mess of blood and brains from the floor into a *képi* with the late owner's spoon.

In our off moments, we told the stories of our lives—usually mythical—and read our shirts.

We had a crude chimney in our dugout and were busy brewing chocolate. Bert, from Kentucky, ex-racing driver, and God knows what besides, was going all out. He finished, and there was a moment of awed silence. His sidekick broke the spell:

"Bert," (scratch) "you know that's a damned lie." (scratch) (scratch).

The answer was disarming. "Well, who the hell said it wasn't!"

Here Bill's wriggling and scratching disturbed the aesthetic artist beside him. Turning his face from the fire, with a dreamy look in his eye, he summed up the whole cootie question:

"Good Lord, Bill! Do you still *scratch?*"

The nights were more fun. The Boches used to sneak out and hang baskets of "delicatessen" on our wire. There was always a note with them, assuring us this was their daily fare, and we need only desert to enjoy the same. Our officers replied in kind. But we felt that Charity began at home, and the baskets were generally empty by the time they reached the German wire.

★★★★★★

It gave us comfort and cheer to see the *château* lighted as we filed through the gates of the park. The glass *porte-cochère* was intact, and so little damage seemed to have been done to the facade that it was hard to realise we were only a few hundred yards from the front line. We turned the corner, and as if by black magic the lights went out, and the place became a gutted ruin. It had only been the moon shining through empty windows. The heavily vaulted cellars had resisted shrapnel and fire; and here our company was quartered. One section was immediately posted at points of vantage along the wall of the park where rude shelters had been built; and the wall itself was loopholed.

Craonnelle must have been taken by surprise in the opening days of the war. I don't know how the inhabitants fared, but a baleful feeling lurked about the ruins. I couldn't wait to explore. The gatekeeper's lodge had not been shelled but the interior was indescribably filthy. The Hun had evidently had one last banquet here. A long table in the main room was piled high with dirty dishes, wine glasses and bottles, and he had left his usual trade mark—excrement—on everything. In the middle of this debris of debauch, lay a small white satin slipper. Evidently Fritz had been true to his traditions of the Kürfürstendam. Had the owner escaped? My mind went back to my mother's place, in France—not so far from the tide of invasion—and I was damned glad I was in the show.

The position at Craonnelle was somewhat precarious. All the streets were heavily barricaded, as half the town was held by the enemy. During the first month of the Legion's occupation it changed hands repeatedly, but we gradually cleared it and consolidated the position.

A barricade at the end of a street is a tricky thing to hold. The attackers have most of the advantage. They mass their forces around the corner and charge in a concerted rush, giving the defenders time for but one shot apiece. Grenades were still unknown, and machine guns too precious to waste on outpost duty. Our major (*commandant*) solved the problem, however, by raking the country-side for shot guns; and these, loaded with slugs, shot and old nails, proved most effective against sudden rushes.

Then the Germans—it was a regiment of *Jägers*—pulled their first raid. Half our section had gone down to draw rations for the week, leaving the other two squads to guard the wall of the park. Vetman, and the man off duty, were in a little shelter in a corner of the wall. Kiffen Rockwell and Alan were doing sentry-go along the wall itself—that is to say, on planks supported by barrels. Suddenly Kiff saw a spark come over the wall from outside.

"You see that, Alan?"

"Yes, I saw that. Do you think it was a bomb?"

"Yes, I think it was a bomb. We'd better call Vetman—" (*B-o-o-o-o-o-m!!!*) "My God, it *was* a bomb!"

Clearly outlined above the top of the wall, they drew a fusillade from the raiders outside, which drove them off their platform. Before they had time to do anything the garden door, on their left, was blown in.

Then there was quick action. The corporal, turning out with the rest of the guard, was met by a howling rush of Germans pouring through the shattered gate. A short hand-to-hand; and Vetman, seeing he was outnumbered, ordered his men to the cover of the park skirting the inside of the wall. As he gave the command his brains were dashed out by the butt of a Boche rifle. The Germans had just time to strip the dead of all their papers, regimental badges, etc., before the section returned from the food detail and drove them out.

Sentinels were doubled and everybody in the section was on guard duty along the wall. About an hour later, we heard something new, but very old. Down from the German lines, on the crest across the valley, came a long wolf-like howl, half human, half beast—derision, triumph, and revenge—straight back across the ages from apeman and wolf-pack. They had found out that Vetman was a deserter, and war and exultation had stripped the Hun of all veneer and boasted *Kultur*.

Phélizot said it first.

"Well, fellows, we're in it for keeps. Let's start a little raid of our own."

Towards morning I disgraced myself. As dawn broke, I was looking through a loophole with the wind blowing in my face, and I made the fatal mistake of resting my chin on my arms. A sniper's bullets smacked the wall just over the loophole, and off I toppled, rolling on the ground. The concern of the sergeant who ran to pick me up changed to wrath when he realised that I had been dozing. Fortunately, the regulations of the French Army insist that you cannot be shot for sleeping at your post after four hours' continual guard, but there is no regulation to prevent every filthy detail of a company being heaped upon you for weeks afterward.

Two nights later we moved up to the "sky parlour," as we dubbed the sector on the hill overlooking the *château*. Here Phelizot organised his raid but did not see fit to inform the *sous-officiers* of his intentions.

I have said before that Phélizot was an elephant hunter, and a successful one, for he had made a fair-sized fortune in ivory. As he explained it the difficulty and danger was not in shooting elephants, but in dodging the Belgian, French and British game wardens over their respective borders in the process of poaching, which crime he freely admitted. His only fear seemed to be of himself, yet he was extraordinarily tolerant of weakness and failings in others.

The first time Phil went out, he tried to bring back a German sentry, smothering his yells in a blanket. There were too many others nearby, however, and he almost got shot up for his pains. He would use all his skill as a hunter to bring himself within striking range of the quarry, but once there, would risk his own life, rather than chance killing a man with a crack on the head. I told him he was crazy to try such stunts, but he only smiled—

You see, Dave, in the game I was in, you're killing, or spilling blood every day. If it isn't an elephant, it's game for the boys, or just slaughtering a goat for meat. It seems to get into you, after a while, the everlasting shooting and blood; and men get what they call Blood Fever. Some of my friends got it—The natives get on your nerves and you start knocking them around with a *jambok* and draw blood. Then one day you lose your temper and shoot one. I felt it coming on, so I quit and came home.

The horror of it was so strong that he could not bring himself to kill a man single handed, even in war.

The next night he took me with him. It was eerie work, crawling toward the German lines, especially when we came to the zone where the corpses of the first big battles lay, still unburied. On we went, freezing when a star shell went up, crawling forward again immediately afterward, in the accentuated darkness. I was no big game hunter, but, by putting my hands and feet exactly in the tracks of Phélizot, managed to slide along quite quietly. Would we ever reach the German lines—? The answer was a sharp clank twenty yards behind me. Looking back, my heart almost stopped. There, large as life, and twice as ugly, was a German sentinel, standing with his back to me. I shook Phil's foot and pointed. But the only reaction was a whispered explanation: "Yes, I know. That's the second one."

My teeth chattered with reassurance.

Finally, we came to a communication trench and here Phil got much excited. He pointed out a fresh spoor of German feet in the mud and proposed to wait, one on each side of the trench, till he, or they, returned. Then I was to crack the last man over the head as he went by, and we would take him back to our lines.

Unfortunately, this plan was upset by the lateness of the hour, so we started back. Nothing happened till we got within thirty yards of our outpost, when considering all danger past we rose to our feet and started walking in, talking as we went. Ordinarily it is easy enough to distinguish between English and German; but after two hours of guard duty, an excitable Italian is apt to confuse the two, especially coming from the direction of the enemy's lines. We were greeted by a hasty "*Halte là! Qui vive?*" giving us just time to flop, before it was followed up by a bullet. Recognition finally established we got back to the lines. Here the plot thickened.

Jaeger, the man promoted to replace Vetman, was a red-headed hot-tempered Alsacian who took his new stripes seriously.

"Where have you two been?"

"Oh, just over the German lines to have a look around."

"Oh, you have, have you! You think you can go out and come back when you like in this army? Did anyone give you orders to go on patrol? *Silence!* Did you ask anybody's permission even? SHUT UP! Am I commanding here, or do you think you are running it? What have you got to say for yourselves? SHUT UP! I'm talking now. I've a good mind to report you as deserters. Never heard of such crust. So, you two think you are commanding this post and I count for nothing. In other words, I'm a flat-footed, lop-eared jackass, *hein?*"

Then came my chance. Drawing myself up with dignity, I quoted, "A soldier should never contradict a non-commissioned officer." He got me later on another count, but it was worth it.

★★★★★★

The whole front became more active. The battalions were shifted without rest from one point to another, probably to familiarise us with the various trenches. Battalion C next occupied *les Tranchées des Moulins* on the left of Berry au Bac. We were allowed to build fires in the dugouts provided we used dry wood, but one night, Flannigan, returning cold from guard duty, stoked his fire too impetuously and set the roof ablaze. When the excitement and shells had ceased I overheard two sergeants talking.

"*Tu sais, mon vieux, je ne suis pas sûr que ce n'était pas fait exprès. Ce Flannigan—je ne dis pas que c'est un nom boche, mais je n'en suis pas sûr.*" ("You know, old man, I am not at all sure that wasn't done on purpose. That fellow Flannigan—I don't say it's a German name, but it all looks pretty phony.")

I laughed, but not for long—fires were forbidden.

The sector had been quiet for a day or two; so a shot from an outpost roused our curiosity. Sergeant Thérisien called me and we went to investigate. We found the lone sentinel, plugged through the left arm, applying a first aid bandage. Thérisien questioned him:

"They got you, did they?"

"Yes."

"Did you see him?"

"No."

"What did you fire at?"

"I didn't fire."

"That's funny. I could have sworn it was a Lebel and not a Mauser."

The man denied it vehemently. I, too, was puzzled. I had been so sure I could tell the roar of a Lebel from the crack of a German Mauser. Still musing, I picked up his rifle and half mechanically threw open the breech. I could have cut my hand off, but the thing was done. An empty cartridge case tinkled on the ground. Thérisien's sharp eyes spotted it. A brief search over the rampart disclosed the tell-tale bandage—wet, burned and bloodstained.

I could not look on death; this being known,
Men led me to him blindfold, and alone.

CHAPTER FOUR

A Cup of Coffee and a Riot

Sergeant Major Lecomte bustled into the farmyard of our billets, and blew his whistle:

Rapport! Tomorrow morning, at nine o'clock, there will be a dentist at the Regimental Infirmary. Any man who needs to see him must apply now. All those doing so will be excused from morning drill.

There was an ugly rush, and some two hundred men scrambled to put their names on the list. Something told me that this dentist was no Painless Parker, so the next morning I hung around the infirmary door to see the fun. There they were—two hundred of them in a queue smoking and laughing, without a care in the world; all but the few who were really suffering. Suddenly the door opened, and the first man disappeared inside. There was an interested silence broken by groans and muffled curses from within.

Finally, the victim emerged, holding his jaw and moaning. He passed down the line spitting blood and spreading terror. The line went forward, but minus some ten or fifteen men. Again, the blood-curdling sounds from within, and again the line was decimated. *Coué* wasn't in it! The nearer they got to the door, the surer they were their toothaches were imaginary. Six saw the dentist. The rest took two days' prison for malingering. Cheap at the price!

Next day another treat. The first company marched off to Maizy, some five miles away, for their first anti-typhoid inoculation. The march back was hellish. I wasn't the only one to crash into a dead faint as we staggered into quarters. Few of us slept that night, and the billets were like a typhoid ward in a madhouse.

Things were looking up in Cuiry les Chaudards. The social season opened with a gathering in the churchyard. For some time past, the general had noticed that this particular church had come in for a flattering amount of attention from the enemy. He organised a Field Day, to settle matters—the event of the afternoon being a tug of war. Battalion C *versus* Church Steeple. As the long rope tightened and the steeple teetered, the inhabitants, headed by the *curé*, protested vehemently, claiming sacrilege. The general, however, was adamant. It was too good a regulating point for German guns, and he reckoned the lives of a thousand men—even godless *légionaires*—more important than one church spire.

Two days later the battalion was marched off by companies to a nearby sugar refinery. Here shower baths had been rigged up and I had my first hot bath since Toulouse.

Just before we went up into line again three entire families were shot for conveying information to the enemy. One old man and his wife had used a pair of white oxen in their ploughing to indicate the position of the French batteries, but his erratic methods of agriculture finally gave him away.

★★★★★★

It was Craonnelle again, this time the Little *Château* and the cemetery trenches. Interesting, but a bit grisly. The family vaults were the *parados* of our trenches. Gradually the walls were broken down by shell fire, and now and then a wrecked coffin would slide into the trench, disgorging its occupant in various stages of decay. This was stopped by boarding up the vaults, but the walls were pierced and the rats came in. It gave us the creeps to hear the greasy rustling of rats feeding inside the tombs. Later, however, chloride of lime was used; and we got no little satisfaction hearing a fat one scuttling along inside the boards, cough, choke, and retire hastily.

The Little *Château* had belonged to an old colonel. Some of it was smashed by shell fire, and ransacked for valuables; but the library had been spared. Long rows of bookcases, sun pouring in on piles of magazines, and big armchairs—a room lived in and loved. Alan and I were enthralled.

"Look here, Dave, a first edition of Jean Jacques Rousseau."

"Yes, but see this Déscartes—My God, here's Montaigne! I haven't read him since I was a kid. I used to sneak him out of the library."

"Dave, what do you make of this?"

"This" was a carefully bound manuscript, evidently the journal of the owner's grandfather, an officer on Napoleon's staff. Jena, Austerlitz,

Beresina, and Moscow—what a saga! But there were other magnets—
Molière, Anatole France, Farrère, Rabelais—I was miles away—

"*Rassemblement! Couvrez sur deux.*" I hurtled down through the
centuries to fall in for the filthiest *corvée* of my whole experience.

The captain had decided the cellar must be cleared, as a shelter in
case of bombardment. During the German retreat, it had evidently
been used as a dressing station, bomb-proof, and finally as an arena
for hand-to-hand fighting in clearing the village. The whole place
was flooded two feet deep in water, for the drains had been clogged
by rotting straw. As a result, the cellar, some fifteen yards square, was a
huge cesspool of foul water, rotting straw and decomposed bodies. It
took us a day to clean it out, but it took me a week to get the stench
out of my nostrils.

Craonnelle was full of charm for the *anciens*. I found Conti, one
day, coming out of the church with a secretive air, and a bulky bundle.
For two weeks, he lugged it around on top of his sack. Then he got
confidential. After swearing me to secrecy on the heads of three generations of grandmothers, he took me into the woods and showed
me the swag: three enormous gold crowns, raped from the heads of
defenceless saints. Conti was gibbering with a mixture of avaricious
glee and superstitious forebodings.

"*Il bello doro,*" he repeated over and over, rubbing his hands.

It was a shame to undeceive him, but I could not let him carry the
crown jewels of Craonnelle any longer. I picked one up, and scraping
the gilt away showed him the plaster of Paris below. The chuckling
ceased and superstition turned to wrath. Deep-seated, sincere rage
shook him; Italian, Arabic and *Lingua-Franca* curses rolled out of his
mouth, as he pulverised the crowns beneath his feet.

God had cheated him! Conti devout Catholic had reason to feel
abused.

But to get back to Craonnelle. Bibouker, the Arab bugler, used
to disappear for hours at a time. Curiosity got the better of me, and
I followed him. He ducked into a house and presently a strange mechanical humming came from the top story. I crept upstairs, and for
a moment had grave doubts of his sanity. There sat this great gorilla
man, grinning like a death's head, and pedalling furiously on a Singer
sewing machine. A few questions, however, made everything quite
clear. Bibouker had discovered a safe and easy way to learn to ride a
bicycle!

It was Bibouker who produced a delicacy most of us had met

ALAN SEEGER, NIELSEN, BOLIGNI, MORLAE,—
LITTLE CHÂTEAU, CRAONNELLE.

before, but *incog.*—that is to say, cat, cooked as rabbit. It wasn't bad, there was really very little difference, but somehow, I lost my appetite for this dish when I discovered another cat gorging itself on a fresh corpse.

★★★★★★

Christmas came and went, not very different from any other day. We worked hard, building trenches and repairing roads, which called forth no little grousing from the English. That night we got extra wine, a few oranges, and rice prepared with chocolate with our supper. The *sous-officiers* congregated in a big room; but the soldiers and corporals, having no place to go, retired to their quarters where they sat in semidarkness—quietly drinking. The volunteers added a new verse to their marching song:

> *As we go working,*
> *Picks and shovels, on our way—Gor' blimee!*
> *You can hear the people shouting*
> *The bloody Legion works on Christmas Day.*

By this time the battalion had lost a good many, besides casualties. Some who had enlisted, just before the war, as Belgians, turned out to be German spies.

Stuart, Paul, a long lanky Southerner, and two or three other Americans had been *reformés* (discharged physically unfit) mostly on account of inflammatory rheumatism. The English had been transferred *en masse* to the British Army, and I found out later that most of them had applied for the Army Service Corps (Strawberry Jam Stealers) and wondered how they fared in that Paradise of military brigands, after four months' training in the Legion—or rather, how their new comrades fared, after their arrival.

Bill and Bert had gone to the aviation. Bill with his previous experience qualified at once as pilot. Bert's debut was typical. He climbed into the machine, had the controls explained to him, and started off just as Bill had done. Full speed ahead, up, and then down with a crash. After they had extracted him from the debris the officer in charge questioned him.

"What went wrong?"

"I don't know."

"You don't know! Haven't you ever been in a plane before?"

"No."

"What in God's holy name do you mean starting off like that?"

"Well, I thought I might be able to fly."

They decided he had enough nerve to be worth training.

Then we lost Phil. It all started over a cup of coffee. Bibouker was ladling it out, and Bronstein, an English-American-Russian, was trying for a second cup, insisting he had had none. Bibouker waxed wroth and swore all Americans were cheats and liars. Given one other Arab, he said he could make the whole American section eat the dung-heap in the yard. He called to a passing friend, an Arab from the machine gun section, to bear witness. Phil, who had been listening, stepped forward laughing and suggested that he and Bronstein take them on. Bibouker backed down, but the other Arab seemed eager, so the fight was on.

Phil generally packed a gun but he gave it to me at the start. The Arab pretended not to know this and to be nervous, and Phil held out his arms to show it wasn't on his hip. Whereupon, the Arab gripped him by the arms and butted him in the face. They both went down and came to grips, and Phil was gradually getting the best of it. They were fighting in a field covered with little piles of manure, and by this time a crowd had gathered.

An Alsacian, a friend of the Arab, broke through the ring and cracked Phil over the head with a *bidon* (water bottle) full of wine. Figured out in physics, this meant a five-pound weight at the end of a four-foot lever, taking into consideration the length of the man's arm and the strap. Phil went down, and a general riot broke loose—our section against the machine gun outfit. An officer rushed in to stop it, calling on the sergeants to help him. "*A moi les sergeants!*" He drew a gun, but before he could fire Thérisien, roaring, "*J'arrive, mon Lieutenant,*" hurled himself at the back of his knees and bowled him over. Finally the guard turned up and stopped the fight, but not before five Americans and six *légionaires* had been knocked cold, and several others mildly marred. Both sides retired, growling at each other, and our billets were changed.

Phil was in a bad way, and growing worse daily. He thought it was a return of African black-water fever, but it was hard to get proper treatment for this sort of thing. The doctor on duty was not impressed, and after painting the wound on his head with iodine, pronounced him fit for service.

I tried to beg, buy, or steal him some hot milk, but to no avail. The good Samaritans slammed their doors in my face, in spite of my offers to pay. Two days later we moved up to the second line. The march finished him. He was taken to hospital, babbling with delirium, and died after three days of agony—tetanus.

The Alsacian was court-martialled, but acquitted on the ground that he was drunk at the time. Why shouldn't we get drunk? Goaded by criticism for having started the row, Bronstein walked over, followed by the section, and picked a fight with the Alsacian. In two minutes, it was general, but the Alsacian was a marked man. While we kept up a milling battle with the others, every one of us concentrated on the Alsacian. When he went down it was all over. It is surprising how quickly hob-nailed Army boots can reduce a man's head to pulp.

Then the guard turned out, and we were all arrested. The major examined the case, and privately sympathized with us. But what could he do? There had been a row between the two sections, and a man had been killed. How could anyone tell who had done it? Anyway, he explained to our sergeants, putting us under arrest was as much to protect us as anything else. Most of the muleteers of the machine gun section carried knives, and in case another row started—?

CHAPTER FIVE

Scraps

May 1915. The train was teeming with Tommies, officers, W. A. A.
C.s, and other feminine military organisations necessary in conduct-
ing a war, and I was a very blue spot of blue in all that khaki. With true
flegme brittanique, I was discussed, but not spoken to.

"I say, old horse, whatever is he?"

"Don't know, must be a bloody Belgian."

"What's his rank?"

"Couldn't say, old bean, must be an officer, travelling first."

I was out of luck; the compartment was full of temporary gentlemen—Flying Corps, at that. I wondered what had happened to that
finest type of man, the pre-war British officer. Had they all gone west
at Mons?

Southampton at last, and I started aboard the leave boat. I was
stopped at the gangplank by an M.E.O., who demanded my travel
warrant. I explained I was not travelling under orders but was a French
soldier returning from leave. The British had apparently never heard of
leave being granted, at least not to a private; and I instantly became a
suspicious character, and was referred to the civilian passport control.

Why had I, a soldier in uniform, come to the civilian authorities?
. . . Because the military police had sent me . . . . Then where was my
passport, and visa? . . . I had neither . . . . Then I came under military
jurisdiction.

Finally, I was turned over to a military embarkation major. I explained the case, pointed out that if I did not catch that boat I would
be twenty-four hours late; and twenty-four hours' absence in time of
war is desertion, the penalty for which is death, in the Foreign Legion.
The major, a decent sort of chap, argued the matter for ten minutes
through a curtain with an irate general who had apparently retired

for the night, but to no avail. Whereupon the highly suspected spy was turned loose in the town and told to look up the French Consul next day.

The consul was furious and gave me a letter stating that I had presented myself in plenty of time, papers in order, and that I was not to blame for the delay. This was fortunate, for the British made amends by a very curt note which would have been about as helpful as a death warrant. I found out later. On arriving in France, I had to go back to the depot of the Legion, then situated at Orleans, and wait for the next draft before rejoining the regiment at the front.

Life at the depot was hell. I successfully resisted the offers of the doctors there to pronounce me physically unfit for a thousand *francs*, but gained the enmity of most of the depot draft by asking to leave for the front with the next reinforcements.

On board a troop train,
July 16, 1915.

Dear Gerald:

...We have been travelling all day and have changed trains four times. The carriage is getting dark. There is a jumble of sleeping men, sacks, rifles, cartridges, belts and haversacks strewn on the narrow benches. Very little talking, except for a drunken sergeant, and no singing. These aren't the gay, carefree men going to the front for the first time. Most of them have been there, as I have, during the long, dreary winter months, and have been sent back wounded or sick. We have been travelling sixteen hours, and as yet have not had a chance to fill our canteens. A stop—everyone wakes—and a rush: for the fountain. A struggle—"*En voiture!*"—and back we go to our wagons, without water. A few curses and a little grumbling, and silence again. But don't make a mistake. If these men don't shout and sing, they are none the less effective. And they are far more useful stone-walling material than the eager, imaginative, would-be bayonet-workmen of the green troops....

...There is a fresh rumour, with some confirmation, that we are going to the Dardanelles. "We ain't got much money, but we do see life!" You' don't know how glad I am to get away from that damned depot. At least I shall be among men. There is no one left but *embusqué* officers and little Jew tailors who have been more or less forced to join. Their one idea is to keep away from

56

the front. They had to dress one by force, and all the time he kept yelling *"J'ai peur de partir!"* God, it must be awful not to have enough pride to conceal it if you are afraid!

I found the regiment at Plancher les Mines, near Belfort, due to a concentration of troops near the Alsacian border, as the powers-that-be were expecting an offensive in that direction.

★★★★★★

For a month, we were in clover. Billets were beautifully clean and fairly comfortable, and the inhabitants more than friendly, and there were two or three *bistros* or inns. There was no work, but manoeuvres, route marches and reviews came thick and fast.

First and Second *Etrangers*, Eighth Zouaves, First Moroccan *Tirailleurs*, Second Algerian *Tirailleurs*, Colonial Artillery, and two squadrons of *Chasseurs d'Afrique*. Twenty-five thousand picked men—the Moroccan Division—to be reviewed by Leyautey.

Long columns of marching troops on the way to the field; *légionaires* in the new sky-blue uniforms; *Zouaves* and *Tirailleurs* in khaki—great baggy trousers and red *chechia* (*fezzes*)—and the *Chasseurs* d'*Afrique* in pale blue *shakos* and dolmans.

The division forms three sides of a square. "Stack arms—stand at ease . . . . Attention!" Bugles and drums sound the *Garde à vous.* "*Rompez les faisceaux! Sacs aux dos!*" . . . . A moment's pause . . . . "*Adroite alignement—fixe!*" Starting with the regiment on the right of the square, orders ripple down the line from one end of the division to the other. . . . "*Baionet-on!*" (*Baionettes au canon*—Fix bayonets). . . .A flash of white steel in the sunlight. "*Présentez armes!*" The division looks like a wheat-field of bayonets.

A slim officer in general's uniform, followed by his staff, rode up to the entrance of the square, and the *clique,* (drums and bugles), of the first *Etranger* crashed out the *Générale.* The drums and bugles of the other regiments took it up as he reached them. He tore along at full gallop with the figure and *élan* of a young cavalry officer. In spite of years of responsibility, he had kept his fire, but the keen hawk face was that of an old man.

He made the round of the regiments and came to a halt in the centre of the square, and the massed bands played *Au Drapeau* and then the *Marseillaise.*

I think most of us had a choky feeling. A day like this made up for a lot. A staff officer went down the line, informing the various captains that the general wished to speak to all those who had served with him in Africa. There is something of the Little Corporal in Leyautey: the cynical, hard-bitten *légionaires* returned to the ranks, shoulders back and eyes shining.

Then the march past began. For the first time, we heard the march of the Legion played by a full band. The *Zouaves*, Moroccans and Algerians filed past with their strange gliding swing, to the air *Sidi Brahim*. Their way of sliding over the ground seemed to fit in with the combination of weird Algerian bagpipes (*nubas*) and bugles. The rumble of guns and caissons, the thunder of cavalry riding by at the charge.

Ça y est—it was over!

★★★★★★

We were getting soft—good food and no work—so forced marches were the order of the day. The first was a little jaunt to the top of the *Balon de Surveillance* and back—fifty-seven kilometres with a climb of fifteen hundred feet. Before re-entering the village, the *clique* went to the head of the column and the Legion marched in with their long, rolling swing as if they had just started. However, in spite of the efforts, to tame them down the men were in the pink of training, and fights and drunken brawls in the various *bistros* were becoming a nuisance.

I was sitting with Bob, the negro prize-fighter, in the most disreputable *café* in the place, when the door flew open and a little Italian *légionaire* tore through the room, like a scared dog through a country village, and out the other side. A minute later, an enormous half-breed Algerian, his pock-marked face lit up like a Tibetan devil mask, and stark raving mad with cheap liquor, lurched through the door. He was followed by a huge Russian in similar condition. Lolling over the nearest table they questioned the little group of serious drinkers as to the whereabouts of Marius, evidently the late departed bar-room sprinter.

"Have you seen Marius?"

"No!"

"You lie! *Bande de salauds!*" (You swine!)

Whereupon, they each grabbed two empty bottles by the neck, broke the bottoms off against the table, and with these improvised glass daggers, blundered down the room slashing out impartially as they went.

Bob's reaction was immediate.

"Look here, boy! Ah seen this befo'. You do like me." And he promptly ducked under the table. I bumped heads with him in my

CONTI,—DOG FANCIER

eagerness to imitate. As soon as the roisterers had swept by, we were out and up; wrenched a leg apiece from the table, and stole after them. Bob crowned one and I the other, and then the guard came.

Next day was pay day and the night was hell. The American section was on guard duty. Three or four *légionaires* had determined to enter a house, and the women were hanging out of the top story, yelling. We arrived in time to see an attack worthy of a battlefield. The Legion Lotharios lined up across the street, bayonets fixed, rifles at the correct angle. As one man, they hurled themselves forward. Piercing shrieks from the women as the bayonets plunged into the door—then we fell upon them before they could wrench free.

Towards morning we were called out for the twenty-third time; but how to cram any more into the bursting jail was a problem. The sergeant of the guard, however, rose to the occasion. Placing the prisoners outside the door, he rapped out directions. We surrounded them with fixed bayonets. Throwing open the jail door, he ordered us to advance. As the points pricked them, the prisoners cursing and howling with fear fought their own way into the teeming clink.

Alan had a new crony, a gigantic Serb called Hupmaja. He was a veteran of the last Balkan war and was probably a brigand before that. But he had abandoned brigandage for the law, and was studying in Paris when the war broke out. When he wasn't cleaning, and crooning to his rifle, he was arguing with Alan.

In the heat of one of these discussions Alan called him an imbecile. Now he might have insulted his ancestors for ten generations, and Hupmaja would have grinned; but to insult his limited intelligence was striking too near home. With a roar the fight began; Alan sticking to the Marquess of Queensbury, and Hup using kill as catch can rules.

"Stick to out-fighting, Alan!"

"Don't let that Gorilla close with you!"

"Use your knee if he does!"

But in spite of all friendly advice they came to grips, and crashed to the ground—Alan underneath. The struggle went on but the Serb had it all his own way, and his thumbs crept towards the corners of Alan's eyes. A fight's a fight, but gouging is mutilation—so we kicked his thick head, and stopped it.

There were other troubles, besides drinking. The first grenades had appeared—cranky things made by women munition workers. They were guaranteed to go off in seven seconds, but occasionally exploding in three, and there were several tragedies during practice. But it was left to a Corsican sergeant to use them for his own private grudge. Hate is never far from love. Torrelli had been thrown down by his girl, and his hot blood demanded revenge. He pranced up to her house with a neat paper package under his arm, and tried to inveigle her to come out.

The gist of it all was to let bygones be bygones but he wanted to make her a parting present. His expression, or perhaps her intuition, warned her something was wrong. Instead of coming forward to take the package, she questioned him through the half-closed door. The more he urged, the more distantly curious she became. The argument ended abruptly—as the present exploded. Marie was considerably shaken. Torrelli disappeared in a fine red mist.

★★★★★★

Alsace was a great disappointment. The *Quand Même* and *Little Bird from France* stuff was useful as propaganda, but we hadn't been there a day before we discovered it was eye-wash—or, shall we say, banana oil! It seemed to me that most of the French Alsacians must have cleared out after 1870. The present population is neither anti German nor pro French; they simply want to be an independent state, like Switzerland or Luxembourg. They were anti Boche for good reasons, but principally, because they are *always* "agin the government."

After I had been there a week, I was convinced they would prove as much of a stumbling block in the Chambre as they had in the Reichstag. The *cafés* were amusing. French was evidently the patriotic tongue of the moment. It was comic to watch the worthy *burghers* come in, raise their hats and solemnly greet the gathering: "*Ponchour dout le monde-Zalut, la gompagnie!*" Their French went no further, but honour was satisfied—and with a sigh of relief they would lapse into guttural German.

CHAPTER SIX

Battle of Champagne

The 2nd Etrangers disentrained at St. Hilaire the night of Sept. 15th. The road was blocked with regiments. I had never seen so many men. At dawn, we moved on, and even as we moved, troops, by this time banked up behind us, took our place. Regiments, brigades, divisions,—Line, *Chasseurs Alpins, Zouaves, Tirailleurs,* Colonial Infantry, what next! Guns, field guns, Howitzers, siege batteries, endless ammunition trains—then cavalry. Our hopes ran high—it was the big offensive—open warfare—Berlin! Still the blue columns rolled on— picked men, shock troops—the lance head of the army. There must be a big show coming and, as if in confirmation, the German guns began a sullen systematic shelling.

We camped in the park of the *château* at Suippes and lost touch with the shifting horde in the intensity of our own preparations. Every day officers went up into line to learn the trenches and returning explained with plans scratched on the ground. A. was our first line, B., C. and D. evacuation trenches, and God help the man who was caught in one of these without a wound. Specialists were trained. Grenadiers with the new contact grenades, whose business it was to put the machine guns out; *Nettoyeurs des Tranchées* with wicked looking trench daggers, to mop up after the first wave had swept over—there was to be no repetition of Arras. And still more troops and guns rolled up.

Our preparatory bombardment began. God what a prelude! It crashed out on a split second, and for three days thundered relentlessly on. In the face of this, how childish our new gas masks and steel helmets. . . .

"Hey, feller, tomorrow's the big day!"

"Yeh—Thérisien just told me."

"Did he tell you we're not going to lead off, after all?"

"Yep—We've got the dirtiest job of all. The Colonial Infantry's going over first. We pass 'em, and take over just where the hardest fighting begins, and when we're shot to pieces the *Zouaves* carry on through the gap."

"Sounds pleasant!" Then Denny's voice dropped, as he sheepishly handed me a bit of paper. "That's my sister's address, Dave, just in case . . . . . Will you write?"

"Sure. Here's my brother's."

Evening came—everything was ready. Huddled around the dying fires we *bleus* were trying to hide our stage-fright, and the *anciens* were singing the traditional songs of the Legion—and over everything the increasing roar of the guns.

"*Rassemblement! Couvrez sur deux!*"

"We're for it now, Denny."

"Yes, feller, but what an experience!"

At 12 sharp we started for the line in column of twos. As we got clear of the woods we could hear troops marching on all sides. Occasionally we got fleeting glimpses of them as the moon came out of the clouds. The shells were beginning to burst around us now, but we were comparatively safe in the shelter of a *boyeau*. (Communication trench.)

Suddenly we came out into the street of a little village. This was Souain, and at that moment no healthy spot. Two of our batteries were in the ruins and the whole place was lit up by the flash of the guns. The German guns were searching for them, and the noise of crashing shells and tumbling masonry was infernal. As we passed the door of a huge barn I saw an artilleryman, hands in pockets, legs wide apart, grinning from ear to ear. He made some remark about it being a bit showery. Another flash—*Abracadabra!* His goblin figure disappeared.

We plunged into another *boyeau* and finally reached the second line, where in spite of a fine rain and the bombardment we slept like logs. At dawn, we were up watching the effect of our shells. They were bursting like ocean breakers on the first and second German line, following each other so fast that they howled like a wind overhead.

On account of poor visibility, zero hour was postponed till nine. At nine sharp the order was passed "*Sacs aux dos*" and we started to the first line, our section in front with Rosé leading. We came to a place where the *boyeau* was cut by a road. Beside us a masked battery had opened up and was working full blast. The Germans were hunting for it and had just got the range. They were dropping big shells at the point of crossing, and were sweeping it with machine guns.

Commandant Rosé climbed out onto the road, looked coolly about him, and walked across with his cane on his arm. I held my breath and plunged after him. Those of us who got across were surprised to find ourselves still alive.

At a fork in the *boyeau* we learned that the Colonial Infantry had led off; already some of the wounded were streaming back. I was so interested in a Colonial with the tops of four fingers shot off that I lost contact with the rest of the section, and found myself with the men behind me, including Lieutenant Pelozza, cut off from the rest.

We blundered into the first line trench as a section of Colonials was about to go over. Out in front of the trench a *commandant majeur* (doctor with the grade of major) was walking up and down. There he was, bullets and shrapnel whistling all about him, swinging his stick as he calmly directed the stretcher bearers. Seeing us he hailed Lieutenant Pelozza. "*Hey, que faites vous là!*" ("What are you doing there?") Pelozza explained that we had lost our regiment, etc. He was bothered for a moment, and then his face cleared. "*Vous allez tous dans la même direction. Vous n'avez qu'a f outre le camp avec les autres.*" (You are all going in the same direction, you'd better jump off with the rest.)

Once out of the communication trench we lost all awe of the bullets which were spatting about us and started across the level ground. A roar of rage from Captain Petaud, on the left, called us back: "What the HELL are you doing out there!" And rejoining the regiment, we meekly waited our turn.

Prisoners began to filter in. Poor devils, half crazed from the effects of the bombardment, they offered us everything they had, from watches to water bottles. Four of them were bearing a Colonial captain on a stretcher. He saw the green 2's on our collars, and raising himself cried, "*Vive la Légion!*"—Then he fell back exhausted, the blood welling from a jagged hole in his chest.

We fixed bayonets. Commandant Rosé jumped out ahead—"*En Avant*" we were off. We crossed their front line at a quick walk, and for the first time got some idea of the effect of our bombardment. Nothing was left but a series of mounds and holes with half-buried men, machine guns, and barbed wire entanglements—here and there a dead Colonial hanging on them.

We began to lose men by rifle and machine-gun fire, as well as shrapnel. A halt to get the men in hand again, and I had a chance to look around. Behind me in every direction came heavy columns of

"Shirt reading" between attacks, Champagne, September, 1916

blue-clad infantry. Regiment after regiment surged over the hill—an overwhelming flood of blue. "Hey! Look at the cavalry!" Sure enough, we could see columns of horsemen. As they came broadside to us we noticed the strange formation in which they were riding—six men by twos—then a gap—then six more. Suddenly we realised they were not cavalry but batteries following up the infantry. Five minutes later they came galloping into the flat sort of valley where we were waiting. The Boches caught sight of both the guns and us at the same moment. The result was a veritable hail of 4.2 inch shrapnel and the famous German 105" shell.

We lay flat with our sacks hunched on our shoulders and watched the guns come into action. A contact shell hit the lead team of one gun and "messed 'em up considerable." In a flash the wheel driver was at the horses' heads calming them, the gunners had cut loose the quivering mass of horses and men, and what was left of the team was on its way again, the driver swinging into his saddle at the trot. A minute later the battery was in action front and had fired its first salvo.

A shell burst just above us and the man on my left gave a little moan. The corporal on my right buried his face in his hands squeaking like a snared rabbit, and my rifle burned my hands. There was no doubt about the other man—he was through; the corporal was weeping in such a high *falsetto* we thought he was fooling, but when we pulled his hands down from his face we found it split open like a ripe melon. In the meantime, I had troubles of my own; the same shrapnel had smashed my rifle so I had to look around for another.

It was not difficult to find one as men were dropping all around and there was one continuous yell for *brancardiers* (stretcher bearers). According to orders they only brought in men of their own regiment; it looked cruel to see them pass a man with his whole side torn out to pick up another slightly wounded, but it saved lives in the long run.

Things were becoming a little too warm in that part of the world so we were ordered to occupy a German position, the "Angelheart shooting trench." Here, however, in spite of the pleasing name things were even worse. They had the range down to an inch, and were only waiting to make sure it was occupied before plastering it with heavy contact shells. A sickening crash, the stench of hot acrid gas—the pelting of rocks sand and clods of earth, and finally the shrieks of the wounded. Two hours of this, and at last the order to advance once more. This meant climbing out, assembling, and calling the roll, under the same murderous fire.

The first, second and third sections fell in and numbered off; only five men and a sergeant of the fourth appeared. Captain Petaud waited patiently for a bit but finally shouted to the sergeant, "Come along, Malvoisin! Where is the rest of your section?" Malvoisin gave a dry chuckle, "We're all here, Captain." Petaud never turned a hair. "Oh, I see. It's like that." And he gave the order to advance. They started shelling us with shrapnel as soon as we moved, but anything was better than being wiped out like ants in that ditch.

A cyclist came up with a message. Colonel Le Compte Denny had been wounded and Major Rosé was to command the regiment. Petaud took over the battalion, and Lieutenant Hallouette, or "Jo Jo, the Dog-Faced-Boy," as we called him, took our company. He had been a reserve officer, but was considered too old for active service when the war broke out, so he resigned his commission and enlisted in the Legion. Within a year, he had won the *Médaille Militaire* and was back in his old rank of lieutenant through sheer efficiency and courage. He was the finest shot in the regiment, and could outlast the best men in his company on the march. He carried a full sack and spurned his horse as an example to the men.

The battalion advanced in open order and, just at dusk, dug in about two hundred yards back of the Ferme de Navarin. The ground was strewn with little patches of newly turned earth covered with straw, and the first man to step on one went up with a loud bang—field mines.

Denny and I were *copins de combat* (battle side-kicks) so we dug in together. As we flopped down, our hearts stopped: we were bang in the middle of one of those sinister patches of straw! Fortunately, it was a dud, so we shifted and went to ground.

Our battalion had advanced too far and was enfiladed on the left flank, so moved back to a little ridge some twenty-five yards to the rear.

The battalion on the right had taken the Ferme de Navarin but our gunners didn't know it and our barrage stuck fast, just in front of the farm. The German barrage was some twenty yards back of the farm, so the battalion was boxed. Fritz discovered their predicament first, and shortened his range . . . . .

Meantime, we were consolidating our position on the ridge. The Germans turned everything they had on us—shrapnel, marmites (H-E shell), aerial torpedoes, and machine guns. It was raining hard by now—it always rained when the allies attacked—so much so, that

AS THEY SWUNG INTO COLUMN THE NIGHT BEFORE THE 25th OF SEPTEMBER we began to think there was something in the *"Gott mit uns"* slogan. As fast as we dug the holes filled with water.

About midnight chaos broke out in the Ferme de Navarin. Wild firing, then the panic-stricken bleating of the battalion holding it, guttural German cheers, and clear-cut commands of French officers trying to rally their men, (it was a line battalion made up entirely of the young class of 1916). The Boches had counter attacked and the kids had broken and scattered.

Suddenly a bugle cut clear and calm through all the noise and confusion—first the regimental call of the Legion, then the rally.

The German shouting stopped. There was a half-hearted cheer from the young troops. The Legion went mad. Every man sprang to his feet and whipped out his bayonet—The bugle began again—clear and inviting it sounded the charge. This was too much! Low growls ran down the line—We started forward with the long swinging *pas de charge*. The officers ran out in front, beating us back with the flat of their sabres.

"Stay where you are! Don't fire! We must wait till they are driven back to us and then counter attack."

Discipline held—the Legion subsided and waited with grim expectancy. Now the bugler had passed to the double time of the charge! The kids pulled themselves together and fairly hustled the Germans out of the farm.

Bugle calls are forbidden in time of war, to avoid traps. When the confusion started Petaud was visiting the defenders of the farm, followed by the regimental bugler. Sizing up the situation, he immediately ordered the bugler to sound the rally and charge—it did the trick.

All the day of the 26th was spent in consolidating our position under heavy shell fire. Alan described it in his poem *Maktoob*.

When, not to hear, some try to talk
And some to clean their guns, or sing,
And some dig deeper in the chalk—
I look upon my ring.

Sept. 27th. Waguenenestre brought mail last night. Got six letters. Too dark to see. Wondered if I'd be killed before I could read 'em. Waked by knapsack landing on me—Morlae's. Roused Ole and Denny and went to investigate. Found same shell buried him alive. Got him out just in time—gasping like fish. Went to sleep again. Attack still going forward. Moved back to reform with Bat. D. Old German trench. Range down pat. Not so good. Raining again. Kitchens came right up into line—Hot food!

★★★★★★

Orders! We were to take the Bois de Sabots, on the right of the line, but had to cross the whole field of battle to get into position to attack. We started off by sections in column of twos, four abreast at distances of fifty yards. The Germans spotted us and turned everything loose, but the columns pushed on. Shells burst full in the middle of sections, annihilating the centre. The remaining men picked themselves up and joined sections to their right or left; the march continued.

Horrible apparitions crawled out of shell holes and looked at us as we went by. A thing with no face—only four caverns in a red mask, where eyes, nose and mouth had been—mooed and gibbered at us as it heard the clink of accoutrements passing. Some strong-minded humanitarian put a bullet into it as we filed by.

We reached a wood. It was like a scene from the underworld—ghostly columns picking their way through shell-torn trees in the smoke and fog of high explosives. A shell burst in the section on the right—it looked like a football scrimmage writhing in agony—a swirl of men and smoke. Shells cracked over our heads—shells tore up the ground in front of us. We took the last gap at the run.

All that were left of us joined the remnants of three previous attacks. We crouched at the edge of the Bois de Sabots and peered through the underbrush. Oh Christ . . . . Two battalions of the Legion and one of *Chasseurs Alpins* were stretched out in skirmish order in front of the German barbed wire. The alignment was perfect—the men were dead.

We felt pretty sober till Ole Nielson began to sing "Ragtime Cowboy Joe." The section took it up with a roar, convulsed with mirth at the line. "No one but a lunatic would start a war." The other *légionaires* grinned, but the *Chasseurs Alpins* looked at each other in horror, convinced we had gone mad.

"*Quatre hommes de bonne volontée!*" Commandant Rosé wriggled forward with them to reconnoitre. The place was stiff with machine guns and the barbed wire was not touched. A brief report to the general, demanding guns to blow a way through the wire—then we waited. Rosé had nerve. Just given command of the regiment, and his first act of initiative was to refuse to order a hopeless attack. He could have covered himself with glory while directing it in safety, from the rear. God, what a soldier he was!

70

Sept. 29th. Back last night where we started from. Repeated whole bloody performance today. Dug in. Shot up by our own guns again. Bois de Sabots outflanked and taken. Few losses.

Sept. 30th. Spent night converting German positions. Prying roof off dog kennel, needed planks. Out bounced Jo Jo, the dog faced boy.

Sept. 31st. Still digging, cleaning out Germ. dugouts. Found amusing p. c. to Germ. from girl—

The troops on the eastern front are performing miracles of bravery and strategy. Why don't you advance? Do you know what people are saying in Berlin? 'In the east is an army of brave men. In the west are the village firemen.'

Wonder how Fritz laughed off retreat. Fred found jar gun grease in dugout. Started to clean rifle—turned out to be honey. Better and better, said Alice.

Oct. 1st. Relieved last night. 30 kiloms. to rear for rest. Everyone dead beat. 50 min. march. 10 min. rest. Dropped in our tracks. Had to be kicked awake. Reformed with remains 1st and 2nd Etrangers—one regiment.

Oct. 6th. Back to line yesterday. In immediate reserve today. Lost heavily . . . .

The work of consolidating the line began, grabbing off sectors still held by the Germans to round out the position, and burying the dead—simple enough once you know the trick. We would dig a hole beside the man and roll him in. As time was short, the holes were shallow. Men take strange positions in death. They did not always fit the grave, and someone would stand on the arms and legs, to keep them down while the others shovelled furiously. But when they have been dead a day or so, they are like enormous dolls with limbs worked by elastics. In some cases the burial party miscalculated the amount of earth needed to hold them down, and as the man standing on the corpse stepped aside, an arm or leg would slowly rise through the loose sand and earth, in mute protest.

★★★★★★

Oct, 19th, 1916.

Dear Gerald:

I'm not going to write you a word about the battle . . . but I managed to snap some photos from time to time, and if they come out, I'll send you some prints. One thing bores me like hell. We were going to work Indian file. A shell burst near us, and my friend, Fred, who was walking just ahead of me, gave a funny little squeak and fell back into my arms, fighting for breath and clutching at his side. There was another man scratched, and screaming like a stallion; as the stretcher men were around him, I picked Fred up and carried him down to the *poste de secours*. The shells were getting thicker and I was making the best time I could, so you can imagine my rage when I discovered he was still hanging onto his rifle. At the dressing station we found it was only a broken rib. Thank God it hadn't penetrated his lung . . .

★★★★★★

The Legion had been so cut to pieces that the Powers That Be had almost decided to send it back to Africa. The volunteers were given the alternative, however, of going into a French regiment. Rosé called us together. "You're leaving the Foreign Legion—for God's sake don't go and spread the usual lies about it. We're not all cutthroats, perverts and sneak thieves. We're men who have had troubles of our own. We're a hard fighting regiment of professional soldiers, and we've won a glorious name. Don't go and smirch it! You've come up to standard—I'm sorry to lose you. Good luck!"

"Jo Jo" shook hands with me twice, and said something I'm prouder of than any of my decorations—and I never even thought he had noticed me . . . . And we marched down to join our new regiment—the 170th Infantry—"*les Hirondelles de la Mort*."

CHAPTER SEVEN

We Leave and Relieve the Legion

Out of the frying pan into the fire—Another attacking division! Thirty-two kilometres down—thirty-two kilometres back, the next day. By irony of fate, the 170th relieved the Legion. No rest for the wicked.

Then began the long drawn-out business of consolidating the ground taken in the advance; not very startling to read about in the *communiqués*. It was a dreary stretch—a blur of cold misery and over-work and mud. The nights were the worst. Two hours' guard or out-post duty with eyes and ears strained—two hours' work—carrying enormous logs, rolls of barbed wire, stakes and *gabions* through tortu-ous mud-filled *boyeaux*, driving posts and stringing barbed wire out-side the lines, filling sand bags and repairing trenches demolished dur-ing the day—then towards morning the long tramp to the kitchens to bring up food for the next day—and at dawn everyone standing to arms.

One of our listening posts was only eight yards from a German outpost. The parapet was made of German and French dead, and the shallow communication trench leading to it was strewn with Ger-mans. The ground above the trench was swept by machine gun fire day and night so that the relieving guard scuttled along it bent almost double—no time to throw the corpses over the side. A huge Prussian grenadier halfway along it we dubbed "Croaking Conrad" for if one stepped on. his middle he still uttered a guttural frog-like croak.

In the post, we sat, slept, even ate, sitting on corpses. But the night we were relieved came my breaking point. In the narrow entrance one of the relief bumped me and I lost my balance. I grabbed the parapet behind me to save myself from falling, and was almost sick as I felt a face come away under my hand. For days, everything I ate or touched smelled of putrid flesh.

The Germans had advanced a machine gun post some twenty yards beyond their lines; very annoying to us. Seven of us climbed over, picked our way through the wire and began the usual business—wriggling through mud and over corpses, a rocket—stop, darkness—we scuttled forward. Our orders were to throw two bombs apiece and then get back as best we could. A black mound loomed up—a whispered command and fourteen grenades were hurled in rapid succession, wrecking the gun. Instantly, machine guns in the German line began to rake the spot.

All the way out I had been doing some hard thinking. "*Sauve qui punt,*" all very well—but where? Lie down till it blew over? Yeh, and be mopped up on the ground—not enough cover for a rabbit. Head straight back? Forty yards, and you can't beat a bullet. I ran parallel to the German lines till out of the zone of cross fire, and then cut back to our own lines. Three lay down and three raced bullets. I got home.

The Germans were strafing us more every day. They would begin at one end of a regimental front, hammer their way along it, let up for half an hour, and then begin again. At this time, Fritz started the retarded fuse shells. We heard the dull thuds of the departure, the menacing *crescendo* whistle, then four more dull thuds. For a moment, we thought they were duds, and cheered hilariously from sheer relief. A second later four muffled explosions, and cubic yards of earth, rock and chalk were hurled into the air. This was something new and nasty!

★★★★★★

I heard the swish and howl of a shell, and ducked behind a traverse. Sudden blackness—and I was struggling desperately for light and air under an avalanche of earth and sand bags. It seemed hours—but it could only have been seconds—before they cleared my head and dug me out. I looked around groggily, my knees trembling, on the verge of horrors. Did the sergeant tell me to go down to the dressing station, to sit down and think over my narrow escape and work myself up into a state of shell shock? He did not. The first thing I heard was a curse and a roar:

> You holy bit of blood sausage! Don't you know there are others buried alive, too? Grab a tool and help dig them out. Make it snappy!

He took control of my mind before I had time to realise the shock, and directed it along normal channels. As I tore around the other traverse where the men were buried, I saw a pick and a shovel. Even as I ran, my mind decided the question which to take. Buried men— might kill them with a pick—better take the shovel. Snatching it up in my stride I got to work.

★★★★★★

Next morning the mist cleared suddenly, as it had a habit of doing at the front, and out beyond their wire was a German working party. I flung my rifle to my shoulder, closing my left eye—blank. What the . . . .? I rubbed my eye and tried again—still nothing. That shell had made trouble after all. . . . Later, the oculist told me that it was due to the concussion. No chance of the aviation now—but after all I had one eye left. In any other army, I would probably have been coddled into a case of shell shock. This being the French Army, I learned to shoot from my left shoulder.

The matter was closed.

★★★★★★

Dec. 5, 1915.

They have stuck me in the *peloton des élèves sous-offs* for 20 days hard, so it looks as if I won't ever get my four days home. Good Lord, they work us hard! Yesterday they had a little endurance race with our equipment and rifles, I didn't shine. And like the damphool I was my cartridge pouches were full. All the others had emptied theirs moons ago. Never again! I have now arrived at the magnificent state of *Soldat première classe*—a distinction, but not a grade. I am entitled to wear one black stripe on my arm, but up to the present have been too lazy to sew it on. Hence earning a reputation of having a magnificent indifference for all military grades and honours . . .

Just at present, I'm leading one hell of a life—neither fish nor fowl nor good red herring. We are *en repos*, waiting and getting ready for the dance this spring. If you want to know what sort of life it is, read Kipling's *Gentlemen Rankers*. Almost all my friends have been wounded or have passed into the aviation. I can't, on account of my right eye. Well, Gerald, if I don't get it this spring, you had better stick close to me all your life, for I bear a charmed life.

They have put me into the 'Chucka de bombsky' squad (Grenadiers); that means that we lead off the attack and try to put the machine guns and crews out before they can get the second wave which follows us. It has its advantages, though. We don't

75

have to carry a sack in action, and there is talk of taking our rifles away and giving us automatic pistols. As I've packed an automatic right through the war, plus fifty rounds, it will relieve me of the damned old blunderbuss and the 250 rounds of rifle ammunition. In spite of what we know is coming, most of us are looking forward to it. Anything but this inactive life away from the front, and at the same time far from civilization ,

This letter is getting so long that I already have grave doubts if the censors will let it by, so I think I will ring off. Don't be uneasy about the spring. I've got the same hunch I've had since the beginning that I will get by without a scratch.

     In haste,

          Affec,

                    Ding.

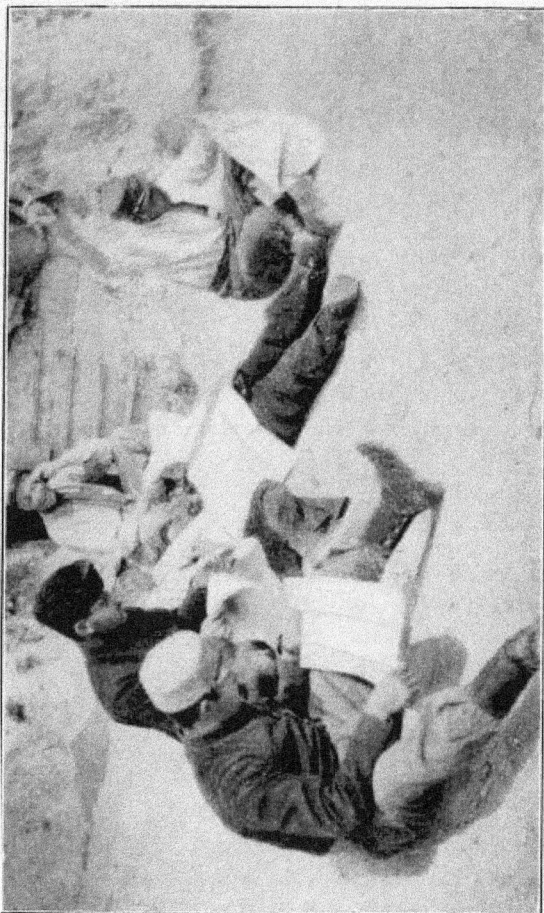

AMERICANS IN THE FOREIGN LEGION RECEIVING NEWS FROM HOME

CHAPTER EIGHT

Verdun—Shock Troops

As fate would have it, the doctor chose the 17th February to inoculate us against typhoid. All morning, long lines of men seeped into the infirmary. Some fainted as they came in sight of the white-aproned doctor and his aides, wiping the needles, jabbing, and then wiping again. One of the *aides* was dealing out aspirin tablets as the victims went out, checking off the names and droning "*un jour exempt d'éxércise*" in a sing-song voice, after each name. That night, the men moaned and tossed restlessly in the hayloft where we were quartered.

About midnight a new element of unrest: towards the northeast, the intermittent rumble of guns suddenly quickened and increased to concert pitch and volume. Even those who had been sleeping heavily stirred in their sleep, and some of the more wakeful lit candles and cigarettes, muttering to themselves, "*Ca chauffe la bàs. Pourvu que nous ne sommes pas appélles demain.*" ("It's warming up over there. Hope we are not called tomorrow.")

The division was supposed to be resting and training for the spring offensive, but an attacking division never knows . . . . We were offensive shock troops, but likely as not to be hurled into the line at any moment, to stop a gap. What we did know was that, once in, we were never withdrawn from a show till we had lost three quarters of our effectives.

At four o'clock came a shout from the farmyard below. "*Allans là Tiaut! Tons le monde en bàs! Faites les sacs. On part à six heures.*" ("Come on, everybody on deck! Make up the sacks. We leave at six.") Instantly everything was in a turmoil.

Candles were lighted and men groped feverishly in the straw for lost possessions and crammed them into their bursting knapsacks. Every few minutes a corporal would appear, followed by two men carrying half a pup-tent filled with things to be distributed: extra cartridges, emergency rations, first-aid kits, and last of all the squad cooking kettles. Finally, the man of the day appeared with the coffee, which he poured into our outstretched cups. Too hot to drink! We set them in the straw to cool, where most of them were promptly upset. The general confusion was increased by shouts from below—"*Allez, allez! Grouillez-vous! Tout le monde en bàs! Les autos vont venir à six heures!*" ("Come on, make it snappy! Everybody down! The trucks are coming at six!")

By now most of us were in the farmyard. Squad after squad stacked rifles and sacks and waited. There were low mutterings. "*Les autos*"— not so good. That meant a particular sort of perpendicular hell when we got there—we only rode up to the show when a specially hot corner was reserved for us. No wonder the motor trucks were called "slaughtermobiles."

By 6:30 the big grey Renaults, Fiats, Whites and Saurers began to roll into the village, and company after company piled aboard, wincing as they put on their sacks. The inoculation was playing havoc with us. Spirits revived though with the dawn and we began to sing, bellowing forth outrageous ribald songs as the trucks rolled through half-wakened villages. We passed peasant girls in *sabots* coming from the bakery with the family loaves clasped under their arms, yawning as they walked—they scarcely looked up, however, as the troops thundered by. The war had been going on for eighteen months now.

It began to snow and then freeze, and snow again. The trucks skidded from the high-crowned roads; soon the three leading ones were in the ditch and the road was blocked. No luck—we were ordered to get out.

"*Allons! Rassemblement! Couvrez sur deux! Sacs aux dos! En avant par quatres!*" And the heavy, grey-blue column got under way, shuffling precariously along the icy road. Every few yards someone slipped and fell. Nobody laughed. It's no joke to go down with a hundred pounds of sharp-edged equipment on your shoulders, particularly after an inoculation. The stumbling, slipping column plodded on and on. . . .

Three o'clock, and a halt is called in a village. We begin to speculate on the chances of soup, and staying there for the night. "*Formez les faisceaux! Sacs à terre.*" Ah, that's better. But hopes are dashed as an order trickles down from the head of the column: "Don't let them undo their sacks or break ranks." Sure enough, a cyclist comes up to the colonel with an envelope. "*Sacs aux dos! En avant par quatres!*" And the

ONE OF A MILLION

weary column gets under way once more. Heads down and shoulders hunched, eyes glued to the feet of the man in front—we stumble after them, hypnotised . . . . .

Four o'clock, and it begins to snow again. The guns grow more and more insistent and the roar is numbing. Suddenly, freakish shapes loom up on the road ahead. They crowd to one side as the column slouches by: old men in queer, heterogeneous apparel—women pushing baby carriages, piled, high with household possessions over and above the wailing occupant.

Terror-stricken, dumb, they drift by like startled ghosts; their wide eyes scarcely see the troops. Women, half pushed, half dragged along, calling for killed or missing babies. Lost children struggling to keep up with forced, uneven steps, moaning pitifully for dead parents! "Where do you come from? What's going on?" we shout in passing. But the only answer is a murmur—"The big shells—oh, the big shells!"

We know we are going to Verdun. But it conveys little, except that it has always been a quiet *secteur*. On we go through the night. At ten, half an hour's halt to eat bread, sardines, cheese. Still snowing, and the going more and more treacherous. The hours string out till there seems no end to this nightmare of a march. The guns are near, now. Occasionally men cock their heads to one side, persuaded they hear the whistle of a shell, but as yet it's only the wind in the telegraph wires.

Five o'clock. Fort de la Sartelle, the first of the group around Verdun. Our march is over. We are herded in and flop on the stone floor half an inch deep in water. Who cares—we may sleep! We have come sixty-five kilometres in nineteen hours' forced marching over ice-coated roads, but no one cares, except the general, who is awaiting fresh troops.

Two hours later, seven o'clock, and the column is under way again. We skirt the city and make for a wood, in which to hide from enemy aircraft while waiting for definite orders. Vain hope. A high-pitched thrum in the air; overhead a French observation plane tries desperately to escape some fourteen German scouts. The moment they spot us they turn back, and flying back and forth over the road proceed to bomb us. A short command, and we scatter over the fields. The planes disappear, whistles blow, and ten minutes later the regiment is on the march again. The seeming loose discipline, for which French troops are criticised, has one advantage—it makes large bodies of men more flexible.

Nervous business waiting for orders under fire, especially in the woods. We can see nothing and the crash of explosion echoes and re-echoes, so that every shell seems to have dropped within ten yards of us. A series of dull thuds as the shells leave the guns—*boooomp, boooomp, boomp.* Then a crescendo wail—*phoo-o-o, phoo-o-o, pho-o-o-o. Bramraram!* A black column of smoke—shrieks from the wounded—and calls for stretcher bearers. A quarter of an hour later a pathetic little *cortège* starts to the rear—four men carrying a bloodstained canvas trough, in which lies a quivering, moaning mass of mangled flesh, in dirty clothes and blood-soaked bandages. A heroic bid on the part of pigmies for a comrade's life, but the odds are on his bleeding to death or the whole *cortège* being wiped out on the way.

Our nerves have readjusted themselves to the noise, now. Mercifully, after several hours' bombardment, high explosives act like a soporific.

Night falls and a move is ordered. Ghostly columns leave the wood and advance along the road. Sibilant orders run down the lines:

You are in sight and perhaps in hearing of the enemy. No smoking. No talking. Keep your bayonet scabbards from clanking, and try to keep your feet from sucking in the mud.

The shelling has ceased for the moment, and the silence of the regiment is almost uncanny. Presently, the leading company tops a hill, and a ripple of laughter floats back to us. We have been pussy-footing it along as if the Boches were just around the corner, and there, in the valley ahead, the other regiment of our brigade is encamped and cheerful pandemonium reigns. Tents are pitched and candles burn brightly. Officers shriek at the top of their lungs for companies and sections, and companies and sections call for their soup kitchens, and shells crash and whine in the midst of it all. "*Troisieme compagnie. Troisieme compagnie.*" "Heh! la cuisine du quatrième!" "*Premiere section a la soupe.*" "Hep, la bàs! Eteindres ces bougies." *Fo-o-o-o-e-e! Crash!* Etc.

An hour later we have had soup and are off. The division is split up between two army corps. The brigade is split, even the battalions of our regiment are lent out right and left. The Boches have attacked unexpectedly and in force. They have taken the first and second lines. Vaux still holds out but Douaumont has fallen. Rumours fly: there has been treachery—the general in command has been shot—two regiments were marched by a *poiteau d'éxécution*, with a general's *képi* on it, as proof.

Now the real work begins. The counter attack has driven the Boches back, and surrounded Douaumont, but it is still held by a battalion of Brandenburgers. An hour's march in the heavy mud and slush, fifteen minutes to marshal the regiment into position, and the whistles shrill out for the charge. The night is stabbed by weird streaks of light as machine guns in the fort open up, and part of the advancing line crumples like burnt paper. But with the snarl of a wounded leopard, the rest dash on and clear the outer ramparts.

Position after position is taken, and the various machine gun crews are wiped out. No quarter is expected or given. A machine gun spits, three or four grenades snap, a rush, a scuffle, thuds and curses, and the attackers go on. As the fort is cleared, the inevitable happens—attacking squads fire into each other. The Brandenburgers fight to the last man; there is no question of prisoners. Finally, the job is done. The regiments left and right send troops to take over the fort and the attackers withdraw to lick their wounds.

Dawn finds us back in the same woods, once more in the position of immediate reserves, for we are still considered fresh troops, and, indeed, we are now thoroughly in our stride.

I wander down the hill to visit Billy Dugan, in the second company. Pipe in mouth and hands in pocket, I register coolness. As I arrive, three or four big shells shake the earth fifty yards off, and give me a cue.

"What are you guys doing? Dumping bricks? I wish you'd quit it. You've spoiled my beauty sleep."

However, in relaxing my jaw to speak, my outraged nerves rebel and the pipe wobbles like a crazy pendulum.

"That? Oh, they're just a few late New Year's presents from Fritz. But, say, old man, would you mind smoking a cigarette for a while? That pipe of yours makes us dizzy."

An ominous whistling rush cuts all conversation as we flop. A 210" bursts slap in the middle of a section, sending men hurtling into the air, sacks on backs, rifles still grasped in their hands. We look at each other, awe-struck. "*C'était la troisième de la quatrième.*" Then as our nerves relax, "*Tu as vu la drôle de gueule Gaillard faisait?*" (Did you see what a funny face Gaillard pulled?) Callous, perhaps, but if we let ourselves go after everything of this sort we would be demoralised in a day. As it is, we save our sympathy for the wounded, and rush to help.

Food is short, but rumours are plentiful. *Agents de liaison* pass with news of the other regiment—strange clipped accounts that somehow tell the whole story. "You should see the 174th. They got theirs. There'll be plenty of extra *pinard* for everyone, when they do draw it again. And as for stripes, we'll be holy zebras—if we get through this show. Look you—a quarter-master sergeant led back all that was left of two companies and a *sous-lieutenant* is commanding a battalion."

"Perhaps—but the new draft from the depot will have too many animals with sardines on their forelegs." (Old soldiers' way of speaking about newly made non-coms. Non-coms are animals till proved otherwise. "Sardines" slang for sergeants' chevrons.)

"The only way to get promotion is to be wounded and go to the depot. At the front, we won't even smell corporal's stripes."

The veterans growl and grouse, but they'd be the first to prevent a newly arrived *sous-officier* from making a blunder in action.

As night falls, all that is left of the regiment reforms, and starts off on a long dreary trudge across country—through shell holes filled with mud and water—quickly past French batteries in action, before the Germans reply—halting for a moment to let the tail catch up. Each stop and start spreads the column out, so now the men at the end are running in a feverish effort to keep up.

Six vicious cracks overhead! The Germans are sweeping the roads with Austrian 88's. and 130's. One or two shrieks, a little confusion; the stretcher men pass along the line to find the wounded, and the column moves on. There is little talking, and that in low tones, as if the men are afraid of starting the shelling again—the same feeling one has on a mountain trail, where avalanches lie in wait for the loud-voiced traveller.

Soon we are at a huge dark mound, and word comes back that it is the redoubt of Vaux; we are to relieve the present garrison. Then begins a weary wait while they bring out their wounded. Pitiful sights—some of them, hobbling along between two friends, then an endless procession of stretchers—among them, the "basket cases." Why they don't put them out painlessly, then and there, is beyond civilized intelligence. Mere trunks, both arms and legs shot off, some of them blind as well, what possible use can they have for life, except that horrible instinct to live? Yet they must be carried for miles, go through torture in hospital, and drag out lives of helpless hell, to satisfy a squeamish sentimentality we called humanity.

Here are the needles. See that he dies
While the effects of the drug endure. . . .

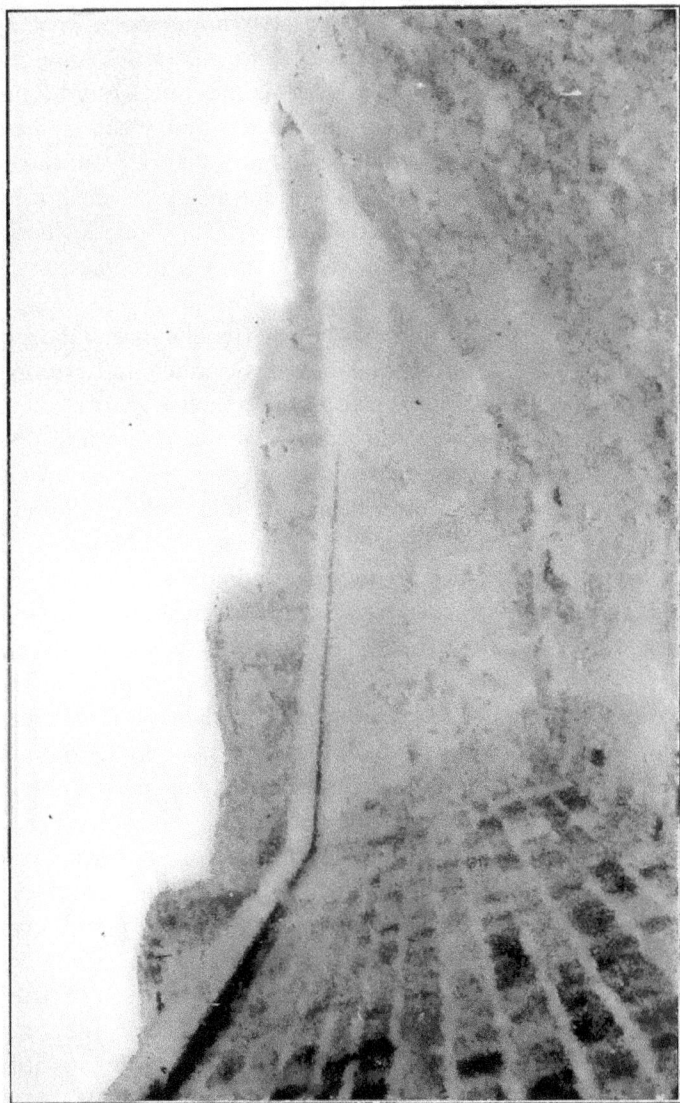

THE REDOUBT OF VAUX, VERDUN MARCH 1ST, 1916

What is the question he asks with his eyes?
Yes, All-Highest, to God, be sure.

The last of the wounded disappear into the night, and we move into the redoubt, while the other battalion files down to the village to dig in and create a first line of defence .... Barricades are built of everything they can find. Houses are ransacked for mattresses to be used as sand bags. Then the clown in all soldiers comes out. Absurd figures dance around the streets dressed up in everything they can lay hands on, from top hats to petticoats. Men in the most fantastic mixtures of full dress uniforms of officers. One soldier dressed as a woman minces along putting up a ridiculous small parasol every time a shrapnel bursts. A wedding procession forms, but the shelling becomes serious, and everyone scuttles for cover.

The village of Vaux and the newly made trenches are raked from one end to the other. As house after house is crushed and crumpled into smoking ruins, the survivors take to the trenches.

All eyes are strained toward the edge of the slope leading up to the village, expecting each minute to see the grey-green wave of the attack surge over it. Then a sinister heart-stopping whistle. A blinding flash—an almost simultaneous series of crashes which dislocate the pit of the stomach, prolonged by the roar and rumble of falling tiles and masonry. The survivors turn to the wounded. Another salvo—the solid, stone house is a gutted shell, one side strewn across the street.

A sharp order to evacuate, and the men spring to pick up their helpless comrades. But a third salvo strikes, and all are buried under a smoking pile of beams and bricks. In the meantime, the trenches are catching it. Retarded fuse shells and shrapnel, a sullen subterranean rumble and yards of the line are hurled into the air—men, sacks, rifles, *gabions* and earth, all falling back in a torn and tortured heap, while shrapnels crack like demon whips over all. The shelling redoubles,— then a nerve-shattering calm. The veterans know—their shrill cry of warning comes down the line.

"*Attention! Ils vont donner!*" As if conjured up by the cry, a solid green-grey mass of men rolls over the rise in front. *Crash!* The salvos once more before their barrage lifts from our front line. Firing breaks out in vicious crackling bursts, and the machine guns take it up with their steady wop, wop, wop, wop, wop. The firing increases spasmodically as the reserves from the redoubt arrive in the first line in breathless handfuls. But the mass of *veld-grau* rolls on. Heavy toll is taken, but they are advancing in the famous mass formation, and as soon as one man drops another takes his place and the line seems impervious.

We are praying for our guns to put down a barrage, and cursing the gunners. A single rocket goes up from the fort. "What the hell's the use of lengthening the range; don't they know we want a barrage!" Ten seconds later, two white rockets go up and almost immediately the 75's come into action. To us it is the most cheering sound in the world, that continuous roll—like drums—the sharp, spiteful crack of the shells! The whole German line is blotted out in gobs of thick white smoke. Great gaps have been torn in the line. The attack wavers, stops, fails.

This lasts all day. Seven times the attack surges over the rise, seven times it breaks, and retires under the combined rifle, machine, and field gun fire.

The four companies in the redoubt are copping it, too. One company is in bomb-proofs under the main rampart, but these shelters are only protected in the rear by a *parados* some twenty feet back. A three-hundred-and-eighty-millimetre shell bursts in the open space and the shelters become a shambles. Of the two hundred and fifty men, only six survive, and the walls are plastered with blood, brains and bits of smoking uniform.

March 2, 1916.

Dear Gerald:

The shelling has become so fierce today that we can't keep anyone on deck, and are all huddled inside the so-called bomb proofs, which the Boches are chewing big pieces out of at each shot. I feel a lot better now, but a few minutes ago the shock of the shell and the blasts made me faint and sick, and I had to lie flat till the blood ran back again. The Boches are attacking now, and our *feu de barrage* of big guns and field pieces and their preparatory bombardments are something hellish.

I hope you don't mind my writing you these things, but I want to register them with someone who can keep them. They should be interesting later. They have just shot away a whole corner of this redoubt—and the damn thing was made of rein-forced concrete and steel plates. The devils have been at it for nearly four hours now with an average of one shot a minute at this particular little redoubt. I mean one big shell of 210 or, 380 mm. calibre. The little ones only help to make a row and sweep the ramparts. *Allah* knows how long this old box will hold together.

We laugh and munch army biscuits and smoke, but there is cold death in the eye of every man. Some of the men are fast asleep—sheer nervous exhaustion. I took some pictures yesterday of this dump before the real riot started. If I can, I'll get some of what it looks like after it's over. Goodbye old man, more later if I can. Keep this.

Affec,

Ding.

The inside of the casemate looked like Goya's picture of a madhouse. No room to lie down and no benches to sit on, we squatted on our heels. Here and there a smoky kerosene lamp lit up a group of faces, hollow-eyed, gaunt. We had to relight the lamps continually as the concussion of direct hits blew them out. Periodically, the silence in the room was broken by a shout from the man nearest the door. "Sentinel's killed! Send up another!" Then a slight commotion as the next man on the list groped his way to the door, and almost certain death.

Suddenly a cry from above galvanises us into action. "They are coming!" The major telephones desperately to the brigade commander asking for a barrage. "*Hallo! La brigade! Faites donner les soixante-quinzes devant Vau!*" No answer. The sergeant telephonist almost tears off the handle in his effort to ring through—the wires have been cut. "Two runners."—They go.—"They are down, Captain."—"Two more." "One of them is through. No, he is down too." "Fire the two rockets." (The signal of the day for a barrage.) One of them misses fire—(Oh, Christ—is everything against us!) At last the signal is given; and as the 75's begin to roll, we pile out of the fort to reinforce the first line.

★★★★★★

March 3.

Dear Gerald:

Well, we got out of that bombardment all right, but I hope I never have to go through the like again. They burned up 1,200 big shells on that little fort alone, all 15 or 10 inch. Good Lord, things are moving fast! Last night we were in reserve waiting to attack. We rushed six miles to get into position, and at the top of a hill were met with gas shells. We had to catch our breaths in our respirators. Like eating a banana under water, it can be done, but it's difficult. . . .

At dawn, we moved out of the woods and advanced toward Fleury. Word was passed around that we were to attack and take it, and then continue toward Douaumont. The usual soldiers' grousing broke out on every side. "What! Attack after two days with nothing to eat! Just let them give the order, they'll see what'll happen. I'm going to throw up my hands and go *kamarad*".... But when the whistle blew we went forward like fresh troops.

French soldiers are a cool lot. We were taking cover behind a railway embankment before the final rush to take the village. Everyone knew we were to attack within the next minute, but each was attending to his own little affairs as if he were in rest billets. I was having quite a struggle with a dead Algerian.

My rifle was broken, and I had a shrewd suspicion I might need it in the house to house fighting ahead of us, so I tried to borrow one from the dead *Bikho* (slang for Algerian soldier). I grasped it firmly by the muzzle and pulled, but the *Bikho's* hands were locked around the trigger-guard and sling, and he clung to it in grim death. Then I tried a little pressure with my foot on his chest, but though his arms gave, he still hung on. So, I borrowed one from a less tenacious stiff. Some of the men were writing postcards; they explained it was not often they had a chance to write just before an attack. Others were busily hunting in the packs of dead men for emergency rations.

At the preparatory command, we crouched ready to spring forward. "*En avant!*" And we flowed over the embankment, like water over a dam; greeted by a murderous fire from the German batteries. The station of Fleury was enveloped in a red haze as shell after shell hit the red-tiled roof. The village was like a gigantic Noah's Ark hammered to pieces by a child. The streets were littered with dead cows and horses, lying on their backs, all four legs stiff in the air. Furniture abandoned by the refugees was scattered everywhere, and chickens and ducks fled squawking before us.

We took the village in a series of short rushes, but the Germans pulverised it with shell fire and as we advanced we lost heavily. Once Fleury was cleared, the regiment was reformed and we started off in the direction of Douaumont. The original intention was to take the village that night, but casualties were so heavy that it was decided to wait for what was left of the second battalion before pushing on. So, we crouched in a valley where we were spotted by airplanes and shelled till nightfall.

At dusk, I took a detail of sixteen men down to bring up food. This not being the Foreign Legion, the soup kitchens were considerably in the rear; in fact, it took us four hours to find them. The comments of some of the old *légionaires* were acid. The negro prize fighter was mumbling and grumbling to himself as he forged through the mud.

"What's the matter now, Bob?"

"Hungry yesterday. Hungry today. Hungry the day before. Don't care how soon my military experience terminates."

Neither did I.

We had to keep to the roads, as the mud was impassable in the open fields; but on the other hand, the roads were being continually swept by a fire from Austrian 88's and 130's, the shells that give no warning. Between Fleury and Souville the road was strewn with broken artillery wagons, exploded caissons, mangled and puffed-up bodies of horses, men, rifles, equipment, baby carriages, mattresses and birdcages.

Finally, we discovered the field kitchens and fell to for a square meal before starting back—natural but imprudent. You can't go three days without food and then gorge: two minutes later we slid our lunches to a man, and compromised on a cup of coffee apiece. The stew might have been edible when we left, but it was nothing but cold grease by the time we reached the line.

Of the sixteen, who started out, seven got back. We arrived at the edge of the wood, just at dawn, and then the worst happened: in the final rush to the trenches, the man carrying the two canvas buckets of coffee was hit, and of course fell on them as he went down. This was bad, for the men in line had been two days with nothing to drink. Some of them scooped up snow and ate it, which only made matters worse, adding dysentery to thirst.

Dawn and fresh complications. The village of Douaumont was not held, as we had supposed, by French Infantry, but by German machine guns, and our line was exposed to fire from the right flank and rear. Sandbags had to be placed—at any price. . . .

The morning mist cleared, and we stared on our handiwork. Line after line of grey-green German dead lay stretched in front of us, piled three feet high in spots—almost as if the slow-rolling waves, that come after a storm, had been frozen as they climbed the beach.

Heads rose from the enemy's trenches. Germans and French stood up and looked at each other at a distance of only forty yards numbed. Nobody fired, nobody spoke. Both sides were fought to a standstill. . . .

At nightfall sounds of arriving reinforcements came from the

German lines, and we prepared to repel a fresh attack. But there was stealthy movement behind us, and *Chasseurs Alpins* began dribbling into the trenches. Our relief had come also—and just in time. We had scarcely dropped over the hill into comparative safety when the German attack broke loose. But they were met by fresh troops, and we could hear the yells of the *Chasseurs* driving forward a counter attack.

All we could think of was our thirst. I waded into a shell hole and drank greedily from the green-scummed water. A rocket flared up— what I had taken for a log, lying in the pool, was a corpse! I didn't give a damn, only glad I had drunk before I saw it. A shell burst unpleasantly close and I lumbered after the disappearing section.

From a letter:—

Next day, we hung around in some woods about three miles back of the line in reserve. As luck would have it, the Boches chose that day for a systematic search of the surrounding country with their big guns. They began at six in the morning and kept it up until five that night. I saw whole squads of men go up twenty feet in the air, sacks on their backs, and come down a shower of arms, legs, heads and red hash. That night, we pulled out for the rear, and marched fifteen kilometres. You may guess what condition we were in when I tell you two men dropped dead from exhaustion.

We stayed a day in a little town, and then marched twelve kilometres, where we took autos, just back of Verdun. Another man dropped dead on the way. The autos took us to a village about 60 kilometres off. We stayed, there one day, and then started marching 25 miles a day. The next three days were like a nightmare to me. I couldn't eat, and I had the colic and dysentery as had over 75% of the men. How we ever marched is a mystery; every day men dropped dead. Anyway, here we are for a few days' rest. The brigade went into it with 5,500 rifles, and came out with 1,100, but we stopped 'em, by God.

Best luck, old man, and write soon.

Affec,

Ding.

CHAPTER NINE

Verdun Again—and Spring

With the fresh drafts, Ole Neilson, a huge Swede who had been wounded in the Legion, joined the 170th. During his long stay in hospital he had got badly out of hand, and I had a job keeping the peace between him and Georges, our sergeant. I finally persuaded Georges that if he would be lenient with Neilson in rest billets, he would find him worth the trouble in line. In consequence, Ole stuck to me like a big overgrown puppy. We shared everything, though I was not partial to the tins of dead fish and other Swedish delicacies he got from home.

25th April. Orders to move up. Verdun again. Bad news. Everyone gloomy. Motor trucks. They evidently need us badly.

26th April. Faubourg Pavé—not so bad. Found pianola—wild night.

27th April. Hear we're to go up into line tonight. Rumours say counter attack. Everyone pretty sober. The very names around here are ominous. *Mort Homme-Ravin de la Mort.* Even Vaux and Douaumont sound like big guns.

The long blue column trudged in silence through the town; shoulders hunched, jaws thrust forward—dogged resignation. On the outskirts of the *Faubourg Pavé* a mechanical piano in a ruined *café* came suddenly to life under the ministrations of some *Zouaves*, and jangled out *Mariette*. Magic! Squad after squad took up the refrain and with roars of laughter waltzed up the road. A hundred yards further on the music died away, and gloom settled down once more.

Past Souville, down through Fleury (now nothing but a hole in the ground), swinging to the right of Douaumont we finally halted on the other side of the valley of the Bois de Chapîtres.

Then came the weary business of a relief. Ten steps forward.

Stop. Ten minutes wait, punctuated by raking shell fire groans of the wounded and curses from the rest of us.

"*Bon dieu! Quest ce qu ils foutrent la bas?*" (Good God! What the hell are they doing over there?)

Finally, however, by shuffling and pushing, it was over. Ole and I found ourselves in a shallow dugout along the Décauville ledge. He had forgotten a lot of his trench warfare cunning, and his rage was comical on discovering that someone in the other regiment had exchanged a filthy, mud-crusted rifle for his own nice clean one which he had left outside the dugout.

All morning shells howled over the crest of the hill back of us and burst in the valley below. Ole was an optimist.

"By yiminy Dave, I tink we're in a dead angle. Dey can't reach us here!"

My gloomy reply, "There ain't no such animal in this God damn war," was drowned by a formidable explosion ten yards off. Three seconds later there was a dull thud just outside and going out to investigate we discovered a 210" shell, which fortunately had not exploded. A slow smile crept over Ole's face and he burst out laughing.

"By yiminy you bane right. Dere ain't no such animal!"

For two days preparations were made for a counter attack. All the work was done under heavy bombardment and losses were according. An old quarry was turned into an ammunition dump and filled with small arms, 37" hand grenades and trench mortar bombs, as reserve ammunition for the attack.

Next day a shell lit bang in the middle of it and the ammunition went skyward in one glorious explosion, taking twenty men with it.

We seemed to be dogged by bad luck. As we stood to, ready to go over, the company on our right was practically annihilated by four 155" shells from French batteries—shorts. Result—when we went over, our right flank was dangling in the air. We gained our objective and dug in, but were exposed to galling enfilading fire and were outflanked by a counter attack of grenadiers of the Prussian guard. They came forward running zigzag, hurling potato-masher grenades. It was a wonderful occasion for sport from the point of view of shooting—either you got the man before he threw the grenade, or the grenade got you.

The support troops came up on the right flank and the serious business of consolidating the position began.

Ole was now in his stride. During a food fatigue once, the detail

VERDUN, APRIL, 1916

ran into a barrage. Six men were killed and one wounded. The others waited in shell holes, hoping for it to lift. Not so Ole. Carefully depositing his soup kettles in a shell hole, he picked up the wounded man and carried him to Fort Souville. The detail was still waiting when he got back. Announcing that the men in line were hungry, he picked his buckets up again, and walked straight on through the barrage. In three days he won three citations.

Meanwhile my backbone got in the way of a bit of shrapnel and I was ordered down with the next convoy of wounded, for treatment and rest. At nightfall we started. Somebody strapped my pack on my shoulders for me, and I followed the walking cases. Down across the valley, stumbling into shell holes and tripping over the corpses that littered the narrow path, now in inky darkness, now in the blinding light of a rocket, we shoved along in fearful haste. The ground was swept, from time to time, by salvos of high explosive shells. Sometimes they took their toll, and the surgeons' work was reduced. The Fort of Souville rose in front of us and in we all crowded. We found ourselves in a jumble of troops, horses and wagons, and stretcher bearers, waiting for the storm of shells to abate before continuing on their divers missions.

I left the fort and wandered back to the *Maison Blanche* a clearing station, hoping for a ride on the running board of an ambulance to *Faubourg Pavé*. The house was dark, but from somewhere in the back came low moans. Groping my way along, I opened a door and stepped into a medieval torture chamber.

On the floor writhed a huge black Moroccan, held down by four *infirmiers*. The sweat of agony was on him. His eyes rolled white—he groaned through his clenched teeth—bright red blood gushed over his black skin from a jagged wound in the groin. Two, white-coated surgeons worked with fiendish intensity. And flickering candles threw grotesque, reaching shadows on the ceiling. . . . The post had evidently run out of morphia. Thirty yards down the road I saw the house go up in splinters as a salvo of heavy shells struck home. All that pain and trouble for nothing!

★★★★★★

At the *Faubourg Pavé* the search for quarters was a nightmare. The place was infested with Algerian troops, none too friendly to a lone French soldier at best; and by now my arms were hanging limp and paralyzed.

I couldn't light a candle; the only way to find a safe place for the night was to try the doors with my shoulder, and if they opened, to listen for breathing. At last I found an empty room, and went to sleep with my feet planted against the door, and my sack still strapped to my back. Next day I found the wagon train and a doctor, who patched me up in record time. . . .

In my absence Ole had been distinguishing himself further. During a German counter attack, he recovered one of our machine guns, turned it on them, and when the ammunition was exhausted, retired carrying it with him.

I was still on the sick list, but had volunteered to take a message up to our major, in line. At Souville I was told the regiment was being relieved, but that the major was still in the trenches. So off again, with two Red Cross men as guides. We had barely started when all Hell broke loose. The stretcher bearers, pointing to the left, shouted some garbled directions and disappeared into the night. For a moment I was completely lost, but the flash of the next salvo showed me the path lined with dead. I was guided across the valley by the flash of shells, and I knew, each time I stumbled over a corpse, that I was on the right road. Suddenly a rocket disclosed a little procession twenty yards to my right. Four stretcher bearers with their usual load, followed by a lanky figure I would have known anywhere.

"Ole!"

"Py yiminy! Is that you Dave? Dey tell me you're dead. See you later." Then, as an afterthought: "Py Christ, I'm glad you're not!"

We passed, on our lawful occasions. I heard the story later. During the relief, the remains of the third section had been practically wiped out by a barrage. Six men had been killed outright, the sergeant and another, wounded. The other man ran for the dressing station, but Georges was badly hit—eye, both wrists, and side.

At this point Ole stepped in. Sitting calmly beside him, he cut the sergeant's equipment to pieces, made tourniquets of the straps, and stopped the bleeding of one wound after another. Then he waited. Presently four stretcher bearers hurried along and he hailed them. Georges was too weak from loss of blood, to walk, but on hearing he was not wounded in the legs, the stretcher bearers refused to carry him. Ole admitted having lost his temper. Georges told me afterwards, he was afraid Neilson was going to clean them up. Anyway, cocking his rifle, he convinced them it was healthier to carry the sergeant in— they were doing so when I passed them.

★★★★★★

Spring—and six whole weeks in front line trenches in a quiet sector. Wild flowers grew along the edge of the trenches, and some little brown birds were nesting in the eave of our dugout. Between bombardments, came the calls of thrushes and blackbirds and finches— once I heard a lark. There were drawbacks of course, other than rats and shells. The Germans had three mines under our lines; we could hear their sappers working at others, and wondered, vaguely, when they would be touched off. The muffled subterranean tapping day and night, might have got on our nerves, but how could we worry with the sun shining! Days of quiet reading, bathing in the canal, endless games of *Manille* and symphonies on cigar box fiddles. Besides, the Battle of the Somme was raging, and we were wondering when our turn would come.

Before the end of July we pulled out of line, and moved up to the Somme sector.

CHAPTER TEN

Battle of the Somme

All around us was activity and hustle; parks of artillery waiting to go up into line, shell dumps, barbed wire duck boards and all sorts of stores, ammunition, and equipment. Narrow gauge railways spread out in all directions, and every ten minutes a toy train loaded with enormous shells puffed busily on its way to the forward ammunition dumps.

The roar of guns was continuous night and day; and from dusk till dawn a flickering, red glare lit the horizon.

July 25th, 1916.

Dear Gerald:

We are moving up again shortly. At present we are in wooden huts about seventeen miles from the front. The band is giving a concert, and over the music you can hear a continual booming—the most devilish bombardment I have ever heard. It makes you feel as if you were at a comic opera, with a storm gathering, while the villagers stroll about the *plaza*. It would be funny if we had not been there before and did not know what all the cannonading meant.

I hope I get plugged this time for better or worse. I'm tired of being the lone, last survivor of gory battlefields, the only human, civilized eye witness, so to speak. God! how those guns are roaring! I have never heard anything like it before. Wish we would hurry up and get into it. Funny—I'll be nervous as a marmoset now till I get right into the first line, and they start bursting over us. Always the same—almost trembling till the riot starts, and then feeling like a kid going home for Christmas vacation

July 28th.

. . . . . The flag was decorated this morning, so we should be on our way ere long! I'm pleasantly confident that I'm going to be wounded this time—My God, it's about time—two years without a rest is enough for any man

July 30th.

. . . . . Here we are, eight miles nearer. We can smell the powder and corpses. One regiment of our division attacked last night. The 174th attacks tonight, and we will probably attack tomorrow

August 2nd.

. . . . . Hell of a big explosion just now. Whole sky red. Shells popping like a curtain fire. . . . It's all hell to pay somewhere and no pennies hot

August 3rd.

. . . . . . Know all about it. One of our shell and hand grenade depots went up in a blaze of glory, and killed about twenty men. Lucky it wasn't the 15-inch shell depot. The Second *Zouaves* of our division have been relieved. Came down cut to pieces, one battalion cut up and captured; the other two with about 150 men apiece left

August 5th.

Seems we are to have the honour of attacking Clery. Whether we take it or not remains to be seen. It is the worse sector on the French front in these parts. This seems to be the devil's own fight, but it can't be one hell of a lot worse than Verdun. . . . .

On August eleventh the regiment moved up. As night fell we trudged along the road, a high hill on one side and a river and marshes on the other. Almost immediately we came under fire of the German long-range guns.

Some of the shells plopped harmlessly into the river; others burst on the cliff above us, and some took their toll. Then we came out on the level, passing through the ruins of Veaux (Somme)—the ghastly skeleton of what had once been a village. Marching along its main street, we clambered out of one big shell hole full of water into another, finally reaching the third line and effected the relief, then out on a work party.

August 13th.

. . . . . Just got back from working between the first and second lines in plain day. Of course, we were shelled out by high explosives. Damn that fool captain of ours. At present we are in reserve for two divisions. If anything goes wrong, we stop the gap. Hell of a job, for we will have to come up under heavy shell fire after the attack has started. There was a little fog this morning, so their fire on our trenches was poor, but now it is a beautiful day, and they are dropping them all around and into us.

11 a. m. Aug. 13 (?)

By golly, they wanted to send us out again. But the lieutenant sent us back. My Lord, those guns are busy. They are beginning to strafe our part of the line now. They move up and down the line, concentrating, and giving each a bit of music for a while, and then move on. This war gets worse and more terrible every day, Gerald. I don't see how flesh and blood stands it. It makes me sick when some bloated profiteer sits in his armchair in Paris and talks about going on to the limit. If those people had to go through 16 hours shelling, and didn't die of heart failure, we would have peace tomorrow.

And don't you believe all those hardy *poilu* yarns. They are spun by men in the reserve who spend all their time in quiet parts of the line, where they have shelters 40 feet deep and get about ten field gun shells a day. I think this war must be getting on my nerves, for every day I get more and more fretful, and I used to like these affairs . . . .

. . . . The attack has started. The minute they saw our men on the parapet, a lot of Germans came running over, hands up, and cursing the *Kaiser*. They were knocking hell out of our trenches.

Aug. 14, 12:30 p. m.

At five prompt, last evening, we started off. We had communication trenches for about 200 yards, and then they thinned out into mere ditches. Imagine lines of men, Indian file, rushing down the ditches, crouching in the deeper places to catch their breath, then rushing over the shallow ones, mouths coated with dust and powder fumes, and hearts as big as toy balloons from the running and excitement. Big shells dropping on each side of the trenches. We climbed out to cross a road and had a glance at what was going on. The first and second waves were 500

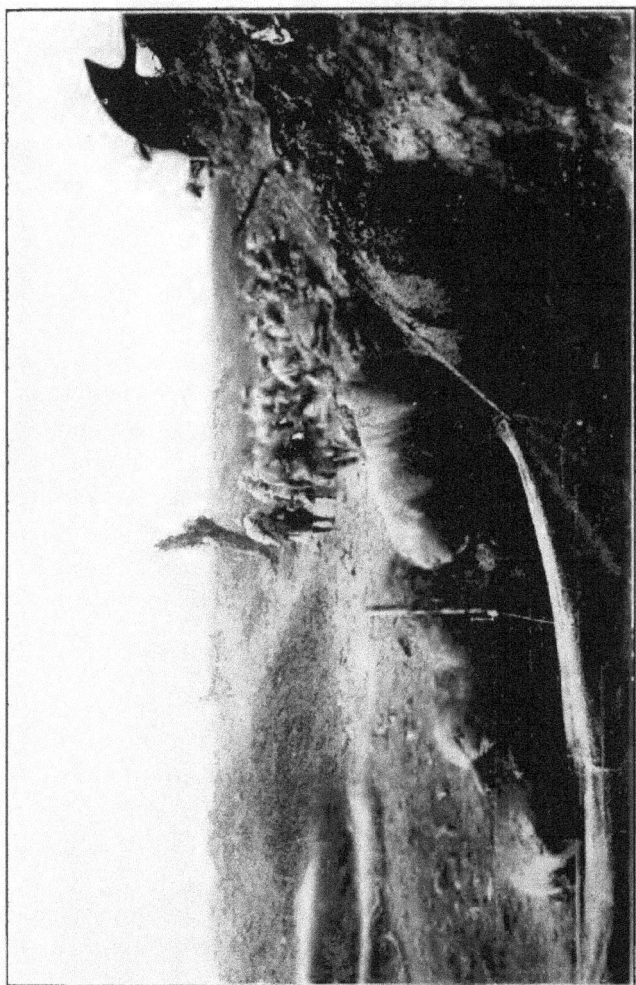

INTO THE FIRST GERMAN LINE, SOMME, 1916

yards ahead, deployed in open order, and going like hell. But there was a machine gun tickling our flank, so we rushed across the road to take advantage of the bank on the other side. Then open country again, and catching it from everything.

The German machine gun nest on the left began to cripple the attack. This meant the regiments on our left and right would go forward, flanks in the air.

Our major sized it up at a glance, and decided to sacrifice his battalion. "Face to the left! Open order! Grenadiers forward! Go and get 'em!" It cost six hundred men, but the battalion coming on behind us went through clear. Finally, we got into position. The 2nd and 3rd battalions had taken the trenches, and we were four hundred yards back of 'em in an open field as reserve. We were told to dig ourselves in as best we could. I went back to some Boche rifle pits to get some big tools. You should have seen the work of our 75's. Every damn pit was full of dead bodies. Disgusting sight—still pink and white instead of the yellow and black they will be—flies all over them. I found my tools and started digging with Neilson, my fighting mate.

Just as we got started he was called away to go on a water detail. At sundown, 8 o'clock, the Boches started a counter attack, and started bombarding the landscape. Their big high explosives were bursting two or three yards from my hole, but I was so tired I went to sleep in spite of them. At midnight, someone landed all fours on my chest, and lay down beside me. I thought it was Neilson, but it was someone else. He lay there for a while, but they landed a couple of big ones near us, and he cleared out. I was just getting to sleep when someone else crawled in. He stayed a while, till they began to get unpleasantly close, and then persuaded me to make a break for some rifle pits to the left. When we got there, he disappeared, and I spent a miserable quarter of an hour trying to find a place.

Just then they began shelling the pits, and men dropped so fast that I decided to go home. There I found a friend who, while I was visiting, had had a shell drop on him, fortunately a dud. We dug out the pit and went to sleep. About 4 a. m. another Boche attack broke loose. Next night Neilson came back. He couldn't get back the night before on account of continual curtain firing. He had hardly arrived before I was called up for a food detail. Two miles there and back. It's bad enough scurrying over bad places, corpses, and marmite holes, with a rifle and equipment, but when you have a couple of soup kettles, as well, it's pure hell. . . .

6:30 p. m.

There is something up on our left. The 75's are rolling like drums, and the Boches are bombarding to keep them quiet and under cover. I think we were to attack, but the Boches may have beat us to it. Their curtain fire is getting nearer and nearer our dugout. God help us now.

August 13th, 7:45 p. m.

Well, they seem to have let up for a bit. They may begin again any minute, and it only takes one shell to do the trick, but it's different from seeing those big shells creep nearer and nearer, exploding in perfect time. Hell, they are at it again. The worst of it is they don't let up at sundown—on the contrary; and shell fire is twice as terrifying at night. At least to me.. . .More later, perhaps.

Ding.

The shells descended upon us, and Ole and I crouched in our shelter, smoking furiously.

"Well Ole, it looks as if we're in for it this time. Do you believe there is anything on the other side?"

"I dunno. I don't believe much in nothing." And, with his usual afterthought: "Anyway, if a shell bane hit this dugout we bane go together."

We were interrupted by a series of crashes and screams from the pits some twenty yards back, and rushed over to see what we could do. One of the young class was standing with his back to the parapet, breathing spasmodically, a glassy look in his eye and the whole back of his head blown off. No time to waste on him—reflex action. (I once saw a man buried with the earth heaving up and down, from muscular convulsion, as they covered him.) The others were in a bad way. One was disembowelled, and the sergeant was screaming—and with cause. Both legs were shattered, but the thing that broke his nerve was a shrapnel bullet through the palm of his hand.

We dug them out and bandaged them. The poor devil started screaming: "Put me out of it! Be good fellows, and put me out of it! I'm done!" We reassured him in one breath and cursed the Boche in the next: "You're all right old man. Steady on. The stretcher bearers will be along presently—God damn those Christ-bitten . . . . . Hope to hell we get another chance at them before we clear out!"

I gave him one of my morphine tablets. That left one for Neilson and two for me; one for a wound, and two to go out with if I were badly crippled.

The morphia began to take effect, and the sergeant quieted for a moment. Suddenly he screamed again, and then, in a strange, small voice:

"Can't you stop that man screaming? He's getting on my nerves."

The stretcher bearers turned up. I scribbled a label that he had had morphine, and stuck it in his tunic. Twenty yards to the rear all five of them were wiped out by a shell.

I had copped it in the groin the first day of the attack, but as Ole was firmly convinced that nothing would happen to him while he was with me, I tried to stick it out. After four days though, the pain was unbearable.

"Sorry Ole. Can't stick it any more. Try and get a light one yourself, and get to the same hospital."

"That's right. You got to go old man. Goodbye. I think I'll get it next time."

I dragged myself along to the clearing station, where I was examined and ticketed. I took such of my things as the Red Cross men had not stolen, and crawled into an ambulance. I never saw Ole again. . . .

★★★★★★

The ambulance jounced over the rough roads.

"Stop! Stop! Oh, for God's sake stop. My shoulder. My poor leg!"

The driver was green and pulled up to see what was wrong. As he appeared at the door, he was greeted by a storm of protest.

"*Bougre de charroigne d' embusqué!* Do you want us to be killed, after getting this far back?—Get on—step on it—beat it!"

They dumped me in a hut on the outskirts of a field hospital, and there I lay, forgotten, in the rush to entrain the wounded. . . . Two days later orders came to evacuate the place, and in collecting the cots, I was discovered—so low, they rushed me to hospital at Amiens. The battle of the Somme was still going full blast, and the town was crammed with wounded and British staff. Every hospital was full—they finally found me a bed in the citadel. . . .

This place was a catch-all for the general overflow—everything from prisoners awaiting court martial, to shell shock cases. One poor devil was muzzled and strapped to the bed, for he bit and clawed furiously at anyone coming within reach. Another was fully convinced that the whole damn war was being waged for the benefit of the moving picture companies. He refused to take his medicine, go to the shower bath or even get up, before he had been reassured that the lights were correct, and camera-men waiting and ready. A third had been blown up in a sapping operation. He was a public nuisance. At any hour of the night or day he would steal through the wards, open a *table de nuit*, tie a string to the vessel inside, and close the door again.

Then came a regular ritual. Holding the string tightly in one hand, and striking an attitude, he would begin: "*Attention! Attention! Couchez-vous par terre, tons le monde. Tirez!*" (Everyone lie down! Fire!) On the last command the string was yanked, the little door flew open, and, *crash. . . .*!!! Satisfied that he had carried out his orders and blown up the bridge, or whatever it was, he would go back to bed and sleep for a few hours more. After the first two or three times, the sight of him creeping through the ward was enough to set up a howl of rage from the rest of us. "*Bon dieu, c'est le fou, encore! Gardes les pots!*" (Good Lord, it's that idiot, again! Look out!)

Military hospitals are wonderful things—in novels. Spotless, sunlit wards, sympathetic doctors, charming Red Cross nurses, and well-behaved wounded. Propped up on fresh pillows, with neat strawberry stained bandages round their heads, they smile in heroic endurance. Emergency hospitals don't come up to scratch. The floors may be scrubbed, the walls and ceilings remain in *status quo*. Spiders have fled from the reek of disinfectants, but their deserted homes still wave gently in the breeze. Doctors are overworked—efficient but hectic; and the charming nurse is replaced by some fat old orderly, who, as a great favour, smuggles in wine—at a price. If rude and unromantic the treatment is effective, and wonderful operations have been done in these improvised hospitals.

CHAPTER ELEVEN

I Change Arms—Then Armies

"Unfit for the Infantry. Send him to the Artillery."

The judgment of three medical colonels, after the doctor had drawn diagrams on me in blue pencil, and the oculist had put in his report. And so to the Artillery School at Satory. . . .

Satory was ten minutes from Versailles and only an hour from Paris. The major's striker sold bits of paper, stamped with the battery's seal, for a franc apiece. Then you wrote your own leave, made a squiggle for the signature, payed somebody three *francs* to replace you on guard duty—*et voilà!* Perfect—unless you were caught. Better still, Satory was only three miles from Buc, where I found many old friends who had transferred to the Aviation. One of them, a schoolmate, was *brigadier moniteur,* (corporals and sergeants in cavalry and artillery are called *brigadiers* and *maréchaux de logis*), in charge of the American *éléves pilots* (cadet pilots).

Pete was having a deuce of a time keeping the new ones in order. It was a different story from running a squad in the cavalry, with the discipline of the whole French Army to back him. They were nice boys and keen on the job. But they seemed to think that, having volunteered before America came into the war, they were released from all rules, regulations, and discipline to which the rest of the French Army might be subject. Quite a problem!

He thought of me. Foreign Legion from the beginning of the war—if I didn't know what discipline was, who did? The very motto, on the colours of the Legion, substitutes "*discipline*" for "*patrie.*"—Just the man!

I was asked over to dinner, and the new recruits were invited to meet and talk with this veteran of two-and-a-half years. I gave a marvellous harangue on duty, discipline, and obligations. I got more smug

106

with each drink. I pointed out that it was a fine act on their part to volunteer, that they deserved a great deal of credit for it, and that I was sure they would do well when they got to the front.

At the same time, the fact that they had come of their own free will was offset by the point that they had been admitted, at once, into the most sought after arm of the service. That their French colleagues now training with them had only gained entrance to the school at Buc through conspicuous bravery, or wounds that incapacitated them for the infantry or artillery. Therefore, they all started on an equal footing, and they should consider themselves just as subject to regulations as the French!

I piled it on till Taps sounded, and started back to Satory. It was a dark night, and after two or three attempts to find my way through the woods, I gave it up and went back to the aviation school, returning to Satory for roll call next morning.

I slid into line just in time to answer my name, but I was told that the captain wished to speak to me, at once. The interview was short but sharp.

"Where were you last night?"

"At the aviation school, Captain."

"What were you doing there?"

"Oh, just talking to some friends."

"Why didn't you return to the barracks in time for call over?"

"I lost my way in the woods."

"Hm! Bad as that, was it? Well, there was a counter roll call last night, and you were missing. I don't care whether you're an American or not—you must be taught that there is such a thing as discipline in the army. You have come from the Legion; somebody should have hammered it into you by this time. No explanations! Shut up! Four days' prison."

So, for four days, the disciple of discipline meditated on the beauty of discipline—for others.

We were trained on the old 155 guns—*Système Benge* breech— obsolete. Almost as dangerous to the gun crew as to the enemy! On the firing grounds . . . . . a recruit pulled the lanyard—no result. Misfire! He opened the breech to see what had happened—the powder sack was smouldering. In a frenzy he tried to close and lock it, fumbling badly. With a backhander, the sergeant knocked him flying, and in the same stride threw open the breech. He yanked out the burning sack, throwing it on the ground, to burn harmlessly.

"Gerbaut, four days' prison! That'll teach you not to monkey with a breech till five minutes after a misfire! If that powder had caught in the gun you'd all have been blown to bits. *Brigadier*, go on with the practice—" and he walked off to the infirmary, to have his burned hand dressed.

★★★★★★

Change of regiments. Due to mathematics at college, I was sent to a sound-ranging section at Vincennes. For a fortnight we did odd jobs around the artillery barracks of the 13th field guns, waiting for our officers and apparatus to materialize. Here I got the reputation of a magnificent horseman. Though fairly well broken and trained, the Canadian remounts did not understand French, so the French drivers were up against it. "*R-r-r-r-r!*" they would say, the mustangs looked interested but unconvinced. "*Salles bêtes!*" They were as stubborn as mules. "*B-r-r-r-r-r-r*"—this time accompanied by a threatening gesture.

The Canadians understood the gesture and registered indignation and restiveness. "*Quils sont féroces!*" Stepping up to a horse, I grabbed the bridle: "Back up, boy—back!" A look of relief came over the mustang's face and he backed gently and gracefully, delighted to oblige. From then on I did overtime handling remounts.

We found a new way to get out of barracks. Forming in line, we would march across the yard, with an obliging corporal shouting fierce orders. "One, two—one, two! Left—Left—Left! Even if this *is* a fatigue, you're going to march in step!"

"Halt! Where are you going?" This from the sergeant on guard, at the gate.

"Fatigue to get hay." And we swung smartly out of the barracks, dispersing two hundred yards down the street, for the four corners of Paris.

It started at the "Hole in the Wall." Billy Dugan, some XVIth Canadian Highlanders and myself. We adjourned to Weber's—more drinks, and decided to hold Grand Fleet manoeuvers on the Champs Elysées. Seven *fiacres* were commandeered. The flag-ship was stocked with ammunition, rum, whisky and H. E. Brandy. Being in blue, I was admiral. I named my captains, and off we went: line ahead formation.

Every light, rakish craft on the horizon wanted to come alongside and board us; but, somehow, when women join a show of that sort, men disappear mysteriously. I signalled "repel boarders." This was neatly done by exploding our gas balloons with cigarettes.

The next evolution, line abreast across the whole avenue, brought down an attacking flotilla of police and *gendarmes*. They caught sight of me in French uniform, and the fight was on. Dugan was in blue too, but having eaten a tube of tooth paste he was foaming at the mouth. Not even the *gendarmes* cared to tackle that apparition. A brawny Highlander saved the day. Kilts flying, heedless of traffic, he tore down the line, bellowing:

"Change carriages! Race around the fleet and back!"

Instantly every one piled out, giving an imitation of a subway rush going to Jerusalem. The police fell back and we steamed full speed ahead for a restaurant in the Bois and scuttled our ships. . . .

. . . . The brawny Scot had been sinking lower, and lower. Of a sudden his eyes became fixed—he sat bolt upright—he bounded from his chair. Out on the road stood two steam rollers, deserted for the night. Inviting wisps of smoke floated from their chimneys. No need to explain—with a whoop they surged after him, and climbed aboard. The French have a huge sense of humour, but most *gendarmes* are Corsican—and I was A. W. O. L. anyway. When I last saw them, they were waddling down the road like outraged hens—the Great Steam Roller Race had started. . . .

★★★★★★

It was at Vincennes that Mata Hari was shot. Every week we were called out for military executions.

"*Mort, avec dégradation militaire*" For desertion in the face of the enemy, or in time of war—Death, with military dishonour. We used to laugh—what difference could it make, if they were going to shoot you anyway? That was in the early days. After we had seen our first execution. . . .

It might have been a parade, or an investiture. Everyone spick and span. The regiment in a hollow square—officers, colours, and band, in the centre. "To the Colours" the band blared out. *Was* this going to be an execution? Must be. There was the prisoner standing between a guard with fixed bayonets. "Right shoulder arms!" Yes, we usually presented arms at this point. Drums and bugles sounded "Attention!"

★★★★★★

Soldier Jean Dubois, class of 1898—married, father of three children. *Croix de Guerre*, two palms desertion while on leave, and attempted escape to Spain. (The voice droned on), absent twenty days time of war tried by court martial Dijon found guilty. *Mort avec dégradation militaire.*

A group of non-coms gathered round the prisoner. When they stepped aside, his coat hung open and ragged—buttons, decorations, insignia were gone. We saw him start at one side of the square, the guard around him, hands clinched, head up, looking as if he'd see us all in hell. I think most of us were sorry for him . . . but he couldn't understand that, and only felt hundreds of eyes denying him. About half way, it began to get him. His head drooped—his hands hung loose. They took him around the whole of that dreadful square. . . . At the end, he could hardly shuffle along. I think he was in a sort of stupor when they put him up against the post, for he never made a sign when they asked him if he wanted his eyes bandaged. Then a squad, from another regiment, stepped up. And they shot him. . . . A little, crumpled heap on the ground. "*Mort avec dégradation militaire.*"

★★★★★★

The life at Vincennes was too good to last. Our lieutenant turned up while we were all A. W. O. L. in Paris, and decided that we had run wild quite long enough. Within a week we were on our way to the front.

There were thirty-five of us in the unit—mixed pickles. Barring those chosen for their mathematics, and kids who had volunteered before their class was called, we were all cripples.

Castagnole was a dark sallow boy, with a saturnine sense of humour. He had stopped a 77 with his back and was pronounced unfit for further service. After working in the Chemical Warfare Laboratory for three months, he volunteered for the front again. Though thoroughly disillusioned, and often in pain, he never shirked his job.

Red headed, hot tempered, Durupt had been a professor at the University of Nancy, but though he examined young officers in Mathematics, was only a corporal himself.

The sergeant was an antique dealer, and our other corporal's chief claim to fame was the fact that he had sung with Mayol. I imagine it was a case of "*Heinie played with Sousa once—but only once.*"

★★★★★★

At Boncourt in the St. Mihiel sector, no one wanted us. They seemed to think a Sound Ranging section would draw fire, so for weeks we were shunted from one farm house to another.

For a while we found shelter in a *barraque Adrian*. It was bitterly cold. We had a miserable little stove, but no coal; even the partitions in the hut were coated with ice. The potatoes froze and in the army when the potatoes freeze there is one result—scurvy. Our gums swelled and oozed black blood, but it wasn't till our teeth began to wobble that we recognised the trouble, and sent for lime juice and tinned vegetables. The hut was infested with cooties and fleas, but the last straw was added when one man spread the itch.

In spite of these little trials, we began the work of installing the section: building dugouts for the advance posts, setting up the microphones, cutting and planting telephone poles. This was great fun as the ground was frozen hard, and a pick was as likely as not to bounce back and crack you over the shins. Then miles of telephone wire was strung out, connecting the posts with the central office; and finally the central itself was ready.

I soon discovered that life in the instrument room lacked privacy and independence, so when the wind and observation station was established, I put in for it.

The idea was to note the velocity and direction of the wind and temperature of the air every time a German shot was fired. When it came to running an *annomètre*, stop watch, telephone, twirl a thermometer on a string, and register everything in a note book, all in the same moment, I used to regret the loss of our caudal appendices.

I lived at the post, on a hill just over a wireless dugout. Somewhat exposed to wind and shell fire, but off duty I was master of my fate.

Boom! A shell would whirl overhead. *Br-r-r-r* would go the party wire, joining the outposts to central. The lieutenant's voice "Hello! Posts one, two, three, four, five, six? Set your microphones." *Ring—Br-r-r-r* "Hello, the wind! They are firing." (You don't say so!)

I would climb out, set up my instruments, put on the telephone receiver, and hang the mouthpiece around my neck.

Boom!

"Shot P 1."

"Shot P 3."

"Shot P 4."

"Yes, Yes—Yes! Hello, P 2, didn't you hear it?"

"No."

"Hello, the wind! What's the direction?"

"40°—speed 60—temperature 10° C."

And so on this way for hours, rain or shine, till the German firing stopped.

Thunderstorms were not so amusing. The lightning would strike the wire and box my ears.

"Hello, Central! there's a thunderstorm overhead."

"Yes—yes! We know."

That was all the satisfaction I got.

I shared the dugout with a wireless operator, Oursan. He was twice my age—a master carpenter—hard boiled on the surface, but one of the whitest men I have ever known. We lived, cooped up together in a tiny room for months, without a quarrel.

Post number three telephoned in one day, that Fritz was putting down a gas barrage and his gas mask leaked. The sergeant, knowing I was headed that way, asked me to take him up a new mask. I passed our dugout on the way. Oursan was watching the barrage between us and post number three.

"Hello, where are you going?"

"Nosal's gas mask is out of commission. I'm taking him up another."

"Through *that?*"

"Yes, I hope so."

"If that good for nothing, slack-jawed fool can't take care of his gas mask, why in hell doesn't he come down and get another, himself? What business is it of yours anyway? You're nothing but a god-damned halfwit, forging through barrages for a fool like that. Here—you stay here—I'll take it."

"Nope, can't do it. Lessure told me to go."

"Told you—told you hell! Don't you know he couldn't *order* you to? It's a volunteer job. Oh, well, go ahead! But I wash my hands of you."

So I went ahead, but Oursan went with me to the edge of the barrage. ,

Half an hour later I found him where I had left him—still cursing. He got distinctly rude when I asked him why he was waiting. But I saw he had his gas mask ready, and I knew my man. If I had been hit, I wouldn't have lain there long.

★★★★★★

I wore *sabots* stuffed with straw to keep my feet warm, and thought myself rather clever. Then I tried to climb down the ice-coated ladder. . . . I landed sudden and hard, and through some strange contortion, probably the same by which men acquire black eyes, stamped on my little finger. My hand got black—two days later I saw the doctor.

"*Tiens, tiens!* How did this happen?"

"I stepped on it."

"Are you trying to be impertinent?"

I explained the circumstances; he grunted, and took up a pair of scissors.

"Look the other way." . . . . . I didn't try *sabots* again.

★★★★★★

"So, you come from America?"

"Yes."

"Did you ever meet my cousin Jean Dupont? He went out to Buenos Ayres."

"No." And the conversation would languish.

When we declared war everything changed, and I was bombarded with questions. About this time I began to think I had better get into my own army. My first application was returned with a note attached: If I would return to America and put in for Plattsburg they would consider my application. "Very much obliged to Jesus," as the British Tommies sang.

Through friends at court, I was allowed to take the exams in Paris, while on leave. The day came, and I presented myself—scared stiff. The three officers, who were to examine me, whispered among themselves; the Major (afterwards General) Nolan spoke.

"Mr. King, we don't know much about the French Army, and you probably know less about the American, so we don't see how we can examine you." My heart sank.

"But we have looked at your record and are proposing you for a first lieutenancy, infantry."

As I left the building, an officer was coming up the steps. In my ignorance I mistook the black braid on his sleeve for a misplaced mourning band. There was something in his face, however, which spelt general, so I clicked to and saluted. Just in time! He seized an unobservant lieutenant by the arm and spun him round.

"You're in uniform! Are you a soldier, or not? If so, why the d—— can't you salute?"

He stumped upstairs, before you could say Black Jack—and General Black Jack himself it was!

★★★★★★

Back with the section—and life dragged along as it can, when you are waiting for an important letter. It was hot on the observation platform and I installed a barrel filled with water. Therein, I spent my time when not actually on the job. The major passed one day just as I stepped out, and ran to tell Lieut. Delva that I had gone stark naked mad. Castagnole told me later, that when Delva explained I was

American, a relieved smile came over the major's face.

"Ah, I see! A redskin!"

From that time on, they spoke to me in the terms of Fenimore Cooper, "Oh, my Red Brother," "Noble Watcher of the Winds," "Rain in the Face!"

Our lieutenant worked us hard, but he didn't spare himself. We were a damned happy section, and I never saw an outfit where rank counted less.

The long expected official envelope finally arrived. Alas, it contained only an unsigned copy of an extract from a cable. True, it said I had been commissioned a 1st Lieut., Infantry, but Delva and others were not convinced. Letters to the adjutant general's department were of no avail. I appealed to friends once more, and a signed and sealed notice arrived.

More complications! The American Army asked for my full record, with all changes of regiments, since enlistment. Delva wrote to the 5th Artillery, at Avranches, who referred him to the 13th F. A., at Vincennes. The 13th F. A. referred him to the 82nd H. A. at Satory. The 82nd H. A. referred him to the 170th Infantry, who referred him back to the 82nd H. A. Thereupon, the 82nd denied all knowledge of my existence, and considered the matter closed. Where was my record since I left the 170th? A day in Paris would have settled it all, but there was no chance of leave for months. However, regulations state that if a man is court martialled, and acquitted, he is entitled to 10 days' leave. I asked to see the major.

"*Mon Commandant*, I demand a court martial."

"On what grounds?"

"Desertion; from the time I left the 170th Infantry till I was transferred to this regiment."

"But this is serious!"

"It is, Sir. I'm in earnest."

"*Voyons, Voyons*, what's the trouble?"

Now a major commanding the artillery of a sector, has troubles of his own. He can't be expected to dry nurse every gunner, unless the gunner makes it plain that the safety pin is sticking into him. The moment I explained, he became human, and started buzzing off dynamic wires . . . .

Midnight—Oursan and I woke with a jump. Hammering on the door—and a liaison runner calling.

"King—King—your papers have come! You're to report at Central

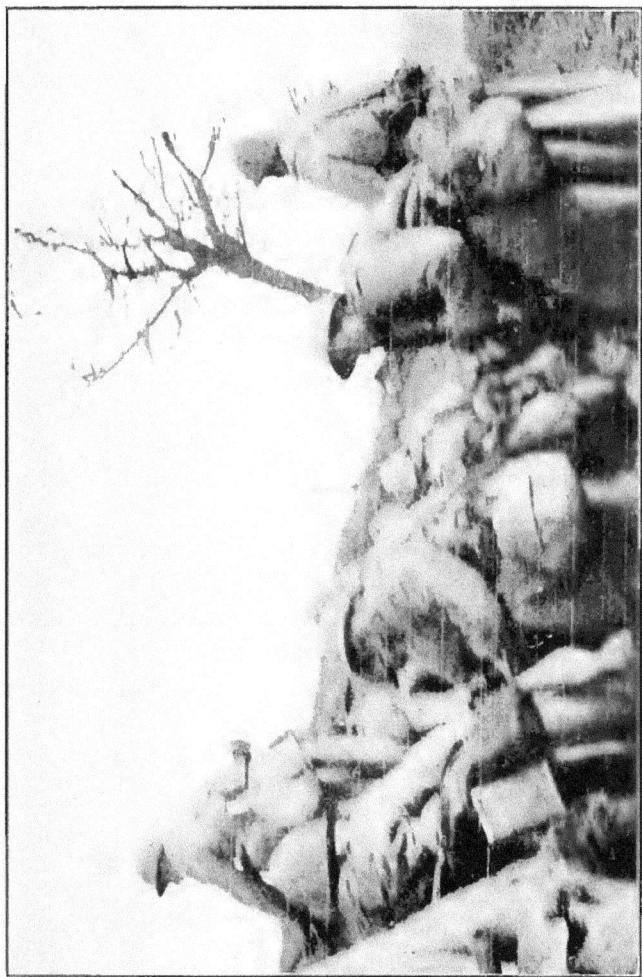

GOING OVER THE TOP, SOMME, AUGUST, 1916

tomorrow, with all your junk, and you leave tomorrow night for the depot. Here—take your orders." He handed me an envelope, then stiffening up, he saluted. "*Bonsoir, mon lieutenant*" and he left.

I turned, to find Oursan with tears streaming down his face, swearing like a trooper.

"It had to happen. I knew you would go, but it's damned hard. Just when I find someone I can get along with, off he goes! Still it's better this way—you'd probably be bumped off if you stayed. You always were a fool!" He grinned.

"We must celebrate! We'll eat up everything we have in the locker," and he set to work making coffee. . . .

The section had planned a send-off party for me, but it had to be shifted to midday, as the officers' mess had asked me to dine with them that night. As the party got under way, I began to have grave doubts if I would ever make dinner. Lieutenant Delva saved the day by calling me into the office to clear up my papers.

"King, pardon, *mon lieutenant!*"—he was only a 2nd Lieut.—"I'm taking the liberty of erasing the eight days prison I gave you."

"But why, Lieutenant Delva?"

"Well, I think you should leave this section with a clean slate. Besides, it strikes me as humorous for a *sous-lieutenant* to wipe out the crimes of his superior officer!"

"*Bien, Saint Pierre!*" I bowed, and emerged with a record white as snow.

Funny to be in an officers' mess after four years in the ranks. I felt shy at first, but I soon got over it, they were so damn friendly. . . A final toast—and Delva, the doctor, who was going on leave, and I started for the train.

Commercy—the station—the doctor and I leaned out of the window, waving as the train started.

"*Vive l'Amérique!*"

"*Vive la France!*"

"*Adieu—bonne chance!*"

"*A bàs les Boches! Adieu! Adieu!*"

Presently the conductor came along. He took one look at my ragged uniform, and scolded.

"Come on, get out of here! You go back to the third class. You have no business on an express, anyway."

I tried to show him my papers, but he wouldn't look. The doctor came to my rescue.

"One moment, conductor. Try to be polite! Can't you recognise an American officer when you see one?"

The *controlleur* gasped, took one hurried look at my orders, and fled. The other officers in the compartment had been mildly curious on seeing a non-com in the first class, but had said nothing. Now, they suddenly came to life, insisted on our dining with them, and we all trooped to the dining car for a drink—to "wet my new stripes."

★★★★★★

If you suddenly jump from two woollen stripes to a silver bar, it is hard to realise that one first lieutenant more or less doesn't matter much in a growing army.

I reported for orders—then I reported again. Still nothing happened; so I wangled a passport, and went to England for Christmas. That did it! Just before I left the French Army I had stepped too near an HE shell and a small sliver stuck in my lip. I pulled it out and thought no more about it. But Christmas dinner must have stirred things up, for within two days my good eye was closed by the swelling. Nothing for it but see a specialist, who popped me into a nursing home—acute blood poisoning.

The operation was a joke, at least for me. The surgeon didn't find it so amusing—as I was going under, I got the idea my gas mask was leaking, and started a free for all fight.

Two days with a wet compress over my face—I could neither see nor smoke. Pleasant, as a premature burial! Then I badgered a nurse till she cut a hole for my mouth, and lighted me a cigarette. The compress dried, and caught fire, and we both got Hell from the matron.

Life was pleasant—good food, friends coming to see the little tin hero, and impromptu dances in the cellar, during air raids.

A telegram from a friend at G. H. Q. spoiled everything.

No authority order you on duty from England. Return France or commission will be cancelled.

Yes, Yes, immediately—but how? My passport was a one way emergency affair, and I had counted on orders to get me back. Then I thought of two friends who were running the ordnance in France on a big business basis, in spite of a few generals and colonels. A telegram, and its reply—the ordnance in London obligingly faked me some orders, and back I went.

Chapter Twelve

.... And Peace?

. . . will proceed to the casual officers depot at Blois and report to the colonel commanding. The travel, etc.

Oh, help! Just what was a casual officers' depot? I soon found it was anything but casual.

The billeting officer handed back my orders.

"All right—report to the O. C. at the barracks tonight, and to Colonel Pulen tomorrow."

"But I've got a room at the hotel."

"Well, you can stay there tonight, but tomorrow you shift. All officers under the rank of major must live in barracks. By the way, you must be in quarters by nine p. m. sharp."

Then and there I realised I would have to get me an independent command. This place was about as casual as a penitentiary.

Next morning I saw Colonel Pulen. He was an old-school artillery officer, with a sense of humour. Ten minutes' talk, and he appointed me chief liaison officer, with an order for billets in town, and a pass to go anywhere any time.

My billets were opposite the *château*,, and fairly comfortable.

Later, the old man from next door, hearing I had been in the French Army, called in state.

"Lieutenant, I come on behalf of my wife and myself, to ask you to stay at our house."

"But, *Monsieur*, I am extremely comfortable, and satisfied here."

"But, Lieutenant, you don't understand. We wish you to come as our guest. I have lost three sons in this war, and I should feel unworthy of them if I did not ask an American, who has served in our army, to use their rooms."

I went.

My first job as liaison officer was to accompany the colonel and his adjutant on their first official call. The French *commandant de place*, a kindly white haired man, received us with a beaming smile. The colonel started to speak in French.

"*Commandant, je vous present mon ajudant.*"

The old gentleman looked blank, and I could guess what was going through his mind. *Tiens, Tiens!!* These Americans are democratic—but is it necessary for a colonel to introduce his sergeant major?

I cut in with a hasty "*Capitaine adjoint, mon commandant,*" and his face broke into smiles, once more. Turning to me, he began the inevitable set speech:

> Kindly tell your colonel that I am not only charmed and touched to be able to welcome the American Army here, but I am also delighted to make the acquaintance of such a distinguished officer. I cannot say how much it thrills me to see the streets of this old town thronged with the khaki clad progeny of the men who fought beside the legions of Lafayette and Rochambeau. *etc., ad lib. . . .*

It was worthy of the opening of a Y house on the fourth of July. I started to translate, but the chief cut me short.

"Stop! Shoot it back to him, and ask him when I can get those motor trucks."

I shot it back strong, finishing up with an impassioned appeal for the trucks.

The *commandant* answered, briefly but to the point.

"What's he say?"

"He says he hasn't got any trucks, but will get some for us."

"Then what the hell was all that spiel you gave?"

"Lafayette, and a few trucks."

The colonel grinned; we made our bows, and left. Outside he turned to me.

"Will he really get 'em?"

"Yes, sir, if I keep after him."

"All right, now listen. I see we can't handle these people as we would at home. I'll tell you what I want, and leave the rest to you. My motto is, *when you've tried everything, and can't make it work, why, go ahead, and do it anyway!*"

★★★★★★

119

If I had had any sense I would have stuck close to that colonel. As it was, I still took the war seriously, and got transferred to Chaumont.

Here I found myself in the G 2 B, or counter espionage section. There was nothing to do but censor field clerks' fiction, and explain to visiting firemen, and generals, how a system of purely mythical control cordons worked.

This would not do. I was wearing out my best cord breeches on a hard wood chair, so I appealed to the sound ranging section. I talked with the officer in charge, who had told me to report to him as soon as I was commissioned. He had become a general, however, so I found myself appointed to the Statistical Department, Prisoners of War Section. You don't understand? Neither did I. There was hidden dynamite in that job. The first time an irate general rang up, and I had to say "Service of Statistics, statistical officer in charge," I knew they would break me for mocking the mighty. Besides, there were too many stars, and eagles, not to mention oak leaves, around Chaumont for a first lieutenant's comfort. Discipline was so highly developed, we used to salute any limousine, on sight, empty or not.

The wildest night club in town was a *patiserrie* with a sign "Exotic Delicacies." I never found out what they were, unless it referred to the two girls who ran it. Here, again, a mere first lieutenant started at a disadvantage. I decided to try for another independent command.

One of my best friends was at our Berne legation, and, unknown to me, was pulling strings to get me up there. One day, the major called me in.

"Do you know Mr. Ellis Dresel?"

"No, sir."

"Do you know Mr. Dolbeare?" (Frederic Dolbeare, 2nd, Secretary, American Legation at Berne.)

"In a way, sir." I was beginning to know my oak leaves, and meant to play safe.

"Well, they want you to go to Berne, and start an office for checking our prisoners of war." "I think I could be more useful here, sir." "Oh, you do, do you! Well, just let me tell you, you will go where we see fit to send you. The trouble with all you young reserve officers is, you don't seem to realize there's a war on . . . ."

"Yes, sir! No, sir!" and I went on my way rejoicing— once the door was closed.

Paris— civilian clothes— a diplomatic passport—and Excelsior!

★★★★★★

Berne was a maelstrom of intrigue and comedy. Most of the diplomatic corps lived at the Bellevue Palace. Allies on one side of the dining room— enemies on the other. Mutual glaring, and hate fests before meals. In the lounge every other chair was occupied by a wide spread newspaper, from which stuck out mysterious legs. If conversation turned to interesting topics, a pair of ears would protrude beyond the paper, betraying the presence of the enemy.

Our chief was a fire-eater, and longed to get to the front. He was a regular officer, and the amateur soldiers about him almost drove him wild. We meant well, but were more interested in results than in regulations.

"Lieut. X., you will proceed as per previous orders, and report to Countess (?) Stejjenska for information."

"Colonel, that woman hasn't a bit of real dope. And, I'm not sure she isn't double crossing us."

"You heard what I said . . . ."

"But, Colonel, it will gum the game!"

"Lieutenant, I've got *just* enough officers here to hold a court martial!"

"Sir, I would welcome a court martial!"

Interference, and business of calming both of them. . . .

When I got to Berne there were three separate fights going on. The French and English were at daggers drawn. Our assistant military *attaché* did not like the English, and wanted to play with the French. The French were afraid we would put our foot in it; and the English were for using us, but mistrusted our intimacy with the French.

Over and above all there was a row in our own camp, between the Military and the Red Cross. Squabbles and petty jealousy seemed to be in direct ratio to the distance from the front. I was, instantly, ordered to take over all arrangements for feeding our prisoners in Germany, but the Red Cross was handling it far better than we could ever hope to, with our limited means, and staff. The head was an international character, and his second is now Secretary of Labour. I had just enough sense to stick to the prisoner enquiry business.

This was only a half time job, and the colonel jumped at the idea of my doing *contre espionnage* work. I broke in a sergeant major to do the desk work in the prisoner game, got a rubber stamp of my initials in case of my absence, and I was off on the trail of the wily spy. But to keep my independence, I made it plain that I was still in the Statistical Department.

Wonderful position! If relations with the colonel became strained I merely had to suggest that perhaps I had better devote myself entirely to my real work. He was the ranking officer in Berne, but I was responsible only to G. H. Q.

For thrilling spy stories read Oppenheim or Buchan. The work of *contre espionnage* is not noisy. In France or England the general method was to spot a spy, censor his mail secretly, and, if possible, insert false information. To arrest and shoot him merely meant that he would be replaced by a new one, who in turn must be unearthed. In Switzerland, however, things were quite different. Anyone doing intelligence work, positive or negative, was liable to arrest. This made the censoring of letters, etc., impossible. There were two ways of doing business: either get all the dope on a German agent and pass it to a friendly Swiss *agent de sureté*, or, lure him near the French border, and Shanghai him across.

★★★★★★

Orders came through from G. H. Q., to try and convince the enemy that the American forces were going to attack in Alsace. The Colonel handed Howe and me the job. . . .

We met heavily, in the bar of the hotel. A fierce, low voiced discussion in a corner—business of scribbling, and comparing typewritten notes. These were lists of pertinent questions as to roads, bridges, etc., in Alsace, implying an offensive in that region. By this time the barkeep was all ears, and interest. He even deigned to bring us our drinks, himself.

When we left, I gathered my papers together and buttoned them into my hip pocket, letting the important one slip out onto the seat behind me. Half an hour later, I rushed into the bar, hunted under the seat, in great agitation. Had I lost anything? Could the bartender help me? No, he hadn't seen any papers, and no one else had been in the bar. I assured him it wasn't really important. He smiled a slippery smile as I left, still agitated. One up to us.

Our next effort was a faked order,—carbon copy, signed true, and everything,—a beautiful piece of work. It took us a whole afternoon to make, and when we showed it to the colonel, he tore around the room twirling his moustaches.

"Ha!! This means business at last! When did this come? Why wasn't it brought to me at once?

Once more, we calmed him down, and explained.

We got in touch with a renegade German, in his own territory, and after giving him a plausible story about being hard up, passed him the papers to show, and return. He may have suspected, but I heard he sold them for a good price.

We got tired of wasting time and energy chasing allied agents. With the English and Italians, we formed a central office, or clearing house, at Geneva. Marvellous! I grabbed the job of intelligence officer in command and became still more independent. Within a week, we found eleven authentic cases of shadowing our own men. Things began to pick up.

★★★★★★

The second in command at Berne, let's call him Bernstein, got in touch with a renegade German—Zero. Then he got the grippe. He had a rendezvous with Zero the next day, but was too ill to go. No one knew Zero, and Zero only knew Bernstein. The connecting link was a postcard, saying he would wait for him in the Station at Lucerne. Fine—at that time Lucerne was practically a German town. The colonel gave me the post card and mumbled something about a message to Garcia—and that was that.

The station was full of interned Germans, in and out of uniform. No use making myself conspicuous hunting for him here. I went straight to the hotel du Lac—Bernstein was a luxurious bloke—I felt sure he would have put up at the best. Half an hour later, allowing Zero plenty of time to walk back from the station, I sat in the garden along the quay. Any number of people were walking up and down. I watched to see which ones passed most frequently. One little German never seemed to be gone for long. I stepped under an arc light and studied the post card just as he was passing. Next trip, he passed closer, looked sharply at the card, and started whistling Tipperary. That was good enough for me. I followed him till we got to a dark place, then tapped him on the shoulder.

"Good evening, Zero."

"Where's Bernstein?"

"He couldn't come. Grippe."

"How do I know you're all right?"

"You don't. You've got to take a chance. I did."

We settled down to work. He talking, and I taking notes. We sat in the dark so I had to guide my pencil with a cigarette.

Next day, I shifted to a quiet hotel, slept during the day, and met Zero at night. This went on for several weeks; I reported at Berne at intervals.

Certainly Zero was in the inner ring. We passed his information to the Swiss police, who, thereupon, arrested Schreck, the head of German espionage in that region. None of Schreck's underlings had a list of his agents, so they could not be warned. As they came to the surface, to find out what had gone wrong, the police netted them. The Germans searched furiously for the traitor. Zero and I had to be doubly careful.

Outside of Lucerne, there are two roads that run along the railway track—one each side. I met him, once, in the daytime on one of these, about a mile from town. We had hardly spoken when he saw German friends coming down the road towards us, in both directions. For a moment I thought we were caught. But luck still held—a long freight train was puffing down the track. Before the agents came near enough to recognize me, I had nipped across, and hidden by the passing train, got away on the other road. We kept to our nightly meetings, after Geneva was filled with deserters, professional spies, renegades, and dope fiends. The cream of the scum of the nations. I had been having difficulty with a suspect and the atmosphere was strained. "Nappy," one of our rough neck agents, took me aside one day.

"Look here. You've been having quite a lot of trouble with M—. Why bother with him? A hundred *francs*, and he goes in the lake to-night."

"No thanks, Nappy. I'm playing my own game, in my own way."

"Well, then, let us beat him up, so he won't get so fresh. That will cost two hundred, though, 'cause he might squeal, and there would be questions asked."

"Thank you, no!"

"All right! Have it your own way, but just let me tell you, if *you* don't, he *will!'*

★★★★★★

The armistice, a Bolshevik uprising, and the flu, hit Switzerland at the same time.

My official work was just beginning. Our prisoners in Germany had all been concentrated at Darmstadt. Some congenital idiot, in charge, sent all the officers by the first train; then for seven days the men and non-coms arrived, a thousand at a time. It was a great game. I climbed aboard the train at Berne, at three in the afternoon, and took over. That was easy—I simply had the doors locked. But arriving at Geneva about eleven, I had to disentrain them, see that they were fed by the Red Cross, and hold them on the platform till the French train came in, about one or two in the morning. Then I must entrain them, check with the O. C. on the train, and catch the six o'clock back to Berne. The last night, I was met at Geneva with a flock of telegrams from Berne.

Understand French train will not arrive tonight. Have men bivouac in station till further orders. Stop. Hold you responsible, *etc.*

Hold, hell! Seven hundred wild Indians just out of prison, and in a big town!

I don't yet know what I would have done, but I got in touch with Bellegarde, and found the train would only be three hours late. . . .

★★★★★★

January 15, 1919.

Orders detailing the following named officers on temporary duty with the Peace Commission, Paris, France, are confirmed as having been necessary in the Military Service. . . . .

By order of the Secretary of War.

Peyton C. March,
General Chief of Staff.

So we were to try a hand at Peace!

The Crillon was a glorious mixture of the University Club and the Eagle House at Concord with the State Legislature sitting, by heck! George left to perch on a heap of coal at Teschen, and I—Oh, I stayed on and helped arrange for bigger and better wars.

Letters and Diary of Alan Seeger

I have a Rendezvous with Death
    By Alan Seeger

I have a rendezvous with Death
At some disputed barricade,
When Spring comes back with rustling shade
And apple-blossoms fill the air—
I have a rendezvous with Death
When Spring brings back blue days and fair.

It may be he shall take my hand
And lead me into his dark land
And close my eyes and quench my breath—
It may be I shall pass him still.
I have a rendezvous with Death
On some scarred slope of battered hill,
When Spring comes round again this year
And the first meadow-flowers appear.

God knows 'twere better to be deep
Pillowed in silk and scented down,
Where love throbs out in blissful sleep,
Pulse nigh to pulse, and breath to breath,
Where hushed awakenings are dear. . .
But I've a rendezvous with Death
At midnight in some flaming town,
When Spring trips north again this year,
And I to my pledged word am true,
I shall not fail that rendezvous.

Contents

POET, ALAN SEEGER

Jeune légionnaire, enthousiaste et énergique,
airaant passionnément la France.
Engagé volontaire au début des hostilités,
a fait preuve au cours de la campagne d un entrain e
t d un courage admirables.—
Glorieusement tombé le 4 juillet 1916.
(Citation à 1 ordre du jour de la Division du Maroc,
25 décembre 1916.)

Alan Seeger in his uniform

Prefatory Note

Those who have read the published poems of Alan Seeger and the sympathetic sketch of his life by Mr. William Archer, in his introduction, cannot have failed to appreciate the motives that led the young American, in his great love for France and her cause, to take up arms in her behalf as a common soldier in the ranks of the Foreign Legion. But it is one thing to yield to a generous impulse and quite another to adhere faithfully to a high resolve through wretched and tiresome hours of unaccustomed hardship and distasteful surroundings. In these pages, written from day to day and from week to week, unchanged and unpolished by afterthought, in the endeavour to make them appear nobler and more consistent than they were when first set down in diary or intimate letter,—no word will be found, either of complaint, of wavering or of discouragement.

The miseries of life in the trenches, the exhaustion from long marches, the ennui of inaction, are related simply and faithfully, but, at the same time, they are accepted as the inevitable lot of the soldier and borne with patience pending the arrival of the hour of battle, for which he longs. Even when cramped in the trenches, this lover of beauty can take keen pleasure in an occasional glimpse of a picturesque *vista* through the *créneaux*; nor, when his endurance is taxed to the utmost to hold out until the end of a march that lays low many a stronger man among his comrades, does he fail to remember and record the sunlit verdure of the meadows bordering the dusty road along which he toils, with heavy burden, weary almost to the point of dropping. In the lonely vigils of sentry duty, during the hours between night and dawn, when the most courageous feel spirit and hope at the lowest ebb, he can find consolation in "a kind of comrade ship with the stars."

So, a knowledge of the character and life of Alan Seeger would not be complete without the revelation of patient endurance and steadfast devotion to an ideal contained in this volume. While they lend a confirmatory value to his later poems, written during the same period, they enhance, by contrast, the beauty of his earlier verse, the product of years when the pleasures of life were his goal, and danger and self-sacrifice unthought of. One has only to turn from almost any page of this book, chosen at random, to the sonnets of "*Juvenilia,*" to discover a new pathos in the lines and to feel more keenly the extent and nobility of the renouncement.

But these pages tell not merely of strain and trial. There are glorious moments of exultation in taking part in the mightiest struggle of history. There is the thrill of the "*Marseillaise*" and the weird martial music of the *Tirailleurs*. There is rejoicing in the contact with other brave and strong men. There is the pride of surmounting toil and hardship, which outlasts the suffering. And in spite of the love of life which endured to the last,—inferior only to his conviction that a life could only be worth living when filled with the most vivid emotions,—we know that the manner of Alan Seeger's death was that which he himself had chosen. It threw a brighter and clearer light upon his word and deed and so dignified both that they will live the longer for the years that were cut off from his life on earth. There is solace, too, in the remembrance of what he had written, when the sight of death had become familiar and the peril of it imminent:

Death is nothing terrible after all. It may mean something more wonderful than life. It cannot possibly mean anything worse to the good soldier.

1: September 27–December 4, 1914

Toulouse, Sunday, September 27, 1914.—Fifth Sunday since enlistment. The arbour of a little inn on the highroad running east from Toulouse. Beautiful sunny afternoon. Peace. The stir of the leaves; noise of poultry in the yards nearby; distant church bells, warm southern sunlight flooding the wide corn-fields and vineyards.

Everything is ready for departure today. We shall leave tomorrow or next day for an unknown destination. Some say Antwerp, some Châlons.

To His Mother

2me Régiment Etranger,
Bataillon C, Ire Cie., 3me Section,
Toulouse, Sept. 28, 1914.

We are still held up here, though all preparations for departure have been made and everyone expected to be off yesterday. We are entirely equipped down to our three days' rations and 120 rounds of cartridges. The wagons are all laden and the horses requisitioned. The suspense is exciting, for no one has any idea where we shall be sent.

We have been putting in our time here at very hard drilling and are supposed to have learned in six weeks what the ordinary recruit in times of peace takes all his two years at. We rise at 5 and work stops in the afternoon at 5. A twelve hours' day at one *sou* a day. I hope to earn higher wages than this in time to come but I never expect to work harder. The early rising hour is splendid, for it gives one the chance to see the most beautiful part of these beautiful autumn days in the South.

We march up to a lovely open field on the end of the ridge behind the barracks, walking right into the rising sun. From this the panorama, spread about on three sides is incomparably fine, yellow corn fields, vineyards, harvest-fields where the workers and their teams can be seen moving about in tiny figures,—poplars, little hamlets and church-towers, and far away to the south the blue line of the Pyrenees, the high peaks capped with snow. It makes one in love with life, it is all so peaceful and beautiful.

But Nature to me is not only hills and blue skies and flowers, but the Universe, the totality of things, reality as it most obviously presents itself to us, and in this universe strife and sternness play as big a part as love and tenderness, and cannot be shirked by one whose will it is to rule his life in accordance with the cosmic forces he sees in play about him. I hope you see the thing as I do and think that I have done well, being without responsibilities and with no one to suffer materially by my decision, in taking upon my shoulders, too, the burden that so much of humanity is suffering under and, rather than stand ingloriously aside when the opportunity was given me, doing my share for the side that I think right. . . .

Letters are taking such a long while to come from America now that I have not much expected to hear from you yet and in fact have heard nothing since I left London last month. But I ought to get something soon in answer to my letter from Rouen. I hope it will show you in good spirits, as you ought to be, for I am playing a part that I trust you will be proud of. . . .

DIARY

Camp de Mailly, Sunday, October 4.—Left Toulouse Wednesday at noon. Marched through the streets behind our *clairons*. Came here *via* Limoges, Bourges, Auxerre and Troyes. Beautiful country last afternoon around Saucerre. Uncomfortable nights.

Mailly apparently was about the furthest point reached by the Germans before the French success in the Battle of the Marne forced them to retreat. There are numerous vestiges of the recent battle. Some of the buildings in the village are damaged by shells, some that we passed yesterday morning in the train completely demolished. Entrenchments in the fields.

Yesterday we heard cannon for the first time. All day long the occasional rumble of heavy siege guns came from the direction of the frontier. The distance must have been 60 or 70 kilometres. This makes drilling interesting.

Last night two Germans were found in the woods near here by a patrol. One was dead from hunger and exposure and the other nearly so. He said the reason they had not surrendered was that their officers had told them that they would be shot. He said also that there were thirty or forty others in hiding in the neighbourhood.

We are four battalions here, two of the first regiment of the Legion and two of the second.

Sunday, October 11, 1914.—Very beautiful fall days during the past week. The atmosphere has been quite clear, revealing the most distant horizons of the open, rolling, sparsely cultivated country of this part of France. The first frosts of nights full of stars have begun to colour the trees so that each tufted top stands out separate in the yellow sunlight that floods out of skies without a cloud. This weather is unusual; the grey winter days will set in soon.

Yesterday we took a seven-hour march that made the most demand on our endurance that has yet been called for. Only one man fell out, however. We pitched our tents in a high field and went through the entire exercise of bivouacking, taking our sacks inside and lying down six men to a tent. I was sure we were preparing to spend the night, when the order was given to break camp and in a few minutes, all the orderly labour was undone. The company was then formed in *colonnes de demi-section par un* and we started back to camp across country, making a wide detour. The whole distance was one continuous battlefield. Everywhere were exploded and unexploded shells. In the woods, we came upon several abandoned French knapsacks but found no bodies, though the woods are probably full of them still.

This morning comes the unexpected news of the fall of Antwerp. This is the most important event of the war to date. It means the entire subjugation of Belgium. The Germans, as far as I can see, occupy all the territory they have coveted and all that they would keep in the event of their ultimate victory. It is my idea that they will now wage a defensive war entirely, limiting themselves to holding what they have. The impending winter will wonderfully favour them in this plan of campaign. The strong defensive lines they have reared on their front will enable them to detach large forces to cope with the Russians. On the whole, their situation seems good and the task of the French and English in driving them back a desperately hard one.

To His Mother

Camp de Mailly,
Aube, France, October 17, 1914.
. . . After two weeks here and less than two months from enlist-

137

ment we are actually going at last to the firing line. By the time you receive this we shall already perhaps have had our *baptême de feu*. We have been engaged in the hardest kind of hard work,—two weeks of beautiful autumn weather on the whole, frosty nights and sunny days and beautiful colouring on the sparse foliage that breaks here and there the wide rolling expanses of open country. Every day from the distance to the north has come the booming of the cannon around Reims and the lines along the Meuse. We have had splendid sham battles, firing dozens of rounds of blank cartridges. Between the *bonds de vingt mètres*, when we lie on the ground, resting the sack on one side and with one's ear in the grass, it has been wonderful to hear this steady pounding of the distant cannonade.

But imagine how thrilling it will be tomorrow and the following days, marching toward the front with the noise of battle growing continually louder before us. I could tell you where we are going but I do not want to run any risk of having this letter stopped by the censor. The whole regiment is going, four battalions, about 4,000 men. You have no idea how beautiful it is to see the troops undulating along the road in front of one in *colonnes par quatre* as far as the eye can see with the captains and lieutenants on horseback at the head of their companies.

I am keeping a diary in a desultory sort of way, but aside from this I am quite incapable of any such literary effort as you suggest, for one simply has not the time. Tomorrow the real hardship and privations begin. But I go into action with the lightest of light hearts. The hard work and moments of frightful fatigue have not broken but hardened me and I am in excellent health and spirits. Do not worry, for the chances are small of not returning and I think you can count on seeing me at Fairlea next summer, for I shall certainly return after the war to see you all and recuperate. I am happy and full of excitement over the wonderful days that are ahead. It was such a comfort to receive your letter and know that you approved of my action. Be sure that I shall play the part well for I was never in better health nor felt my manhood more keenly.

CARTE POSTALE, POSTMARKED VERTUS 20 OCT. 1914

This is the second night's halt of our march to the front. All our way has been one immense battlefield, little villages that are nothing but heaps of ruins, fields torn with artillery fire and heaped with the fresh graves of the soldiers, buried where they fell, a rude cross above and the *képi rouge*. It was a magnificent victory for the French, that the world does not fully realise. I think we are marching to victory too, but whatever we are going to we are going triumphantly. Reims is 47 kilometres away, the Germans 15 beyond.

DIARY

Vertus, October 20, 1914.—Made a short morning's walk of 16 kilometres,—still through the great battlefield. The Germans retreated along the road we marched over. Everywhere in the fields on either hand were the holes made by the *obus* and the graves beside them where the men fell. Extraordinary evidences of the artillery fire. Pine woods with the branches all ripped to pieces; large sized trees broken clean off in the middle. Though several weeks have passed since the battle, the fields are still littered with debris. Today we passed through the villages of Marsain and Bergères. The first was completely destroyed, not a house on the main street had escaped the fire. Nothing but blackened walls and here and there the inhabitants standing with sullen faces in their ruined doorways. The scene of the marching column down the ruined street,—a scene that will become familiar to us,—was imposing.

We are in Champagne now and the hillsides, covered with yellowing vineyards, made lovely landscapes along the road, although the weather is still grey and melancholy.

Hautvilliers, près d Epernay.—Made a march of about 28 kilometres. Foggy weather that spoiled the beauties of what would have been a charming landscape. No more signs of battle; everywhere the yellow-green vineyards of Champagne. Passed through Chonilly. Expected to be cantoned in Epernay but kept on in spite of considerable fatigue to this lovely little village on the hilltop. Lodged in a most delightful place, a *château* which seems once to have been a cloister, right behind the old church.

We are to sleep in the loft of a barn, where the straw is plentiful. There is a pleasant terrace-garden here, full of flowers, overlooking the valley; the view must be beautiful on sunny days. It seems we are going to Reims tomorrow, or close to it. We are attached to the *cinquième armée*. Lots of troops in Epernay; they lined the sidewalks and watched us pass. Paris autobuses in the streets. All bridges had been blown up and were replaced by temporary structures.

Verzy, October 22, 1914.—Made an early start from Hautvilliers and marched here, a distance of about 30 kilometres, with only hour halts. A hard walk; a great many fell out from fatigue. Passed through many villages; the road between Louvois and Verzy, over wooded hills brilliant with autumn foliage, was particularly lovely. Passed camps full of African troops; automobiles filled with officers and autobuses with provisions showed us that we were approaching the front. During our last halt in the woods the colonel passed along the lines with a group of officers and three generals. Shortly afterwards the sergeant returned and announced the extraordinarily unexpected news that we were to stay in Verzy till four o clock and then leave immediately for the trenches that are only five or ten kilometres beyond here. It is two o clock now. We are actually to be under fire then immediately. A cloudy, dismal day with occasional drizzling rains. No sound of battle here; everything quiet.

Verzenay, October 23.—Half of the regiment was sent to the trenches last night, a battalion of the first and a battalion of the second. Our men slept in Verzy in their harness, that is, wearing the cartridge belt, with sack and gun at our head. At four we got up and, assembling, marched here, a distance of only a few kilometres, where we were billeted again, in a stable at the end of the Rue Veuve Pommery. On the way, we passed lots of wagons and cavalry. There were three graves by the roadside at a place where we stopped, a post above each and a placard reading: *Espion, traitre à son pays.*

To His Mother

October 23, 1914.

It will surely interest you to get a letter from the front though I have only time to write a word. I cannot tell you the name of the village where we are cantoned, for reasons of expediency. We are about 17 kilometres southeast of Reims. I am sitting on the curbstone of a street at the edge of the town. The houses end abruptly and the yellow vineyards begin here. The view is broad and uninterrupted to the crest, ten kilometres or so across the valley. Between this and ourselves are the lines of the two armies. A fierce cannonading is going on continually and I lift my eyes from the sheet at each report to see the puffs of smoke two or three miles off.

The Germans have been firing salvos of four shots over a little village where the French batteries are stationed, shrapnel that burst in little puffs of white smoke; the French reply with explosive shells that raise columns of dust over the German lines. Half of our regiment

IN THE TRENCHES

have left already for the trenches. We may go tonight. We have made a march of about 75 kilometres in four days and are now on the front, ready to be called on at any moment. I am feeling fine, in my element, for I have always thirsted for this kind of thing, to be present always where the pulsations are liveliest. Every minute here is worth weeks of ordinary experience. How beautiful the view is here, over the sunny vineyards! And what a curious anomaly. On this slope the grape pickers are singing merrily at their work, on the other the batteries are roaring. *Boom! Boom!*

This will spoil one for any other kind of life. The yellow afternoon sunlight is sloping gloriously across this beautiful valley of Champagne. I must mail this now. There is too much to be said and too little time to say it. . . .

DIARY

Verzenay, October 25, 1914.—On guard from four to six this morning. *Mitrailleuse* and rifle fire from the lines. Our company assembled this afternoon and we took a fine walk through the woods on the heights above Verzenay. From the open crests, there were wonderful views across the valley. Reims was plainly visible in the middle distance, to the northwest. Could see the cathedral clearly and the church of Saint Remy and the heights at the east of the town where the Pommery works are and where I stood on an evening a year ago, this summer when I visited Reims with A. G.

The autumn foliage on the hills, the vineyards on the slopes, the delicate tints in the eastern sky, all under a pale afternoon sun, were very beautiful. I think we were going to have some manoeuvres, but the appearance of some German aeroplanes coming directly towards us and passing overhead put an end to this plan. We ended by gathering wood for the kitchen. Afterwards we sat a long time on the grassy knolls, watching the lines across the valley. Aeroplanes circled continually overhead on reconnaissance and were bombarded with shrapnel from the lines below, without any apparent damage.

Cuiry-les-Chaudardes, Aisne, October 28.—Yesterday our *9me escouade* was waked early and hustled off into the darkness before the rest. Our sacks were taken and lifted into a wagon; we found that we were to be the escort of the pack train and the *mitrailleuse* section. A long day's march was promised us to counter act the comfort of marching without sack. It was in fact the hardest day we have had. We marched with small and few interruptions from 6.30 in the morning to 10.30 at night, in which time we covered probably about 55 kilometres. No food except the scraps we had in our *musettes.*

We passed over roads that wind along the southern slope of the valley where Reims is situated. For miles, the city lay on our right, but passing at the closest not nearer than six or seven miles I could not see clearly the extent of the damage to the cathedral. The villages lie close together here; the Prussians had passed through them all, but we saw no signs of war except at Marfaux, which had been completely destroyed by fire. Arrived at Fismes after nightfall and exceedingly fatigued, expected to be cantoned there, but kept on marching through the town and out into the dark country again. The cannonade that had been very violent all the afternoon grew louder as we advanced northward directly toward the lines. At 10.30 we halted and were told to spread our blankets in the field beside the road.

I was given sentry duty immediately on arriving and remained in front of the wagons until midnight. During this time an attack by one side or the other took place on the lines only a few kilometres from our encampment. For twenty minutes or so the rifle and *mitrailleuse* fire was continuous, broken every few seconds by the booming of the artillery, while magnesium lights were shot off from the trenches to light up the battlefield. Very impressive in the darkness.

Only a few hours before, a soldier of the *127me* had been telling me at Fismes how his regiment had made such a charge a couple of days ago, and had been practically wiped out, leaving 700 dead on the field. At midnight, I lay down on the wet ground and managed to get some sleep before three, when we got up again and continued the march 10 or 12 kilometres to this wretched village, where we are lodged for the day in a dirty stable. Here we are just behind the lines. We are resting and go into the trenches tonight. At last we shall be under fire.

October 29.—Slept here last night, contrary to expectation. We were all reviewed this morning, in the fields lining the road to Beaurieux, by the general. He showed the captains a new method of marching in single columns under artillery fire and we returned to Cuiry in this formation. Hope to go into the trenches tonight; they are only four kilometres over the hill from here. We have come to the point where fighting is the only thing to do. In this little village, there is not a thing to be bought of any kind, not even a morsel of bread or a drop of wine. We have a foretaste of what we shall have to go through in the future. All that we shall have to eat will come from the kitchen of the regiment, and that in small quantities. The poor will be as well off as the rich and money will be the most useless thing we carry.

November 4, 1914.—Back in Cuiry again. We marched away a week ago, through the forests under a moonlit sky. The road was merely a recent clearing through the trees to move the artillery over and was almost impassably muddy. Arrived at the outer line of trenches I was sent forward into a little trench in the fields to stay awake all night with a half-dozen others on sentinel duty. *Rien signalé*. Next day was peaceful and we spent it perfecting the little bomb-proof shelters along the lines. It was a day well spent, for the Germans that up to this time had been content to direct their fire over our heads on the French batteries behind us began now to turn it on our trenches, informed no doubt by their aeroplanes that buzzed continually overhead. The salvos of shrapnel began bursting in the woods all about us and we were compelled to stay under cover all day long.

Darkness would hardly begin before a fusillade would start from the lines nearby, the cry of *"Aux armes, aux tranchées!"* would run from door to door and we would hasten out into the night to wait in the muddy ditches while the bullets whistled about us. But these fusillades would always die out, provoked probably only by German patrols seeking to discover our position. After the first experience, we were forced to stay up all night, but later we became used to it and were allowed to go back to our holes to sleep. In this way, we would hustle out into the darkness four or five times in a single night, at first a little uneasy, but in the end only bothered. In the daytime, we slept, oblivious to the shells that burst around us. Cannon of all calibre and at all distances—occasional rifle fire and *mitrailleuses*—continual whirring of aeroplanes overhead—whistle of passing shells peculiar report of those bursting high in the air, directed against the aeroplanes.

Four days and four nights of this, in which our company lost two killed and nine wounded. Van der Veldt was killed instantly by a shrapnel ball in the doorway of his hut, only 15 or 20 yards from ours. The position of our trenches was the border of a wood facing the crest where the little village of Craonnelle is situated. Returning here we had a day of repose and then spent the last two at hard labour, digging trenches behind the outer lines. Tonight, we go up into the woods again, it seems, this time not to the first line but as reserve. The company that relieved us has had a hard time, they say, and has already lost four killed.

November 10, 1914.—Fifth day of our second period in the trenches. Five days and nights of pure misery. We came up here Thursday evening, a foggy, moonlit night, bright enough to show the fields through which we ascended, spattered with shell-holes as thick as mole hills, and the pine woods full of shattered trunks and broken branches. The Germans had been trying to destroy the Château des Blancs Sablons, below which our kitchens are situated, but by some miracle it has escaped. It is here that the *état-major* is lodged. Our position this time has been a claypit on a high summit above the *château*. Owing to its exposed and dangerous character very formidable bombproofs have been built at this point of the line. To these we have been confined for five days from morning to night.

A big hole here in the pit, a few yards from our door, marks the place where three men of Bataillon D were killed by a shell only a few days before our arrival. We expected a heavy bombardment, but five days of continuous fog have made the firing very infrequent, though we have heard heavy cannonading at other points of the line. A *brancardier* was killed a few days ago, and there have been a few wounded. It is a miserable life to be con demned to, shivering in these wretched holes, in the cold and the dirt and semidarkness.

It is impossible to cross the open spaces in daylight, so that we can only get food by going to the kitchens before dawn and after sundown. The increasing cold will make this kind of existence almost insupportable, with its accompaniments of vermin and dysentery. Could we only attack or be attacked! I would hear the order with delight. The real courage of the soldier is not in facing the balls, but the fatigue and discomfort and misery. Tonight, we are to be relieved, but whether we are going back to Cuiry or just to the last line of trenches down by the *château* I don't know. What a winter's prospect if our campaigning is only going to be to alternate between these two phases of inaction and discomfort!

To His Father

November 12, 1914.

. . . I am writing you from our encampment in the woods, a few miles behind the first-line trenches, from which we have just returned for the fifth time. We usually go to a little village where the headquarters of our regiment are, but the Germans bombarded this at long range a few days ago, and seem to have done considerable damage. The church has been knocked down and about thirty were killed among the population and the artillerymen quartered there. A shell entered the hay-loft where we had slept only a few days before, killed five and wounded thirteen. So, we are camping in the forest now in a big dugout that we have helped to build in other periods of so-called repose.

This is what is distressing about the kind of warfare we are up against,—being harried like this by an invisible enemy and standing up against all the dangers of battle without any of its exhilaration or enthusiasm. From Belfort to the sea now it is the *guerre des tranchées*. I have tried to describe a little what this means in an article that I have managed to accomplish amid the worst of conditions for writing and which I will send you when it appears. In comparison with it a bayonet charge would be desirable and the command welcome to us all.

I am glad to hear that Mother does not worry too much. You probably can follow things well enough to know that I have not been in the North, where the losses have been heavy, but in the centre where there has been more or less of a deadlock since the Battle of the Marne, and the infantry has not figured much except as artillery support. As long as this condition lasts the danger is very slight and it may last all winter. If it does it will be more to your satisfaction than mine...

To His Mother

November 17, 1914.

I haven t seen any more of the little cards I sent you, so I will write a few lines to let you know that I am well and take the risk of the letter getting through. As you may see by the stationery, I have already received the valise and the contents were most welcome. It arrived by the wagon while we were camping in the woods. I just had time to mark the things, to transfer what I could carry to my sack and give the rest to comrades. Thaw took the *zarape*; I had a good blanket already. It was out of the question to carry the extra weight; you see all the property we now have must go on our backs on the marches and the weight would astonish you a little could you lift it. I am now well equipped for any weather. Yesterday we had our first flurry of snow, so you see how opportunely the things arrived. . . .

Unfortunately, I left my MS. with a printer in Bruges, which is now in the hands of the Germans and the centre of the fiercest fighting. After the war, I shall return there and look it up. And then I shall think of America again. With my volume and my *médaille commemora-*

tive I fancy I should have enough to account for my European visit in point of thought and action. This experience will teach me the sweetness and worth of the common things of life. The world will be more beautiful to me in consequence. So, wait and count on my being with you next summer.

DIARY

December 4, 1914.—Back in the same trenches. Matters have improved here. A well-to-*fermier* sends a *fourgon* in to Fismes every few days, which brings back abundant provisions that the soldiers can buy at moderate prices. In this way, we were able to fill our sacks with chocolate and canned stuff in sufficient quantity to tide us over the six days.

The trenches have been much improved by the last section. The roof has been made water-tight, more barbed wire has been strung in front, and the earth out of the deepened ditches has been piled round the walls, making the dugout much warmer. By stuffing the *créneaux* with straw we are now allowed to make fires at night, so we can heat our *gamelles* and lie down to sleep in a warm atmosphere. This emplacement is on the whole the pleasantest of any we have been in. The dugout is not uncomfortable now, for we have widened it sufficiently and covered the earth deep with straw; the view in front through the *créneaux* is very cheerful, a broad field and orchard stretching from our position to the crest; behind is a little stream in the woods where we can wash, and there is a spring close to a ruined mill where we can fill our canteens.

Here there is a post of the 73rd regiment and one can fraternise with the soldiers and hear the narratives of men who have been in the thick of it since the beginning of the war. We went on a patrol a few nights ago, advanced well in front of the lines and walked to the outskirts of Craonnelle, where we entered an old barn and brought back armfuls of straw for the dugout.

CHOUMU MARITZA
Choumu Maritza okrvavena
Platché oudovitza
Liouto remiena.

Marche, marche,
Zarigrade ie nache.
Raz, dva, trie,
Mladu boulgarie.

147

Boulgari mili
Napred da vrvim
Ca svitchku cili,
Gueneral ie c nac

Marche, marche, etc.

(Translation)
Coule Maritza ensanglantée,
Les veuves pleurent
Grièvement blessées.

Marche, marche,
Constantinople est à nous.
Un, deux, trois,
Jeunes Bulgares.

Chers Bulgares
Nous devons avancer
Avec toutes nos forces,
Notre général est avec nous.

Marche, marche, etc.

This is the Bulgarian national hymn. My *camarade d armes* Hulmaja taught it to me and we used to sing it on the marches around Mailly and coming here to the front. He wrote this out for me one day in the trenches and I wrote for him four *stanzas* of the "*Marseillaise.*"

2: December 8, 1914

December 8, 1914.

This is our fourth period of service in the trenches since coming to the front a month ago. We left our camp in the woods down by the *château* before daybreak this morning and marched up the hill in single file under the winter stars. Passing the second line trenches we walked for some time down a road, torn up here and there with shell holes and obstructed now and then with shattered trees. Through openings in the woods we could see that we were marching along a high ridge and on either hand vaporous depths and distances expanded, the darkness broken sometimes by a far light or the momentary glow of a magnesium rocket sent up from the German lines.

There is something fascinating if one is stationed on sentry duty immediately after arrival in watching the dawn slowly illumine one of these new landscapes from a position taken up under cover of darkness. The other section has been relieved and departs, we are given the *consigne* by the preceding sentinel and are left alone behind a mound of dirt facing the north and the blank, perilous night. Slowly the mystery that it shrouds resolves as the grey light steals over the eastern hills. Like a photograph in the washing its high lights and shadows come gradually forth. The light splash in the fore ground becomes a ruined *château*, the grey streak a demolished village.

The details come out on the hillside opposite, where the silent trenches of the enemy are hidden a few hundred meters away. We find ourselves in a woody, mountainous country, with broad horizons and streaks of mist in the valleys. Our position is excellent this time, a high crest, with open land sloping down from the trenches and plenty of barbed wire strung along immediately in front. It would be a hard task to carry such a line, and there is not much danger that the enemy

149

will try.

With increasing daylight, the sentinel takes a sheltered position and surveys his new environment through little gaps where the mounds have been crenelated and covered with branches. Suddenly he starts as a metallic bang rings out from the woods immediately behind him. It is the unmistakable voice of a French 75 starting the day's artillery duel. By the time the sentinel is relieved, in broad daylight, the cannonade is general all along the line. He surrenders his post to a comrade and crawls down into his bombproof dugout almost reluctantly for the long day of inactive waiting has commenced.

Rather than imitate my comrades, who are filling the chamber with all the various noises of profound slumber, I shall try to while away some of its tedium by giving you a description of the life of a volunteer in the French Army at one of the least exciting points of the present front—that is the mid-centre.

After the brilliant French victory in the Battle of the Marne, the Germans, defeated in their attack on Paris, fell back to a line about midway between the capital and the frontier and entrenched themselves strongly along the crests well to the north of the River Aisne. The French, following close on their heels, took up whatever positions they could find or win immediately behind and sat down no less strongly fortified along a line separated from that of the enemy by distances of usually only a few hundred meters.

A deadlock ensued here, and the theatre of critical activity shifted to the north, where the issue is still at stake in the tremendous battle for the possession of the seaboard and the base for an enveloping movement which may be decisive. Toward the east, the operations have become pretty much confined to the artillery, pending the result of the fighting in the north, which must be decided before an advance can be undertaken by either side on other points of the line.

True, occasionally a violent fusillade to the right or left of us shows that attacks are being made and at any moment are likely to be made, but these are only local struggles for position, and in general the infantry on the centre are being utilized only to support the long line of batteries that all along this immense front are harrying each other at short distances across field and forest and vineyard.

This style of warfare is extremely modern and for the artillerymen is doubtless very interesting, but for the poor common soldier it is anything but romantic. His role is simply to dig himself a hole in the ground and to keep hidden in it as tightly as possible. Continually under the fire of the opposing batteries, he is yet never allowed to get a glimpse of the enemy. Exposed to all the dangers of war, but with none of its enthusiasms or splendid *élan*, he is condemned to sit like an animal in its burrow and hear the shells whistle over his head and take their little daily toll from his comrades.

The winter morning dawns with grey skies and the hoar frost on the fields. His feet are numb, his canteen frozen, but he is not allowed to make a fire. The winter night falls, with its prospect of sentry duty and the continual apprehension of the hurried call to arms; he is not even permitted to light a candle, but must fold himself in his blanket and lie down cramped in the dirty straw to sleep as best he may. How different from the popular notion of the evening campfire, the songs and good cheer.

Cramped quarters breed ill temper and disputes. The impossibility of the simplest kind of personal cleanliness makes vermin a universal ill, against which there is no remedy. Cold, dirt, discomfort, are the ever-present conditions, and the soldier's life comes to mean to him simply the test of the most misery that the human organism can support. He longs for an attack, to face the barbed wire and the *mitrailleuse*, anything for a little freedom and function for body and soul.

My comrade in arms is a young Servian, who went through all the Balkan campaign until the war broke out with the Bulgarians. Then he deserted at Salonica, for he was unwilling to fight against his brother people, and his mother too was a Bulgarian. After the triumphs of the campaign in Macedonia the present method of fighting is almost insupportable to him, and he frets pitiably under the forced inaction. In the Balkans, there was no fighting behind earthworks, but all was in the open field and at the point of the bayonet, and seldom did the Turks await the fury of the shock.

In the evening, there was no lying down in the cold and darkness, but around blazing campfires the soldiers sang the ancient victorious paeans of their people and danced their national dances. Sometimes they would kindle a big bonfire at some distance from their camp and keep only a lot of little fires among themselves. The Turks would bombard the big fire all night, but around the little ones the soldiers would be left in peace. In the squalor and darkness of our subterranean quarters he tells me often of the glories of those days and of the wonderful exploits of his people—the onslaught at Kumanovo and the charge at Dibra, where he was shot through the body and laid up in hospital for a month and a half.

It is ignoble, this style of warfare, he exclaims. Instead of bringing out all that is noble in a man it brings out only his worse self—meanness and greed and ill temper. We are not, in fact, leading the life of men at all, but that of animals, living in holes in the ground and only showing our heads outside to fight and to feed.

Amid the monotony of this kind of existence the matter of eating assumes an importance altogether amusing to one who gives it only very secondary consideration in time of peace. It is in fact the supreme if not the only event of the day. In France, the soldier is very well cared for in this respect. In cantonment and under all normal conditions he receives ordinarily coffee and an ample day's ration of good bread the first thing in the morning; then at 10 and at 5 he is served with soup, meat and a vegetable, excellently cooked, coffee and wine, not to mention such little occasional luxuries as chocolate, *confitures*, brandy, etc.

In the trenches this programme is necessarily modified by the distance from the kitchens and the impossibility of passing back and forth in daylight on account of the artillery fire. When we first came to the trenches we made the mistake of having our kitchen too near in the woods. Whether it was the smoke that gave it away or one of the hostile aeroplanes that buzz continually over our heads the Germans soon found its range and with one man killed and half a dozen wounded the cooking brigade was forced to move back to the *château* and take up its quarters at a point in the woods at three or four kilometres from the line of the trenches.

Since then the matter of *ravitaillement* is arranged as follows: every morning at 3 o clock a squad of men leaves the trenches and returns before daybreak with the day's provisions—bread and coffee, cheese and preserved foods, such as cold meat, pates, sardines, etc. The ration is very small, but the nature of life in the trenches is not such as to sharpen one's appetite. In the evening, another squad leaves immediately after sundown. Everyone waits eagerly to hear the clink of the pails returning in the dark. It is a good meal, a soup, or stew of some kind, as hot as can be expected in view of the distance from the kitchen fires, coffee and wine, and we all gather about with our little tins for the distribution.

These nightly trips to the kitchen are sometimes a matter of considerable difficulty, for frequent changes of position often find us unfamiliar with the course of the paths through the woods, which are newly cut, impassably muddy and ill defined. Notwithstanding the danger of going astray in swamp and thicket and the labour of bringing back a heavy load in the dark it is considered a privilege to be assigned to this duty because it gives a little activity to relieve the day's tedium. Single file, with rifle strapped to shoulders, we flounder on, wet to the ankles, the black forest all around, each man carrying half a dozen canteens besides his other burdens. Our water comes from a spring down by the *château*.

To supplement the regular rations with little luxuries such as butter, cheese, preserves and especially chocolate is a matter that occupies more of the young soldier's thoughts than the invisible enemy. Our corporal told us the other day that there wasn't a man in the squad who wouldn't exchange his rifle for a jar of jam. It is true that we think more about securing these trifles than we do about keeping our rifles clean. Nor is it an easy matter to get such things. The country where we are now has been thoroughly fought over, so that the poor inhabitants and their stocks of goods have suffered severely from the continual passing of troops in action. The countryside is stripped as a field by locusts.

In the village where we are billeted during our intervals of rest between periods in the trenches there is not a thing to be had for any price. Our pocket money is so much waste paper. By sending to remote towns, paying commissions and exorbitant prices, one can manage to get a few things. Once in the trenches these articles are precious beyond gold. In the course of bartering services are paid for in chocolate, for money is held as worthless for wages.

Though modern warfare does not allow us to think more about fighting than eating, still we do not actually forget that we are on a battle-line. Ever over our heads goes on the precise and scientific struggle of the artillery. Packed elbow to elbow in these obscure galleries one might be content to squat all day long, auditor of the magnificent orchestra of battle, were it not that one becomes so soon habituated to it that it is no longer magnificent. We hear the voices of cannon of all calibres and at all distances. We learn to read the score and distinguish the instruments. Near us are field batteries; far away are siege guns. Over all there is the unmistakable, sharp, metallic twang of the French 75, the whistle of its shell and the lesser report of its explosion. When the German batteries answer the whistle and explosion outdistance the voice of the cannon.

When one hears the *sifflement* the danger has already passed. The shells which burst immediately overhead and rattle on the roof of our bombproof dugout come unheralded. Sometimes they come singly, sometimes in rapid salvos of two or three or four. Shrapnel's explosive report is followed by the whiz of the flying balls. Contact shells or *marmites* explode more impressively, so that the earth trembles. Shrapnel shatters trees and snaps good sized trunks as if they were twigs; contact shells dig holes eight or ten feet across all over fields. When lines are close, as ours are now, sniping goes on all the time, especially from the German side. At night, sometimes a violent fusillade will bring us to arms; out of our burrows we tumble to find the hillsides ablaze with the Bengal lights from the German trenches, where our enemies are as alert and mystified and uneasy as we are.

None of these alarms has come to anything where we were, but we hear prolonged roars of rifle fire, punctuated with steady booming of artillery, from the line alongside us sometimes, which make us realise that a desperate attack is always possible.

In clear weather aeroplanes buzz overhead all day long. Both sides bombard at them with shrapnel, which makes a queer little whir when it explodes high in the air. Never have I seen the lines bring an airman down, for the puffs of yellow smoke break too low, and high up in the clouds the machine goes humming on, contemptuously dropping its signal fuses. A few days ago, I did see a German aeroplane sent to the ground by a French monoplane.

We were in camp in the woods behind the lines when the familiar outline of a Taube against the winter sky drove us into hiding in our cabin. Suddenly, without having noticed its approach, I saw a French aeroplane close with its enemy. There was the popping volley of a *mitrailleuse* and the wounded German machine dipped abruptly and came down in a long volplane, but I could not see whether the pilot had height enough to make his own lines before his wheels struck the ground.

It is toward evening that the cannonade is always fiercest. With darkness, it almost completely subsides. Then the sleepy soldiers, cramped and dishevelled, crawl out of their holes, rouse themselves, stretch their legs and take the air. Everybody turns out like factory workmen at 5 o'clock. The kitchen squad departs, others set to work repairing smashed defensive earthworks and the night's first sentinels go on.

Sentry duty, which may be all that is melancholy if the night is bad and the winter wind moans through the pines, may bring moments of exaltation if the cloud banks roll back, if the moonlight breaks over the windless hills or the heavens blaze with the beauty of the northern stars. It has been so for the last few nights, since I commenced these notes. A cold wave has frozen all the bad ways; a light snow has fallen and at night the moonlight flooding out of a frosty sky illumines all the wide landscape to its utmost horizons. In the hollow the white shell and chimneys of the ruined *château* stand out among the black pine groves; on the crest opposite one can trace clear as in daylight the groves and walls and roadways among which wind the silent and uncertain lines of the enemy's trenches.

Standing facing them from his ramparts the sentinel has ample time for reflection. Alone under the stars, war in its cosmic rather than its moral aspect reveals itself to him. Regarded from this more abstract plane the question of right and wrong disappears. Peoples war because strife is the law of nature and force the ultimate arbitrament among humanity no less than in the rest of the universe. He is on the side he is fighting for, not in the last analysis from ethical motives at all, but because destiny has set him in such a constellation. The sense of his responsibility is strong upon him. Playing a part in the life of nations he is taking part in the largest movement his planet allows him.

He thrills with the sense of filling an appointed necessary place in the conflict of hosts, and facing the enemy's crest above which the Great Bear wheels upward to the zenith, he feels, with a sublimity of enthusiasm that he has never before known, a kind of companionship with the stars!

Six days is the regular period for service in the trenches under normal conditions. Often enough it seems close to the limit of physical and moral strain which a man can bear. The last night the company packs up its belongings and either in the twilight of evening or dawn assembles and waits for the shadowy arrival of the relieving sections, to whom the position is surrendered without regret. We march back over the wretched roads and pass our three days' interval of so-called rest either billeted in the stables and haylofts of the village or encamped in the woods around the *château*.

In bad weather, the first is the more agreeable, for one has a tight roof over his head, can wash, and fraternise with the artillerymen and the soldiers of other regiments. But if the skies are clear it is pleasant to camp by the *château*, where a steep hillside in the forest is covered with the rude little cabins that the soldiers put up when the leaves were still on the branches. Here one may make fires at will, and at night fall, with the smell of wood smoke and the twinkle of lights among the trees, the conditions of life in the army come closer to what we imagined they would be when we enlisted.

Such then is the part that has been assigned us in our first month of field service a not very active part so far but one which novelty has made interesting. How long will it continue? What change will the future bring us? This is the most frequent subject of surmise and discussion in trench and cantonment. If our winter is to be nothing but a series of alternations between the discomforts of crowded dugout and squalid village there is not one of us who would not be glad to be shifted immediately to the north to bear all the rigors of an open campaign in order to share some of its action. But if victory in the north determines an advance all along the line it will be as well to be at this point as at any other.

North of us, behind the bristling crest, the frontier is not far. Between and directly on our road is the cathedral city on the hill. Little more than a year ago, I walked in its ancient streets and from its lofty ramparts in the shade of its cluster of Gothic towers, looked off east ward at twilight over the broad, beautiful land scape. To dream of re-entering this city as we would re-enter it has filled many a night's watch. The crest opposite us would have been carried at the point of the bayonet, our ranks would have been thinned, but the flag would still wave in the undulating line of blue and red as it winds up the hillside to the town and rolls through the antique gateway, and our officers would look never so gallant riding at the head of each battle-worn company.

The midwinter afternoon would bathe in ruddy splendour the beautiful towers and flag bedecked balconies. From the one would peal forth the thunder of welcoming bells, from the other the acclamation of thousands. The army of deliverance, we would enter the narrow streets of the ancient city, the first stage of our long victorious advance would be accomplished, and amid the benedictions of a ransomed people our hearts would dilate with that supreme emotion that life can offer, that emotion idealized on the fields of France, of her revolution and empire, whose name is that of the winged figure that her soldiers love to picture at the head of their victorious battalions—*la Gloire!*

3: December 14, 1914-January 11, 1915

December 14, 1914.

We have been camping in the woods for the last three days. These intervals of rest between our periods of service in the trenches are usually passed in cantonment at X——, a few kilometres behind the lines. During our last absence, the Germans got its range well and bombarded at long distance across the hills. The precision of their fire seems to have astonished those who witnessed it. At half past 10 at night the shells began to fall on the peaceful little village. When they ceased thirty soldiers and inhabitants had been killed.

In the hayloft where we had slept a few nights before a *marmite* crashed through the roof and killed five outright and wounded thirteen of our comrades of another company. So we did not return to X—— this time. Those who remained in the village spent their time pulling down what was left of the church tower, whose peaked belfry, showing across the ridge, gave away the position of our headquarters to the hostile batteries. We halted half way and went into camp in a huge bombproof hut in the sand under the bleak branches of the winter forest.

This morning we came back to the trenches for the sixth time. I happen to have kept track of our periods of trench duty (though I have lost count of the days of the week and month), but there is really nothing to distinguish this from the other stages of the monotonous existence that this *guerre des tranchées* imposes upon us at present. Once more the *reveil* in the dark, the hasty packing and departure, the march out of the woods and up the hillside, this time under the last quarter of the last moon of the year. A screen of driven clouds pales its radiance and hides the stars.

Crest after crest the forested hills spread out beneath and around us in the vast twilight. A pine grove crowns the ridge that we are mounting under cover of darkness. We have been told that the position we are going to occupy is one of extreme danger from artillery fire. It is not the gruesome recitals of the ambulance men that make us believe it. It is not the riven branches nor the craterlike holes half full of rain water in the fields. On the border of the grove are the fresh graves of our comrades. They have written the soldiers names on the bars of the little crosses; on the poles droop their red *képis*.

The section to be relieved is waiting for us in the shadow of the pine grove. Once more the hasty transfer, the descent into the black dug out, the jostling and disputes as the men get placed in the dark. A chill wind sweeps through the underground gallery. Someone strikes a match and tries to rekindle with straw from the floor the embers that smoulder here and there in holes picked out of the wall. The sergeant stops him before he has gone very far. It will soon be daylight, when no blue smoke must be seen curling out of the pine trees.

And while we are getting settled a brusque voice of command calls in through the doorway. Formally forbidden to go out during the day. It is a sinister confirmation of the reports of the peril of our situation. Certainly, shivering here in the unfamiliar dark, the prospect of the six days before us is not cheerful.

Guerre des tranchées! What is it that this word "trench" conveys to those who read it continually in the war bulletins—those who are disinterested, with curiosity; those whose hearts are at the front, with anguish? Probably much of what it would have conveyed to me before the war a kind of open irrigation ditch where the soldiers had to fight up to their knees in water, how they slept and how they ate being questions I did not ask myself. Certainly, the condition of the combatants is not anything like this, yet on the other hand the comfort and elaborate construction of some of these works of defence, such as I have seen them described by soldiers in their letters home, are of examples which I at least have never had the good fortune to inhabit.

The typical trench dugout resembles catacombs more than anything else. A long gallery is cut in the ground with pick and shovel. Its dimensions are about those of the cages which Louis XI. devised for those of his prisoners whom he wished especially to torture, that is, the height is not great enough to permit a man to stand up and the breadth does not allow him to stretch out. Down the length of one curving wall the soldiers sit huddled, pressed close, elbow to elbow. They are smoking, eating morsels of dry bread or staring blankly at the wall in front of them. Their legs are wrapped in blankets, their heads in mufflers,

Slung or piled about them, filling every inch of extra space, are rifles, sacks, cartridge belts and other equipment. A villainous draught sweeps by. Tobacco smoke and steaming breath show how swiftly it drives through. The floors are covered with straw, in which vermin breed. The straw is always caked with mud left by boots which come in loaded down and go out clean. To get new straw we sometimes make a patrol in the night to the outskirts of a ruined village in front of our lines and take what we need from a deserted stable. It is our most exciting diversion just now.

The roof of the dugout is built by laying long logs across the top of the excavation; felling trees for these coverings occupies a large part of our rest intervals. On the completeness with which these beams are covered with earth de pends the comfort and safety of the trench. Wicker screens are often made and laid across the logs, sods are fitted over the screens so as to make a tight covering and then loose earth is thrown back on top. This is an effective protection against all but the heaviest shells. If the roof is badly made, out of branches, for instance, the rain drips through and makes life even more miserable inside.

Where the lines run close together the soldiers sleep in the simple trenches and fire through small holes in the wall of the combined trench and dugout. Generally, there is room to build the trenches out in front of the dugout or alongside. There is a section of a company of infantry for each trench, and between the trenches there are deep communication ditches.

A squad has stayed behind in the woods to bring us the day's provisions. Before daylight it arrives and the distribution takes place. Great loaves of bread are handed down the line; each man takes his ration of half a loaf. There is one box of sardines for each two men. A cup of coffee, a small piece of cheese, a bar of chocolate must last us all day, until darkness permits another squad to leave the trench to go down after the evening soup. After food comes mail. Too much praise cannot be given the government for handling the soldiers mail so well. There are daily distributions on the firing line.

The short winter day has dawned. Its feeble light falls through the narrow doorways and all is now clear in the crowded dugout. The sound of voices grows less and less as the men fold themselves into their blankets, and one by one, tired out by the night watch, go off to sleep. I never could do this and have always fought against sleepiness in the morning. For with our life of darkness and chill I find a little sunlight, even if all I can get is through a narrow dugout door, is indispensable for the brightening of one's hours of reflection. I usually wait until the first *cheee-pann-pann-pann!* of the shrapnel bursting overhead marks the opening of the artilleryman's working day before I tumble off to sleep.

The smell of the wicker screens and the branches in the dirt on top of the trench reminds me of Christmas door's in American houses decorated with green things for the holidays. Then the smell of powder from the shrapnel kills the holiday reminder. I dare say Christmas will pass here without any change in our style of life. The insolent crest across the valley will still stand up, inviting steel to come and take it, and we shall go on waiting as patiently as we can for the day when we shall be ordered to advance against the shell and steel of the invisible enemy.

It will be a happy day for all of us, for uncomfortable inaction has more terrors than shell and steel.

DIARY

December 22, 1914.—Returned to Cuiry after five days in trenches. Will be here, it seems, until Christmas. Great things seem to be brewing. Rumours of a general advance in preparation. Last night a violent cannonade and rifle fire all along the line,—the first about eight o'clock, the second at midnight just after I had come in from guard. Hope this means business.

Went to a farm near by today and, waiting for coffee to be heated, missed *rassemblement* of company at noon. May get into trouble for this later but it has given me at least a free afternoon. An afternoon of memorable beauty; mild, sunny weather and loveliest blue skies. Sitting enjoying it on a pile of *betteraves* in the field behind Cuiry. It is so seldom one can get off by oneself to have a little solitude and time for uninterrupted reflection. I shall never forget the beauty of this winter landscape, the delicate skies, the little villages under their smoking roofs. Am feeling perfectly happy and contented. This life agrees with me; there will be war for many years to come in Europe and I shall continue to be a soldier as long as there is war.

December 31, 1914.—Spent a unique and agreeable kind of Christmas in Cuiry, brightened by thoughtful friends in Paris, who sent us all packages laden with everything good to eat and wear. Christmas Day itself was one of the most beautiful of cold winter days. Rose early and walked up to the farm over the frost-whitened hillside. Hot coffee and bread. Beauty of dawn, white landscape and steaming village. Pleasure of opening packages and reading letters in the hayloft. After morning soup, *rassemblement* and march off to work. But I played truant again and slipping off with gun slung over shoulder walked alone (not without considerable risk) to Beaurieux.

The soldier to whom I had given my wash the week before had been moved to Beaurieux, and as it was absolutely necessary to have the change of clothing, I had to be so far unscrupulous. Beautiful walk through the sunny fields. Accomplished object in Beaurieux and enjoyed walking about town, buying the few little things that were to be bought and talking to soldiers of other regiments. Home at sundown. Heated plum-pudding and made hot chocolate after supper and stayed up late talking in candlelit loft.

January 5, 1915.—We left the Moulin trenches and marched back to Cuiry on New Year's Eve. Spent a pleasant four days there. On New Year's Day, we rose before daybreak and the whole section was marched off to take a bath. We walked to Maizy and then turned off down the Canal de 1 Aisne. At a point, several miles beyond where the *poteaux* read about 16 kilometres to Berry-au-Bac and 34 to Soissons we came to a big sugar refinery. Here were excellent facilities for bathing and each man had a fine hot shower and the cold-water hose turned on him afterwards if he wished. In a barge moored on the canal-side a woman sold us hot coffee and bread too. This little excursion was a pleasant diversion taking us for a moment out of the narrow circumscription we had been moving in for the past two months.

I had always been anxious to visit the little neighbouring town of Chaudardes, whose picturesque belfry peeps up over the hillside only a few kilometres to the east. This was a good occasion and so in the afternoon, which was one of lovely skies and mild weather, I walked over. The little church proved to be exquisite both in line and in the patina of the old stones. It had not been desecrated either, like the poor little church at Cuiry, where the legionaries are quartered regularly now, sleeping in the pews, eating off the altar and raising a laugh sometimes by going through vulgar mockeries of the Catholic ritual. On the contrary, all was neat and well kept up inside. There was no one there when I entered except a soldier of the *36me*, who was playing very well on the little organ. I sat long and listened to him in the peace and quiet of the little white-washed interior.

Wandering about the village later I came across another soldier in a black sweater with an American flag pinned to it. I remarked in accosting him that it was the *drapeau de mon pays* and by so doing made a charming afternoon acquaintance. It appears that the man, who was an Alsatian, had become liable to military service in the French Army in some way, but going to the United States when he was 14 had escaped doing it. He was given amnesty, however, on condition of being mobilisable in case of war. Travelling on the Continent there fore at the outbreak of hostilities, he went immediately to his depot at Caen when the order to mobilise came out and became incorporated in the *36me de ligne.*

He was made cook for the *sous-officiers'* mess, in which capacity he was serving when I met him. He took me around to the kitchen and, seeing that his battalion was leaving for the trenches that evening and soup was early on that account, he made me stop and gave me a warm meal before returning to Cuiry. He gave me all kinds of provisions too and took me over to a *ferme*, where I met a young sergeant who spoke English well. We had coffee together and he told me all kinds of anecdotes about the experiences of the *36me*. I returned to Cuiry at sundown.

To His Father

January 11, 1915.

After weeks of inaction in trenches where the danger of attack was slight and there was nothing worse to be feared than the constant artillery fire, our company was moved last time into the little village of C——, the most dangerous part of the sector we are holding, where the line runs too close under the crest occupied by the Germans to be menaced by bombardment but where the patrols come down every night and harass our outposts in the most nerve-racking kind of warfare. Four days almost without sleep, constant assignment to *petit poste,* sometimes 12 out of 24 hours on guard in the most dangerous positions.

It was in one of these that I came for the first time in immediate contact with the enemy in a most unfortunate affair. I was standing guard under the wall of a *château* park with a comrade when a patrol sneaked up on the other side and threw a hand grenade over, which sputtered a moment at our feet and went out without exploding. Without crying to arms, I left the other sentry on the spot and walked down to the *petit poste*, about 100 metres away and called out the corporal of the guard. We walked back to the spot together and had hardly arrived when another bomb came over, which exploded among us with a tremendous detonation. In the confusion that followed the attacking party burst in the door that covered a breach in the wall at this spot and poured a volley into our midst, killing our corporal instantly and getting away before we had time to fire a shot.

On the 20th we shall have been three months at the front. Persistent rumours have it that we are going to be sent back to Orléans for a while on that date to rest. The English and Belgians in the regiment are going to their respective armies and the battalion is going to be generally reorganised. . . .

4: February 5, 1915

To the "New York Sun"

February 5, 1915.

We are back in cantonment after eight days on the firing line. This is the longest stretch we have yet done without relief. The reason? The *Kaiser's* birthday. We looked for trouble on that day and there was no lack of indications that we were going to have it. There has been talk of a mysterious paper thrown into the lines with the warning that a general attack was to be made. And in the still winter nights behind the hostile crest the continual noise of distant trains and motors could be heard, bespeaking a concentration somewhere along the line.

The preceding night I was out on sentinel duty. In a clear sky, the moon, a few nights from the full, flooded the hillsides, making it impossible for patrols to circulate. Not a shot was being fired. The sinister silence confirmed every suspicion that something was under way. At midnight, a French battery behind us broke it rudely and ironically by firing twelve times in succession over the crest as a birthday greeting. The enemy did not respond. And so, the long night wore away and the day came and passed without incident for us.

The blow had fallen on some other point of the line. Strewn pitifully along the summit of the crest opposite we who were on guard could still see the bodies of the French soldiers where they have been lying ever since September, when the magnificent *élan* of the battle of the Marne finally broke on this bleak hillside and ever since when both sides have been sitting facing each other, neither risking the perils of a further attack. Once more we have been cheated in our hope for action, but it may not be for long.

The greatest change has come over our life here lately. In my last letter, I described the soldier's days and nights in the trenches, and I am afraid I drew a rather gloomy though by no means exaggerated picture. For the last month, however, we have not been living in trenches at all, but in a ruined village. It has been much more romantic. Along the vast battle-line from Belfort to the sea each regiment has its sector of a few kilometres to defend.

Ours is a corner of field and forest fronting on the semi-circular crest of the plateau where the enemy are entrenched—a good foot-hold on one end of the crescent, too. Here the soldiers live in the earthen dugouts, amid all the discomforts I described. But at the foot of the hill, corresponding exactly to the position of the stage in a Greek theatre, lies the village of C——. From all the various points of the sector that we have been assigned to its battered houses and great burned down *château* have been visible. Other companies, though, had held it up to a month ago, when it came round to our turn.

It was under the full moon of a month past that we marched into C—— for the first time. I shall never forget the impressiveness of that stealthy, silent entrance. We had left our cantonment at midnight. Five or six kilometres through the forest and the road came out into a pleasant open country, covered with orchards. Sharply silhouetted in the moonlight against the black slopes of the plateau behind were the bright walls and peaked tile roofs of the typical little French town. I had become familiar in our march to the front from Mailly with the tragedy of these pretty centres of peace and happiness made desolate by war. But no scene of ruin that we passed through exceeded the spectacle that met our eyes here.

There had been no general conflagration in C——, it is true, for the Germans had not had time to fire it as they have done system-atically wherever they could. But there was literally not a house that had not been riddled with shrapnel or disembowelled by the deadly "*marmites*" that must have fallen on it in a perfect inferno of fire. Picking our way through the debris that littered the streets we filed in through that picture of desolation that makes always so striking a background for a column of infantry advancing.

Poor ruined villages of northern France! There they lie like so many silent graveyards, each little house the tomb of some scattered family's happiness. Where are the simple, peace loving country folk that dwelt here when these windows were squares of yellow lamp-light, not, as now, blank as holes in a skull? The men away at the war or already in their graves; the women and children refugees in the south, dependent upon charity. The pity of it all is that the French guns have done and have had to do the material damage.

When the Germans marched back in August there was no resistance to their advance. But it was with the artillery close on their heels that they were chased out in September. It is frightful to think that only at such a price can the French regain their conquered territory. If the enemy are to be driven across the frontier does it not mean that every town and village between must be laid in ruins? The alternative is staggering. . . .

At C—— our quarters are most picturesque. They are the wine cellars of the village's two *châteaux*. Here the soldiers have been able to bring straw, coal and candles, and with a good roof over their heads, safe from shells and from rain, enjoy a degree of comfort quite exceptional for a position where the crack of the German *mausers* as they snipe at sentinels seems at our very doors and where the *mitrailleuse* upon the hillside could rake our cellar door itself were it not for the encircling groves.

The big *château* has been completely burned down. Nothing remains but the shell. It sits in the midst of an immense, heavily wooded park, the wall of which, several kilometres long, forms part of our line of defence. Pretty paths intersect the dense groves. There are benches here and there, fountains and summer houses. The lawn that encircles the *château* slopes down behind to a charming little artificial lake. Everything bespeaks the pleasure retreat of some man of wealth and taste. Before the ruined mansion, truly *seigniorial* in its proportions, stand ancestral pines.

Nothing could be more romantic on a moonlit night than the view of these silent walls gleaming amid the great black cones; nothing more eerie than the silent grove, in which there is never the complete assurance that the park wall completely separates one from the lurking enemy.

The little *château* is in the town itself, surrounded by no considerable estate. It has been ripped open with bombardment, but was not set on fire. Strange enough, the pillaging of six months has not begun to exhaust the loot that litters its floors knee deep. Here all the possessions of some once comfortable family lie scattered about as they have been pulled from desk, cupboard and bureau. Sheets and pillowcases lie mixed up with family photographs and correspondence in a chaos of disorder.

Most pathetic to me was a little girl's postcard collection—cards from all over Europe, with their little messages of love or greeting. But most precious were the remains of a beautiful library, the last thing to be violated by the rude hands that have ransacked everything else and left not a bottle of wine in the whole town. Here, stacked just as they were before the invasion, I found finely bound, immaculate sets of Rousseau, Voltaire, Corneille and Racine. The wind and rain that blew in through the immense rents in the walls had not yet harmed them in the least. They were as fresh as the day they left the famous early nineteenth century presses of which they were the choicest examples.

I took away a few of these volumes, esteeming that the pious duty of rescuing an old book doomed otherwise to certain destruction might absolve me from the gravity of the charge that such an act made me liable to.

The advanced position that we hold in this village and the fact that we are far in front of our own batteries minimises the danger from artillery fire. Few shells, in fact, fall on C—— nowadays, then only when a group of soldiers expose themselves unnecessarily. But every night the patrols come down from the hillsides, and we are out against that war of ruse and sur prise, of treachery and stealth, which is most trying to the strongest nerves. Under these conditions sentinel duty ceases to have the air of a mere formality; it means a grave danger, a terrible responsibility. And seeing that the guard cannot be too rigid at this point we are all forced to undergo with heart-breaking frequency the ordeal of the *petit poste*.

The *petit poste* is the outpost which furnishes the most advanced sentinels before the enemy. Its composition and general arrangement may vary according to circumstances, but typically they are as follows: At daybreak, a dozen men and a corporal go out to the position and install themselves behind the rude shelters or defences that have been constructed.

During the day, the guard is simply two men on two hour watches. At night, however, the post is broken up into three little posts of four men each. These are in turn divided into relays of two, which alternate at intervals of one or two hours, as they choose, so that each man has six or seven hours on guard during the night. At daybreak, the whole squad is in turn relieved, for picket duty on *petit poste* is always twenty-four hours. During that time, whether on guard or off, no one is supposed to sleep.

To us, who are lodged now regularly in the cellars of the big *château*, guard usually falls at points along the park wall. At sunset, in little groups of four, we take up positions at a door, on a scaffolding rigged up inside, or in a little trench dug without. "Guard" means standing here with every nerve strained on the dark world outside; relief, sitting huddled in a blanket nearby, walking up and down to shake off drowsiness or stamping the feet to drive out the cold.

When moon or star light makes it possible to see some distance into the orchard, field, or grove outside this job is not so bad. But when the sky is covered and complete darkness draws the lurking menace down to within a few meters of this post then the sentinel creates for himself a thousand imaginary dangers.

As the night wears on the tension begins to tell. The senses of sight and hearing become subject to strange hallucinations. Surely someone is whispering out there in the darkness. Or else it is a low whistle, or such signals as pass between the members of a patrol. A black spot in the night takes shape and seems to move. A human form detaches itself from a tree trunk. As a shot rings out nearby along the wall the sentry's hand tightens on his rifle.

The very suspicion of a sound, a broken twig or a trodden stone, may startle him so that he can hear his heart beat. And so, with finger on trigger and every nerve tense he waits, alarmed enough to entertain the illusion but master enough of himself not to fire till the mark is sure.

"More than he who looks for the morning!" Never have I realised the force of this verse as in the interminable fourteen hours of these winter nights. It is heralded now by the morning star. In the last hours of darkness, amid the summer constellations just beginning to appear, the beautiful planet rises, marvellous, resplendent. Not long after the green glow of dawn mantles over the east. The landscape begins to grow visible, the black spots come out in all their innocuous detail. The little groups of men return to the central post. Here the relieving squad comes up before the stars have completely disappeared and the tired watchers are free to return to the *château*.

If the ordeal has been hard the compensation is delightful. I have said that the degree of comfort we enjoy in the cellars of the *château* far exceeds any that we had in the trenches. In these subterranean quarters, completely hidden from the enemy, nothing prevents us from burning as many candles as we like. The village cellars provide us with all the coal we need; its haylofts are still full of beautiful sheaves of un- threshed grain, just as they were stacked in midsummer last. By means of the little lake in the park close at hand we are able to keep at least comfortably clean. With these simple necessities attended to we have been able to make ourselves perfectly at home in the great stone vaults of the ruined mansion.

Here in the first hour after dawn the scene is most animated and picturesque. One by one the *petits postes* return. The men throw down their sacks and by candle light arrange their places for the day and hang up their rifles and equipment. The long, nervous tension finds, relief in a hubbub of conversation. "Did you fire?" "What did the volley mean at such a place and such a time?" A hundred questions pass as comrades reassembling seek to piece together the incidents of the night. Perhaps we ourselves have had a patrol out, and the adventures of these men are eagerly sought after and listened to.

Meanwhile the distribution of food takes place. A hot sup of coffee awaits the soldiers returning from *petit poste* in the morning. The soldier also "touches" his day's rations of wine, which, heated with a little sugar, makes an excellent sleeping potion. But most precious is the little measure of amber *"taffia,"* or sweet rum, that is doled out only in the trenches and at the front. There is nothing like it for reviving the spirits after a night in the cold. A delicious languor steals through the limbs. Gradually the conversation subsides. One by one the candles are blown out. The soldier lays out his sleeping place carefully, lingers over his preparations, so as to know in its fullness of sensual delight the bliss of falling to sleep.

How insipid beside it seem all the refinements of comfort that peace permits! Though we return to them once more we will never think without fondness of the luxury it was in these days of strenuous toil and robust health to lie down after a night's watch, in the straw covered cellar bottom of our ruined *château*.

Life, then, in C—— is infinitely more picturesque, more interesting, and more comfortable than life in the trenches, which is the lot of by far the greater part of the troops along the present battle front. What it gains in these respects, however, it loses in excitement. The village itself is without strategic importance, so that the likelihood of an attack *en masse* at this point is less than at most others. The German position on the plateau above is so strong that, on the one hand, they have no reason to want to better it here, and, on the other hand, the French have more advantageous things to do than to risk a frontal assault.

Their lines at this point, then, are little more than the maintenance of contact with those of the enemy, their real defensive works, in case of need, being well in the rear. This ground has not been very closely contested and there is plenty of latitude to circulate in between. Con fined to the underground shelters during the day by the artillery that thunders continually all around, yet little parties are free to go out at night and pursue more primitive and more ex citing methods of warfare. If prolonged inaction becomes too exasperating there is always this nocturnal man hunting to break the monotony and no lack of volunteers for it. The simplest form of it is what we call "shooting up a *petit poste.*"

Under the big pines in the *château* park we left a little mound and cross the first time we returned from C———. In modern warfare, where the chances for individual prowess are so reduced, one must give credit to the man who can achieve it one way or another, even if he be an enemy. And it was a little *coup d'audace*, well-conceived and well executed, that cost us the life of our corporal the first night at the *château*.

The third guard had just gone on. Two sentinels were placed at a point in the wall where the breach made by a shell had been rudely barricaded. Enough of the hole was left open to command a view of the hillside approaches by which an attack might be delivered, but of the ground immediately on the other side nothing at all. The moon had just risen.

The sentinels had hardly been on long enough to reconnoitre their post when a grenade fell at their very feet. The fuse sputtered a second and went out without explosion. A bolt out of the blue could not have astonished the two men more. With sickening certainty, the realisation came upon them that the enemy had approached without their knowledge and were standing there two yards away without their being able to strike a blow in self-defence.

It was a moment for quick decision. Yet no course of action that presented itself seemed very satisfactory. To fire was useless, for no possible angle commanded the ground just behind the wall. The call to arms might have precipitated the danger, which still hanging in suspense offered a better opportunity for overcoming. Leaving his comrade at the breach, therefore, the mobile sentry ran down to the *petit poste*, which was only about fifty yards along the walk, and called up the corporal of the guard, warning him of what had occurred.

A little incredulous, the old soldier buckled on his equipment, took his rifle, and preceding the sentinel, walked up the path toward the barricade. Before he had time to arrive another fuse appeared spinning over the wall at the same spot. Realizing the danger, he cried out to the sentinel who had remained, to save himself. He had hardly spoken when the bomb burst with a terrific explosion. Turning toward the *petit poste* the corporal shouted "*Aux armes!*" These were his last words. Almost simultaneously with the explosion of the grenade the enemy burst in the barricade, fired down through the smoke, and were off again before the bewildered men inside had time to answer. They shot well, for almost with the first ball the old veteran of Morocco and Tonkin fell, struck in the temple, and never moved again.

That night there was not much difference at *petit paste* between the two hours on guard and the two hours off. Everyone was on the alert, keyed up with apprehension. But nothing happened, as indeed there was no reason to suppose that anything would. Only about midnight, from far up on the hillside, a diabolical cry came down, more like an animal's than a man's, a blood-curdling yell of mockery and exultation.

In that cry all the evolution of centuries was levelled. I seemed to hear the yell of the warrior of the stone age over his fallen enemy. It was one of those antidotes to civilization of which this war can offer so many to the searcher after extraordinary sensations.

5: February 17–March 24, 1915

To His Mother

February 17, 1915.

You are quite wrong about my not realising what I was going into when I enlisted. I had not been living for two years in Europe without coming to understand the situation very well and I was under no illusion that the conflict which was to decide the fate of empires and remake the map of Europe would be a matter of a few months. I knew that it would be a fight to the finish, just as our Civil War was. The conflagration, far from diminishing, seems to be spreading. The lull during the winter has allowed each side on this front to fortify itself so strongly that, in my opinion, the dead lock here is permanent.

On the Eastern front the Russians under French direction may be able to accomplish something, but so far, the Germans seem to have had all the best of it. The easiest solution to see is the entrance of Italy into the hostilities, which might have the same effect as Roumanians action in the Balkan War. But personally, I can see no end at present. It will probably come about through influences other than military and such as are quite unforeseen now. At all events I do not expect to be liberated this year. . . .

Our Jan. 20 rumour of going to Orléans evaporated into thin air. Now it is Feb. 27 to Vincennes. Someone has suggested that they really meant Feb. 29th. But I do hope we shall have a little change of air soon. Will stop now for it is hard writing amid a Babel of conversation.

To His Father

February 26, 1915.

We have been here for six days in the trenches, out beyond the ruined village of C—— and halfway up the hill to the enemy's lines. It is quite the most advanced post we have held so far. We are not in fear of an attack here but the danger from patrols out looking for trouble has kept us on the alert these last nights. Guard all night, sleep all day,—that has been the programme. The moon has made the strain much less than it would have been had the nights been dark. These advanced posts are really the least dangerous, for one is not exposed to the artillery fire, can sleep all day in peace, or, standing at the door of the dugout, watch the shells raising the mischief with the lines in the rear.

I was shot a few days ago, coming in from sentinel duty. I exposed myself for about two seconds at a point where the communication ditch is not deep enough. One of the snipers who keep cracking away with their Mausers at anyone who shows his head came within an ace of getting me. The ball just grazed my arm, tore the sleeve of my capote and raised a lump on the biceps which is still sore, but the skin was not broken and the wound was not serious enough to make me leave the ranks.

The Germans are marvellous. You hear their rifles only a few hundred metres off, you feel them about you all the time, and yet you can never see them. Only last night when the moon set behind the crest, it silhouetted the heads of two sentinels in their big trench on top.

Rumours continue to circulate about our going to be relieved and sent to a third line position for a while for a rest. It is four months now that we have been on the firing line,—four months with the noise of the cannon continually in our ears. The latest is that the whole 18th Army Corps, of which we are a unit, is to be replaced by a division of the new English troops. I shall like a little change, but I am becoming resigned to this life and accept with equanimity anything that comes along. I see no end to the thing; it may go on for years. . . .

(ON BACK OF PICTURE POSTCARD SHOWING
FRENCH INFANTRY CROSSING C———)

March 3, 1915.

Here is the way we look marching, *l'arme* à *la bataille.* After six days' *repos*, we are going back again to the trenches tonight. In the course of a few weeks we expect to be reviewed by General Joffre, after which we shall probably go back to a second-line position for a rest. There is no chance of serious work before this time. We are just night watchmen at present, which does not please me, but which ought to comfort Mother.

March 12, 1915.

From today on, no more letters nor correspondence of any kind goes out until further notice. As this rule seems to apply to all regiments, it is probably motivated by military reasons. But if it were caused by nothing except a disgraceful article like that of ——'s that you sent me it would not be too severe. I should not think that I would need to tell you that that article is simply the low joke of a mind that thinks it funny to tell lies. If his lies did nothing worse than belittle his comrades who are here for motives that he is unable to conceive, it would be only dishonourable. But when it comes to throwing discredit on the French Government that in all its treatment of us has been generous beyond anything that one would think possible, it is too shameful for any words to characterize.

This man like many others of his type was long ago eliminated from our ranks, for a person buoyed up by no noble purpose is the first to succumb to the hardships of the winter that we have been through. A miserable weakling, in capable of feeling any generous emotion or conceiving any noble ideal, among the first to surrender in the face of suffering, he gives full rein to his perverted American sense of humour now that he can warm his feet amid the comforts of civilization again and it is his comrades who remain in the face of danger and suffering that must bear the odium that an act like that will throw on the name "American" as soon as it is brought to the notice of the authorities.

I should long ago have pulled strings to get into another regiment were it not, as I say and as I expected, that the winter's trials have pretty well weeded out the objectionable specimens and that the depots have sent us up to replace them men that are men and an honour to fight beside. . . . We have many Belgians with us here. Some French boys came up with the last reinforcement who were to commence their service this year or next and who were caught in conquered provinces when the Prussians came in. One was a prisoner in Lunéville three weeks until the French came back and drove out the invaders.

Another was the youngest of six sons in a little town near Valenciennes. His five brothers were mobilised at the beginning of the war. When the Germans entered his village, he was taken prisoner with all the other young men of military age and made to dig trenches for his captors. He managed to escape one night in the fog and cross the lines. There was nothing left for him but to engage in the Legion, for all his papers were lost. His mother and father remain behind in the village which is still in the hands of the Germans. If you can figure to yourself that mother, whose six sons are in the French Army, not one of whom she has had any news from since August, you will have some idea of what is being gone through with over here. . . .

To the "New York Sun"

On the Aisne, March 24, 1915.

Among so many hours in the soldier's life that modern warfare makes monotonous and unromantic there come those too when the heart expands with accesses of enthusiasm that more than compensate for all his hardships and suffering. Such was the afternoon of the review we passed the other day before the general of our army corps.

All the morning in the hayloft of our cantonment we laboured cleaning from rifle and equipment, clothes and person, their evidence of the week in the trenches from which we had just returned. At noon under the most beautiful of spring skies we marched out of the village two battalions strong.

It was pleasant this little promenade, to escape for a while from the narrow circumscription to which we are so strictly confined and get a glimpse of the outer world again from which we have been so long and so completely isolated. Here the littlest things were novel and charming—to pass through new landscapes and villages, to look on women and children again, to see automobiles and get a whiff of gasoline that has the strongest power of evoking associations and bringing back the life that we have left so far, far behind. In contrast with the sinister lifelessness and suspense that reigns along the front, here, as soon as one is out of the zone of artillery fire, all is bustle and busy operations.

Along the roads were the camps of the engineers and depots filled with material for defence and military works—piles of lumber, pontoon bridges in sections, infinite rolls of barbed wire, thousands of new picks and shovels neatly laid out, that raised groans from the men as they passed, for Caesar's remark about the spade having won him more than the sword holds curiously true in the Gallic wars of today, at least so far as our experience has gone.

The roads were teeming with life, lumbering wagons and mule trains mingling with thundering motor lorries and Paris auto buses in the immense work of *ravitaillement*, motorcyclists whizzing back and forth with despatches, *chic* officers lounging back in the depths of luxurious limousines that were once the pride of the *boulevards*. Whereas

175

on the firing line each unit has a sense of terrible detachment, here we could feel reassuringly the nation working behind us, the tightened sinews of that great, complex system of which we are but the ultimate points of pressure in the mighty effort it is making.

For fifteen kilometres or so we marched back over hill and vale, singing the *chansons de route* of the French soldier—along poplar lined canals where the big *péniches* are stalled, through picturesque villages where the civilians, returned to their reconquered territory, came to their doors and greeted us as we passed. Once we passed a group of German prisoners working on the roads. They looked neat and well cared for and took good-naturedly enough the stream of banter as we marched by.

On the sunny plateau, we were joined by the two relief battalions of the regiment that holds the sector to our left, and all were drawn up on the plain in columns of sections by four, a fine spectacle. We had not waited long when the general appeared down the road. He was superbly mounted, was followed by a dragoon bearing the tricolour on his lance and an escort of about a dozen horsemen. Four thousand bayonets flashed in the air as he rode by.

Then the band struck up the march of the Second Chasseurs and under the mounted figure, silhouetted on a little knoll, we paraded by to its stirring strains. At the same time, with a great fracas, a big, armed monoplane rose from the fields nearby and commenced circling overhead to protect us from the attack of any hostile aircraft to which our serried ranks offered so tempting a mark.

Again, we manoeuvred in position and while the *états-majors* were conversing we stacked rifles, laid down our sacks and broke ranks. I took the occasion to seek out a soldier of the ——*ème* and learn something of the kind of life they are leading on the plateau to our left. It is much more thrilling than ours apparently. The position is one of considerable strategic importance, so that the lines run within a stone's throw of each other. Sapping and mining go on incessantly. The noise of rifle firing never stops up there on the crest, and the nights are lit up continually with the glare of magnesium rockets. As if the menace of having the trench blown up at any moment under their feet was not trial enough, the proximity of the lines at this point subject the French soldiers to the fire of the "*minenwerfer*," or bomb thrower, those engines of destruction that were one of the several novelties that German prevision introduced into the present war.

The projectiles, as I understand it, are thrown from a spring gun, and not by explosive force, so that there is no explosion on their leaving the cannon. A sentinel with a whistle stands in the French line; whenever he sees one of these bombs arrive he gives the signal and anybody that is outside in the trenches dives into the nearest shelter at hand till the terrific explosion that they produce is past. Fortunately, the fire of these machines cannot be trained with much accuracy.

I asked this soldier if they had been attacked lately and he described to me their last engagement, a typical assault in the desperate kind of struggle that goes on at these points of close contact along the front. A ditch has been dug previously to the very edge of our lines of barbed wire. For hours before the attack is to be delivered the trenches are deluged with artillery fire so intense that the French are unable to man their first line defences, but must remain back in the communicating galleries waiting the decisive moment.

Suddenly the guns are silent and simultaneously the enemy pours out of the ditch forty, thirty yards away. Some carry wire cutters, others hold the rifle in the left hand and with the right shower the trenches with grenades that they draw from sacks slung over the shoulder. The French rush to their *créneaux*. The roar of rifle and machine gun fire bursts out, and a brief, ferocious struggle ensues, which is simply a question of the speed and number of balls that can be discharged in a given number of seconds and the speed and number of men that in the same time can be rushed against the position.

The attack in question was a complete failure and only resulted in piling higher the heaps of dead that lie where they fell in the continuous battle that at this point has been going on now for six months, with alternations of success that in no case can be estimated in more than fractions of a hundred meters.

Before I had time to gather details of this affair from my comrade of the ——ème the order "*Sac au dos*" ran through the ranks. "*Baïonnette au canon!*" "*Presentez—armes!*" went from captain to captain. Again, the flash of the 4,000 bayonets. And while the battalions stood there, silent, motionless, the band broke out into the "*Marseillaise.*"

At the first bars of the familiar strains even the horses felt the wave of emotion that rippled over the field and whinnied in accompaniment. There was something sublime about it there in such a place and under such circumstances. Unconsciously our lips framed the words of the wonderful song. Instinctively our eyes turned to the north. There on the furthest ramparts of the bare hills was the faint white line that marked the enemy's trenches, and two hundred, one hundred, fifty yards below, our own, where the comrades of our alternating battalions were even then engaged in the grim conflict pressing always on, desperately, determinedly, heroically.

Quoi, ces cohortes étrangeres
Feraient la loi dans nos foyers!

How marvellously every phrase of the song of 1792 applied to the situation of 1915!

Entendez-vous dans nos campagnes
Mugir ces féroces soldats?

The crisis was the same, the passion the same! May our hearts in the hour when the supreme demand is to be made on us be fired with the same enthusiasm that filled them as we stood there on the sunny plateau listening to the Battle Hymn of the Army of the Rhine!

All were in high spirits as we marched home that evening. We took a short cut, cross country, for it was already getting dark enough to traverse without danger the field where we passed a while exposed to the distant artillery. The last glow of sunset shone down the grey valley, illumining with a brazen lustre the windings of the river as we tramped back over the pontoon bridge and into cantonment again. Something breathed unmistakably of spring and the eve of great events.

And that night in our candle-lit loft we uncorked bottles of bubbling champagne. Again the strains of the noble hymn broke spontaneously from our lips. And clinking our tin army cups, with the spell of the afternoon still strong upon us, we raised them there together, and we too drank to "the day."

6: April 15–April 28, 1915

TO HIS SISTER

(Written in pencil on the fly leaves of "*Les Confessions de J.-J. Rousseau*," Genève, MDCCLXXXH.)

April 15, 1915.

We have just come back from six days in C—— where we were *cantonnés* in the caves of the petit *château* that I described in my last letter in the *Sun*. We put in a very pleasant week here,—nine hours of guard at night in our outposts up on the hillside; in the daytime sleep, or foraging in the ruined villages, loafing in the pretty garden of the *château* or reading up in the library.

We have cleaned this up now, and it is an altogether curious sensation to recline here in an easy-chair, reading some fine old book, and just taking the precaution not to stay in front of the glassless windows through which the sharpshooters can snipe at you from their posts in the thickets on the slopes of the plateau, not six hundred metres away. Sometimes our artillery opens up and then you lay down your book for a while and, looking through a peek-hole, watch the 75's and 120's throw up fountains of dirt and debris all along the line of the enemy's trenches.

Here is a volume from the library. I hope it will become one of the treasures on your shelves. It must be a very early if not the first edition of the "Confessions." You see it is only the first half, published probably before the work was completed. I have never read the "*Confessions*" except desultorily, but I am very fond of the "*Promenades*," which you will also find here, especially the fifth, about the Ile St. Pierre.

Spring has come here at last and we are having beautiful weather. I am going in swimming in the Aisne this afternoon for the first time. In fine health and spirits. . . .

To the "New York Sun"

On the Aisne, April 28, 1915.

I have delayed writing in the hope that something would happen here exciting enough to make really interesting reading. The *London Times* brings vivid accounts of the fighting at Neuve Chapelle and the copies of the *Matin* and *Journal* have personal narratives of the men who saw action in the Woevre and in Champagne. Besides these, full of the real flavour of battle, what is there for one to say who belongs to those units that have only been waiting inactive, preparing for the great events that advancing spring ought to be bringing nearer and nearer?

Yet on the other hand these units form really the great majority of the forces now on the front, as the scantiness of the official *communiqués* readily shows, and a description of our life during this interlude may have the interest at least of being typical of that of most of our several million other French and English comrades.

My Servian friend was telling me last night how at one time in his country's history there was a class of soldiers who remained continually mobilised on the frontier, always on a war footing ready to defend their land. These were the Granichari, around whom popular imagination has woven a whole cycle of poetry and romance. By means of signal fires they gave warning of the Turks approach. As we stood on guard back in the reserve trenches, alert for the fusillade that would mean the calling to arms of our company, it seemed to me that much the same thing was the case in France today. Only, whereas in old Servia these defenders were a picked corps of men, here it is practically the entire able bodied male population who make a living wall across the country that they are there to protect or perish for.

In this line our situation is about as agree able as is consistent with a state of war, which indeed, we are often able almost to forget. Our earlier discomforts were largely due to ignorance and an inevitable inability to adapt ourselves to the conditions of a kind of warfare that even to the old soldiers among us was a novelty. Six months have taught us all many things; our life is now arranged with methodical regularity and proceeds along a fixed schedule.

By a system of reliefs by alternating battalions the disposition of our time is as follows: Six days in the first line trenches, six days' repose in our village headquarters ten kilometres back; then six days' reserve in the woods; six days again in the village, and so the routine recommences. Thus, we have three distinct kinds of existence. I will give you a description of each one of these.

Of the three periods, every one of us would agree, that at the outposts is by far the pleasantest. For one thing, we are fairly free from bombardment, being at a difficult angle under the enemy's crest. And even more important, we are entirely free from work. The soldier does not object to danger, which it is his business to face, but he does decidedly object to the hard labour incident to trench warfare, which he feels is really not his affair at all, but that of the engineer corps, whose number, however, is quite inadequate to the immensity of the task. The pleasantest of our life here is due also to the fact that our company's sector is not open country, but the ruined village that I described to you in my last letter, where we are able to provide ourselves with comforts which our comrades in the trenches must do without.

At C—— nowadays we are housed in a little building that was once the stable or garage of the *petit château*. During the night, everyone mounts guard in the trenches up the hillside; in daytime, the sentinel furnished by a single post is all that is necessary, making it possible for the rest of us to enjoy complete repose and freedom.

At sundown, we assemble in the court of the *château* with blanket and tent cover and march out to the posts. Some of these are in a cemetery that got in the way of the flood tide of the Battle of the Aisne. The retreating Germans must have made a stand behind the mounds and grave stones, for the place has been fright fully bombarded. The shells that do not respect even the dead have shattered the monuments and burst open the sepulchres. Quantities of chloride of lime, liberally sprinkled about, are a remedy that is not much better than the evil, and the rats as big as rabbits that scurry under the banks and hedges and discourage one from lying down between watches make this the least desirable of all posts.

Better are the trenches further up the hillside, where in the calm of night, disturbed only occasionally by a fusillade or the cannon's double boom, one can contemplate at his ease the vast panorama spread out below, dim under the circling stars or emerging in the pale lustre of beautiful dawns.

Further up the slope the voices of the enemy are plainly audible. Even wider to them stretch those magnificent horizons, and I often wonder with what feelings they regard them. Beyond the utmost ridges, they had once penetrated, before our victory at the Marne threw them back to the bitterly contested plateau, strewing all the fields and roadsides between with their dead. There below them southward—tempting, provoking—lies expanded, almost coquett-ishly, the fair realm of France, and over behind the sunset hills—Paris! Violators outwitted, is it the regret of an irretrievable defeat that fills their long watches up there, or the hope of making another and more successful assault?

All our outposts now, no less than our main lines of defence, are protected by formidable barbed wire entanglements, behind which we can rest secure from the surprises that cost us lives in the early days of the campaign. The Germans have done no less on their side. In fact, night resounds with the hammering of stakes from all directions and in the quiet of his lone some watch the sentinel imagines with amazement what will be the cost of life for either army that attempts to break through a line which seven months of continuous work have fortified with all the murderous defences that ingenuity can devise.

At 3 o'clock now the east begins to pale, and an hour later the posts can return. Picking up our blankets we hurry down the hillside, through the cemetery and back to the *château* on the edge of the vil-lage. An hour of animated conversation ensues as the day's distribution is made and the places laid in the straw. Then a fine *siesta* until the cry of "*soupe*" calls us all out again around 11 o'clock.

In the long afternoons, no one has any desire to sleep. Warm sun-shine fills the enclosed garden of the *château*. Here the birds are singing and the buds swelling. Shielded from the sharpshooters up the hillside, one can write, sew, clean his gun and equipment, or attend to the hundred little things that fill the soldier's idle hours. Or he can walk in the *château* through a shell hole in the wall, climb to the first floor over a staircase level with debris, and picking his way through the lit-ter of insecure floors find out the little library, where beautiful books still line the shelves. Here he can read under the strangest conditions imaginable Rousseau's *Confessions* or Voltaire's *History of Charles XII*.

On the evening of the seventh day, when we are to be relieved, we go out into the village and bring back loads of unthreshed grain that American harvesting machinery has bound into most convenient little bundles. These we strap on our sacks to take back to the village in the rear for bedding. I was curious to know the weight we carried on these marches, and finding a twenty kilo weight I balanced a plank and placed this on the other end. Sack, cartridge belt and portable pick more than tipped it up, besides which one must add rifle, two haversacks strung over each shoulder and two canteens. But such is the hardening of a winter's campaign that one can carry this load of well over sixty pounds ten kilometres (six miles) back over a sandy road with only one stop and feel none the worse for it at the end.

Our life during the six days in the rear is of a nature designed to counteract the effect of the six days of enforced inaction at the front. It means chiefly work and field exercises. There is always one afternoon of target practice when, after many a period in the trenches without seeing a mark, it is a pleasure to hear the Lebel speak and to get a line on one's marksmanship. In a big abandoned sugar refinery, some eight or ten kilometres down the valley some fine hot showers have been arranged for all the troops in this section and a march down here with soap and towel comes on every visit to the rear and is greatly enjoyed by all.

Though these weekly returns to the rear are a relief after the strain of outpost work the element of danger is not really any further removed, for the village is well within the range of artillery fire, though hid by an intervening ridge, and shells came whistling into it occasionally, especially in reprisal for some misadventure on the firing line. Thus, the depot of the regiment on our right, who had wiped out a German post a few days before, was bombarded the other evening, and the pretty village whose old Gothic church peeks over the green ridge a mile east of us was veiled for half an hour in clouds of black smoke and the dust of the explosions in the narrow streets. A chance shell that came through the roof of a building where an artillery regiment was cantoned in our village one night cost more lives than were lost during their whole retreat from Belgium.

The third period—that in the reserve trenches a mile back in the forest from the front line—is the six days that are looked forward to generally with least pleasure. This is because it is the duty of the companies in reserve to work on the defences and the labour is infinite. Here we live in earthen dugouts, like all the rest of the trenches, the bottom covered with straw brought from C—— and the roof made of bags heaped over with branches and dirt.

Though the week in the second line is the period of hardest work it also brings opportunities for the most excitement, for the companies in reserve are also those which furnish the night patrols of reconnaissance. *Patrouille!* How the heart beats to hear the word go round in the afternoon and to learn that one has been chosen to take part in it. To escape from the eternal confinement of the trenches, to stalk out into the perilous zone between the lines and there where death may lurk in every thicket and uncertainty encompasses one close as the night, to court danger for several hours under a fine starlit sky, this is the one breath of true romance that we get in the monotonous routine of trench warfare.

I have always thought that in a sense this night patrol work was the most exacting on the nerves of all soldier's duties. In great actions where comrades fight elbow to elbow there are all sorts of external stimulants and supports. Each man is his neighbour's prop, there is the spoken and the unspoken encouragement, and borne up on a wave of contagious enthusiasm, individuals act no longer as such but in mass and everyone is as brave as the bravest. Besides one sees clearly, knows from which direction the danger will come and pretty much what to expect, and usually has ample time to prepare himself and muster up all his forces for the shock.

To the member of the little company creeping out over a battle-field in cold blood in the dead of night, all this is lacking. From every side the menace points, behind every turn the ambush may be hidden. He has nothing to rely on but his own *sang-froid*. Advancing over the ground strewn with bodies he faces in every shadow the possibility of the sudden volley at point blank that will lay him cold among them. It is a kind of adventure that the true sportsman will appreciate.

We went out, fifteen men, a few nights ago, to reconnoitre a new ditch that had appeared on the face of the hillside high up under the German lines. The moon in its first quarter, highly veiled by clouds, made the conditions good. We left about 9 o'clock, marching by twos down the wood road to C——. Once more the familiar passage through its barricaded streets, between its riddled walls and skeleton roofs and we walked on beyond and up the hill through a communication ditch to the outer trenches. Here a few brief instructions were given and the *chef de poste* was advised to tell his sentinels of our sortie and so we waded out over the barbed wire, for all the world like launching off over the surf from the security of land into the perilous unknown beyond.

The night was warm and windless. There were fruit trees all about this part of the hillside. They were clouded with bloom, reminding one of Japanese prints. But another odour as we advanced mingled with that of the blossoms, an odour that, congealed all through the winter, is becoming more and more intense and pervasive as the warm weather increases. Among the breaths of April, fragrant of love and the rebirth of life, it intrudes, the sickening antithesis—pungent, penetrating, exciting to madness and ferocity, as the other to tenderness and desire—the odour of carrion and of death.

We had not gone fifty steps when they began to appear, these disturbing relics of the great battle that terminated here on September 20 last, when these hillsides ran with blood. From that day, when our present lines were established, not a living soul had been in this area in daylight, and the rare few who have crossed it at night have been only the fugitive patrols like our own. What wonder then if the dead lie as they fell in the fighting seven months ago. Shapeless, dark masses as one approaches them in the dim moonlight, they come out suddenly at a few steps off in their disfigured humanity, and peering down one can distinguish arms and legs and, last and most unspeakable, the features.

Single or in heaps or files they lie—in attitudes of heroism or fear, of anguish or of pity—some shielding their heads with their sacks from the hail of shrapnel, many with the little "first aid" package of bandages in their hands, with which they have tried to stanch their wounds. French men and Germans alike, rigid bundles of soaked cloth, filling the thickets, sodden into the muddy beet fields, bare and exposed around the trenches on the bleak upper slopes and amid sacks, broken guns and all the litter of the battlefield.

The sight is one which may well be unnerving the first time, but one soon gets used to it, and comes to look upon these images of death with no more emotion than on the empty cartridge cases around them—which, indeed, in a way they do resemble. Having served their purpose, the material shell remains, while their vitality has been dispersed into the universe to enter into new combinations in that eternal conservation of energy which is the scientist's faith and that imperishability of anything that is beautiful in the human personality, which is the poet's.

In general, our patrols try to avoid useless collisions, which, as the English manual puts it, "serve no good end, give rise to reprisals and disturb the main body." But of course, there is always the chance of running into an enemy's party, and this not infrequently happens, as the sudden fusillades along the hillside show. If a patrol comes close and an enemy's post is alarmed they throw up a *fusée*—one of the many German innovations in this war which go to show their superior preparedness. The repeated flare of these on a dark night outlines in white fire their battle fronts across the continent.

They have perfected two varieties, both far better than our own, which appeared on this part of the front only a short while ago. One is simply a ball of magnesium or calcium light that is thrown like the ball out of a Roman candle, its brilliance beginning just as it reaches the apex of its curving flight and lasting just during its slow fall, thus lighting up all the surrounding country for several seconds with the most intense glare. The other is the same kind of light, only of longer duration. It is projected by a bomb thrower to that side of the zone to be examined from which the wind is blowing.

At the height of about a hundred feet a little explosion lights and at the same time liberates the fire ball, which is ingeniously suspended to a little parachute. It floats therefore horizontally on the wind back over the field of danger, lasting for several minutes and illuminating the country for miles around with a brilliance in which every blade of grass can be seen. When this occurs the *patrouilleurs* flop into any shelter they can find or, lying among the dead, escape detection as best they may.

The progress of a patrol is necessarily slow and much of the time is spent flat on the ground. As one's position is often enough right next to a body, curiosity may overcome his scruples, and so he can bring back souvenirs that will the next day be the admiration of his comrades—enemy's rifles and other insignia. A notorious pilferer among us brought in five pairs of new shoes that he had found strapped to a German sack the other night.

The most interesting finds of the kind that I have seen were some letters that a man brought in a few nights ago, from a German body up on the hill. They were postcards, dated the last of August and the first of September last. I wish I had taken them down textually so that you could share some of the emotion that was mine, contrasting with the poor shell of humanity up there in the grass these so living tokens of the ties that once bound him to earth. It was Austin Dobson's *After Sedan* exactly.

The cards, that were wonderfully preserved, were addressed to a certain "Muskatier Maier, bei Strasburg, the 136th Regiment of Bavarian Infantry," if I remember correctly. They were headed "*Mein Lieber Bruder*," "*Lieber Sohn*"—simple little family messages, reflecting a father's pride, a sister's love, a mother's fears. Far away in some German village they have long since found his name in the lists of missing. But soon we will go out in the night and bury these bodies nearest our lines as a sanitary measure, and the manner of his death or the place of his nameless grave they will never know.

Patrol work is the only way of winning laurels in the absence of actual fighting, and the little parties that go out have no end of adventures that make the conversation of the camp for days to come. Seven weeks ago, two Polish deserters came into the lines and gave us valuable information. That night the patrol that went out left the prisoners menu card for that day stuck on the barbed wire in front of a German post. A few days ago, another patrol passing the same spot found a basket in which the Germans had placed two bottles of Munich beer, a box of cigarettes, some chocolate, sandwiches and other samples of their diet, which, it must be said in justice to them, was not bad. On top were three letters addressed to us, "Dear Comrades," and couched in excellent French.

The tone of these was most polite. They said that they had been there all the winter in front of us and felt we were quite old friends now, though they had never seen any of us except at the end of bullet flight. They said that they had seen in our press reports to the effect that they were suffering from hunger and so enclosed this specimen of their daily fare to show what they were really enjoying.

The rest of the letters expressed much the same sentiments as those which are frequently shot into other parts of the French lines with bow and arrow, namely, that if we wanted peace all we had to do was to come out and sign; that England was their real enemy—why should France go on fighting and suffering terrible losses to pull England's chestnuts out of the fire? They hoped that peace would soon be signed and that a friendship and alliance would follow between France and Germany which would leave their hands free to deal with England, who for her selfishness and greed was really the common enemy of all mankind. They had three mobile posts up there in the woods, they said, and knew every time that we approached (which I don't believe), but did not fire, only signalled to each other and waited.

Firing as a matter of fact is becoming rarer and rarer along the line now in comparison to what it was in the winter, when Mauser and Lebel sputtered at each other all through the night. I have no doubt if we were to remain here much longer under the same conditions that there would be a kind of tacit understanding not to fire at outposts and that there would even develop neutral zones and surreptitious commerce between the sentinels, as I have heard from veterans was the case in the latter years of our civil war. For the evolution of hostility is naturally toward chivalry, not toward unmitigated ferocity.

The hymns of hate, the rancour and vindictiveness are the expressions of non-combatants whose venom has time to accrue in the quiet of studies far from the noise of the cannon. To the actual combatant the sense of the *grandeur* of his calling is too strong upon him to let such ignoble trivialities intrude. Without striking any the less strongly when the time comes he is yet ready enough to pay tribute to his enemy where tribute is deserved, and glad enough to be able to say of him as the old Spanish romancer said of his country's deadliest foe:

Caballeros granadinos,
Aunque moros, hijos d'algo.

7: May 10-June 15, 1915

May 10, 1915.

We all had our third typhoid inoculation yesterday and everyone is laid up, weak and feverish. There is a big bombardment going on up the river at Berry-au-Bac and we are all hoping not to have an alert, for it would be hard to do any work under such conditions. I do not imagine we shall have anything doing here, however, for the main operations seem to be in Flanders.

Summer has come here almost without any spring at all. The valley is very beautiful, all the orchards in bloom. Up in the woods the birds sing all day and I love to listen to the cuckoos, particularly in the early dawn at the outpost.

We have all been very excited about the news of the *Lusitania*. I suppose American public sentiment is terribly wrought up, but I have no hope that Washington will do anything and I was not surprised to see that Ambassador Gerard had been instructed to ask for an official report, on the basis of which a new note will be drawn up. Why in the name of all dignity does not the American Government act or shut up, for the *Gazette de Cologne* explicitly states that all indignant protestations will be received with absolute coldness?

I cannot understand the American state of mind, nor why Americans have the temerity to venture into a declared war-zone, much less let their wives and children go there, when anyone with a grain of sense might have foreseen what has happened. They might just as well come over here and go out Maying in front of our barbed wire.

I think we are here in this sector for good now and no one talks any longer of repose. All the regiments around us are in just about the position where they crossed the Aisne in September, the life on the front is being admirably organised and we enjoy a degree of comfort

189

now really inconsistent with a state of war. There are two shops in the village and we can buy practically everything we need.

To the "New York Sun"

At the French Front, May 22, 1915.

Night of violent attacks. All yesterday we listened to the hum of aeroplanes overhead and watched them cruising about amid their little satellites of shrapnel puffs as the vertical batteries bombarded them. About an hour after nightfall the firing began on a sector a few miles to our right, at first the abrupt fusillade, then the rumble of grenades, then the cannon entered into the medley, and the rattle of rifle and machine gun was completely drowned in the steady thunder of high explosives. At regular intervals, a terrific explosion as a heavy piece bombarded a village behind our lines to embarrass re-enforcements coming up.

From our outpost on the hillside we had a fine view of a magnificent spectacle. The German *fusées* kept shooting up like the "flower pots" to which we are used on the Fourth of July. The French fire rockets, mounting twice as high, let out their ball of vivid light that floated on the wind a minute or so over the battlefield. Beside the white glare of the fireworks the explosions of shell and bomb are momentary pinheads of red. A while and the lights become lurid and blurred in layers of smoke. The big guns far from the main scene of action begin to take up the chorus, firing on the flashes. Our own heavy batteries several kilometres back begin to thunder and we listen to the projectiles whistling overhead among the stars. . . .

Went out on guard this morning at dawn. An angle of buttercup field and forest. One would never have thought that it could be so beautiful, this world of green and blue that suddenly, almost without perceptible gradation, has succeeded the world of black and grey which has made winter so discouraging here, the air sweet with exhalations from the heavy, dew drenched grass. From the forest the sweet call of cuckoos and wood pigeons. May morning, rustle of leaves, sunshine, tranquillity. . . .

Today was the sixth and last at second line *petit poste*. Fine weather, warm and sunny. Some of the men, careless after a week without bombardment, were up on top of the turf-covered bombproof playing cards. Suddenly the distant boom of a cannon, and then, half a second later—*whang!* A shrapnel had burst twenty yards away in the branches of the grove that screened us from the enemy.

The sudden stampede into the dugout, then a heart-rending cry, and the frantic voices: "Pick up ——! pick up ——!" Two men go out, braving the momentary recurrence of the danger with that unassuming courage which is a matter of course in the trenches. They bring in the poor comrade, cruelly, mortally wounded. Another, less badly, has had his shoulder torn. We wait till the next shell bursts immediately overhead with a deafening crash. A man has been waiting for it, crouching in the doorway like a sprinter waiting for the signal. By the time the third shell comes he is far away in his race for the litter-bearers half a mile back. Until they arrive we who are not necessary to tend the wounded sit with downcast eyes and shaken nerves, trying not to look or listen, while six other shells in regular succession burst outside, the fragments pattering on the roof of the dugout and the acrid smell of the powder drifting inside.

This is the most distressing thing about the kind of warfare we are up against here. Never a sight of the enemy, and then some fine day when a man is almost tempted to forget that he is on the front—when he is reading or playing cards or writing home that he is in the best of health—*bang!* and he is carried off or mangled by a cannon fired five kilometres away. It is not glorious. The gunner has not the satisfaction of knowing that he has hit, nor the wounded at least of hitting back. You cannot understand how after months of this one longs for the day when this miserable trench warfare will cease and when in the *élan* of open action he can return blow for blow.

How is it that the enemy know so well our positions, for we are well hidden and they probably see no more of us than we of them? One principal way was explained to me by a friend who had visited the aviation fields a few days ago. While we take pains to keep concealed from the enemy's lines opposite, the aeroplanes are so much a matter of course that one scarcely takes the trouble to look up when the hum of a motor is heard, much less of ducking underground.

But here is a very real danger. It is not so much from the bombs that they occasionally drop on the lines and on the villages in the rear, but the observer up there with a camera of powerful telescopic lens is photographing all the time the country underneath. The film is developed that night and the prints scrutinised under a microscope. Details show up in this way that would escape the naked eye. It is thus that batteries and camps, posts and all kinds of military works are located.

The next day the gunner, in possession of the exact knowledge, can point his piece at leisure, and the moment when he thinks he can do most damage, sends us a few shells when the humour takes him and when we least expect them.

In billets, again. Was out on guard early this morning. Suppressed excitement in the little village as the streets begin to fill with officers and soldiers. Then a friend passes. "*Eh, bien! On y met,*" he calls out. Who that prides himself on his knowledge of French can translate that? It is an abbreviation for "*on met les cannes,*" which, I will probably still have to explain, means that we are going to clear out. The rumour is soon confirmed. Yes, after just seven months in this more or less tranquil sector we are actually going to get the change we have all been longing for, and on twelve hours' notice too. We leave tonight. Where? Nobody knows; but nobody doubts that it is to be into the thick of it.

I should like to give you some impressions of the state of mind before going into action, but unfortunately there is no time. The sacks must be made right away. Let me only say that I am heartily glad, and this feeling is increased when the news comes that poor little ———, who was wounded the other day, has died in hospital. Poor boy! It was the best thing for him.

It is good to get away from the constant danger here of dying thus ingloriously. If it must be, let it come in the heat of action. Why flinch? It is by far the noblest form in which death can come. It is in a sense almost a privilege to be allowed to meet it in this way. The cause is worth fighting for. If one goes it is in company with the elite of the world. *Ave atque vale!* If I write again it will no doubt be to tell you of wonderful things.

We are all in fine form, fit and eager for the assault. I think it will come soon.

Le jour de gloire est arrive!

DIARY

May 24, 1915.—Left Cuiry-les-Chaudardes after almost seven months on the Aisne. Were replaced by the *34ème* that came over from Beaurieux. Marched out at midnight. Stopped at dawn on the roadside on the plateau of Merval and had breakfast. Waited here for the autobuses. They arrived by hundreds about noon and, embarking, we came back over about the same route we traversed in October. Got out and had supper in a spot that looked out over the plains of Champagne, a wonderful picture, with Reims and the Cathedral in the distance. Marched from there by night to Ludes, where we passed the night in the stables of a Mumm *établissement*. Leave tonight for the trenches.

Puisieulx, May 25.—Spent a pleasant day in Ludes. It is like getting back into civilization again after seven months in the woods on the Aisne,—plenty of civilians, women and children, stores open. *Rassemblement* at sundown. Marched here over the plains and are to spend six days here in third line and then go up to the first, near the Ferme d Alger. An important sector with the trenches very close. The regiment has been broken up, it seems, and distributed along this part of the front. Our battalion, at least, (which is generally recognised to be the best) is detached and is alternating with the 38th battalion of *Chasseurs à pied*. Beautiful spring weather. Glad to be in Champagne.

May 29.—After some days of *repos* in Puisieulx, came up to the first line trenches yesterday evening. Full moon rising. Passed through a romantic forest, then out over the open fields to the Vesle. Crossed over an improvised bridge, then passed the canal and the railroad tracks. Here the *boyau* began. A fine piece of work, seven feet deep in the chalky ground and wide enough to walk in with ease. Came to first line which is very elaborately organised, and went out immediately on *petit poste*. Only a hundred yards from the German line. A great deal of firing at night. Both sides do plenty of bomb-throwing, but very little artillery fire here. Today went out to the outpost also from 4 to 12 m.

We are right on the national road from Reims to Châlons, at a point near the fort de La Pompelle, between the *Chasseurs* and the *411e de ligne*. The *génie* are doing some sapping here; they have made a lateral gallery some distance out to intercept any German saps, in case they try to repeat the manoeuvre that cost them so dear at the Ferme d Alger a few months ago. Here they exploded mines under our trenches and occupied the crater, but later were chased out by the *Tirailleurs Algériens*, since when the place has remained in our possession. The lines here are so near that the two sides can talk to each other easily. We told them a few nights ago, that Italy had declared war and they yelled back: "Yes, but against you!" Won't they be furious when they learn the truth!

June 3.—Are spending four days of repose in the *cagnats* on the railroad tracks. The canal with its high poplars where the wind rustles all day long is very pretty. It is pleasant here where we are in close contact with the French soldiers, the 38th Chasseurs, the 86th Territorials and the 411 *de ligne*. Not much likelihood of action, for all that is happening now is around Arras. Here the *1er Etranger* was engaged in the charge at Neuville-Saint-Vaast and suffered heavy losses. Rockwell, who was transferred to the *1er* a few months ago, took part in this affair and was wounded in the thigh.

June 10.—Spent six days in second line on the railroad tracks, then came back to a sector on the first, near the Auberge d'Alger. I went up yesterday and looked at the famous *entonnoir*. It is a huge crater, in the depths of which lie buried who knows how many Germans, *Sénégalais* and Algériens. The *Chasseurs* have strongly organised the defences here, which form a veritable little fortress on a height of ground that completely dominates the Germans. They have pushed in very close however, at one point less than 100 meters. There is a continuous fusillade at night and the echoes that crackle back from the woodsides and distant hills, in all kinds of fantastic modulations, never have time to die into a complete calm.

Once in a while a German cries out—"*Hey—Français—kaput, kaput.*" Then piquant dialogues begin, either in French or German, for not only are the two sides near enough to talk back and forth with ease but we can hear them talking among themselves and playing their harmonicas and accordions, a kind of music which the German soldiers seem very fond of. From our little height, we can see the towers of the Cathedral of Reims. Smoke often comes out of the chimneys of the factories, operating under the fire of the German heavy guns that let scarcely a day pass without throwing shells into the un fortunate city.

The French offensive around Arras seems to be extending to the south and there have been attacks the last few days at Tracy-le-Mont, between Compiègne and Soissons, and at Ville-aux-Bois, which is only a few kilometres to the right of Craonne. This may explain the sur prising announcement circulating this morning, that we are to leave again tonight for a *destination inconnue.* This pleases me. After the long *séjour* at Cuiry-les-Chaudardes and Craonnelle, one craves a little variety, and the more the better. These changes are exciting, for no one knows, when we leave, where we are going to end. All kinds of rumours start. Here are some of our destinations as different rumours have them on different authorities this morning: the Dardanelles, the Sucreries de Souchez, Hurtebise, la Ville-aux-Bois and Châlons. *Vamos à ver.*

June 13.—Left La Pompelle at midnight and walked in the early summer dawn to la Neuville, behind Verzy. Spread blankets in a field, had coffee, lay down and had a good *siesta*. Automobiles arrived at noon. Crowded into them, eighteen men to a wagon. Started back west and soon came into same road that we had walked over in October when our squad was escort for the *convoi*. Held this to Fismes and so back again to the plateau of Merval. Here *sac au dos* and we marched down to Œuilly on the Aisne, where we went into billets for the night.

Had a fine swim in the Aisne yesterday after noon, then early soup, *rassemblement*, and we started off again. Turned up the Laon road and through Moulins, came to Paissy on the plateau, where we relieved the *6e de ligne*, who have been here since October. Picturesque village built along the road that crowns a deep horse-shoe ravine. Bottom filled with poppy fields, tumbling stream, distant vistas, Back in the heroic battlefield of the Aisne, with its ruins in the villages and ancient trenches in the fields. Some of the *18e de ligne* are also billeted here and it was they who suffered so badly in the German attack on January 25th. I talked with men who were in this affair. It seems the Germans, the morning after the attack, paraded their prisoners on the crest opposite the French.

The second and fourth companies went into the trenches some 1,500 meters beyond. Evidently, they made too much noise making the *relevé*, for the Germans began launching bombs, which killed four men and wounded several others, including the captain of the second company. We stayed in the village in reserve.

Our section was on guard. Mine fell in the night from 12 to 2. Kept watch at a point on the edge of the plateau right beside the emplacement of a 75 which was cleverly concealed. An artilleryman of the 140 slept in a hole in the ground nearby. *Consigne* to wake him if anything happened. Very quiet in comparison with Champagne, where there was a continual fusillade at night and where we amused ourselves in the daytime shooting through the *créneaux*. Those shots that were fired, however, whistled uncomfortably near the sentinels' ears, cracked in the branches and fell in the ground nearby.

The villages in this part of the country are very old, built in stone blocks taken from the famous quarries of the Aisne. These are all about here, immense grottoes in the solid face of the hillside. It was in one of these that the two companies of the *18e* were trapped while sheltering themselves from the bombardment.

June 15.—Came up to the reserve trenches a mile northwest of Paissy on the plateau. Here the English fought in September—it was about the extremity of their right wing—and there are many graves of British soldiers in the fields all about. We are at the head of a deep ravine which commands a pretty triangular *vista* of the valley of the Aisne through a frame of foliage and of the plateau beyond. Hot, sunny summer weather. A lazy period of almost complete repose. The artillery does a little close range work occasionally, but otherwise the utmost calm prevails here. They call this war!

It seems we are going to make another move tomorrow. They say we are going back to Aï, near Epernay, where we shall form part of a division of reserve. This news pleases me immensely. If true it means almost certainly that we shall have henceforth no lack of action and movement and variety. These troops will probably be thrown in to attack at any point along the front where they are needed.

Here then is a fitting place to close this first chapter of my experiences. That we have been eight months on the front without having once attacked or been attacked need not cause any surprise, for a great part of the troops now in the trenches are in the same position. It seems to have been pure hazard that an easy sector fell to us, just as it was good luck that our battalion and Bataillon D had the low sector at Craonnelle, whereas F and G, who were on the crest of Ouldres, suffered almost daily losses during the winter from bombardment. The winter in the trenches was certainly hard, but it is already far enough away for the miseries to fade out of the picture, and for the rest to become tinged with the iridescence of romance.

What is Virgil's line about the pleasure it will be sometime to recall having once done these things? I have known that all along, through no matter what fatigue and monotony. Never have I regretted doing what I am doing nor would I at this moment be anywhere else than where I am. I pity the poor civilians who shall never have seen or known the things that we have seen and known. Great as are the pleasures that they are continuing to enjoy and that we have renounced, the sense of being the instrument of Destiny is to me a source of greater satisfaction.

Nothing but good can befall the soldier, so he plays his part well. Come out of the ordeal safe and sound, he has had an experience in the light of which all life thereafter will be three times richer and more beautiful; wounded, he will have the esteem and admiration of all men and the approbation of his own conscience; killed, more than any other man, he can face the unknown without misgiving—that is, so long as Death comes upon him in a moment of courage and enthusiasm, not of faltering or of fear; and that this may, if necessary, be the case, I shall strain all my will the day that it comes round to our turn to go into the furnace. I have a feeling that that day is near at hand.

8: June 18–August 8, 1915

Magneux, June 18, 1915.

Received your letters and clippings yesterday on the march. I am not thinking of anything else but the business in hand, and if I write, it is only to divert the tedium of the trenches and to get a little intellectual exercise of which one stands so much in need now. You must not be anxious about my not coming back. The chances are about ten to one that I will. But if I should not, you must be proud, like a Spartan mother, and feel that it is your contribution to the triumph of the cause whose righteousness you feel so keenly. Everybody should take part in this struggle which is to have so decisive an effect, not only on the nations engaged but on all humanity.

There should be no neutrals but everyone should bear some part of the burden. If so large a part should fall to your share, you would be in so far superior to other women and should be correspondingly proud. There would be nothing to regret, for I could not have done otherwise than what I did and I think I could not have done better. Death is nothing terrible after all. It may mean something even more wonderful than life. It cannot possibly mean anything worse to the good soldier. So do not be unhappy but no matter what happens walk with your head high and glory in your large share of whatever credit the world may give me. . . .

DIARY

Magneux, June 19, 1915.—Left the reserve trenches above Paissy yesterday at 2 o clock. Relieved by the *218e*. Marched down the picturesque ravine through Moulins into the valley of the Aisne. Crossed the river at Hautes-Rives, then past the sugar refinery where we have been coming to bathe during the winter. Sunny, very hot afternoon.

Came pretty near to dropping on the climb up to the plateau of Merval. Stopped halfway up and had supper in the fields. Then continued through Merval and Baslieux here to Magneux, near Fismes, where we have spent the night. Many civilians here and conditions apparently quite normal. Saw electric lights and railroad trains for the first time in eight months. German aeroplanes have been dropping bombs on Fismes regularly of late and a while ago killed seventeen soldiers *d'un seul coup*. Our protection against aeroplane attacks is very inferior to the Germans, whose special aeroplane guns shoot very accurately, whereas our ordinary field pieces, turned on so difficult a mark, go very wide.

Chalons-sur-Vesle, June 20.—Left Magneux at 3 o clock this morning. Marched down the *route nationale* through Jouchery and Muizon here to Châlons-sur-Vesle, where we arrived at 8.30. Fine summer weather; stood the march well and enjoyed it. A fugitive glimpse of the cathedral towers. I am afraid the Germans are going to bombard Reims and the cathedral as a reprisal for the recent French air raid on Carlsruhe. This morning as we left Magneux we saw a Taube and a few minutes later heard the explosions of the bombs it let fall on Fismes. Why can't the French stop this?

Do not know how long we are going to stay here or whither we are going. Would that we could take part in an assault on the Fort de Brimont, where the Germans have placed the heavy guns that fire on Reims and the cathedral. Fitting death for an artist, to fall avenging this outrage to Art in one of its most perfect manifestations.

Appel this evening at nine. Took a solitary walk about a mile out of the village. Found a high spot that commanded a wonderful view toward the east, with Reims and the cathedral about 10 kilometres off and beyond Nogent and the heights from which the enemy dominate it. Very beautiful country. The first harvest has been reaped and the tan of the haystacks and stubble and the scarlet of the poppy-fields mingles with the fresh green of the early summer landscape. In the distance could be heard the rifle shots and the occasional booming of cannon, but here all is peaceful and quite normal. The women and children have all returned, the men work in the fields, the church-bells toll the hours and quarters. Sat for a long while looking eastward, till the city and the roofless cathedral faded out in the twilight and the waxing moon brightened in the south. Tomorrow we go to the trenches.

June 23.—Came up to the first line trenches at sundown day before yesterday. Marched single file through what seemed miles of *boyau*. An immense labour has been spent upon these long zigzag ditches, often six and seven feet deep in the chalk. Went out immediately on *poste d'écoute* until midnight.

A very quiet sector here, with practically no artillery nor rifle fire. There seems to be a kind of *entente* not to shoot on either side. But the reason may be that the trenches here are on a level plain and the tall grass makes each line invisible to the other. The guards, in the daytime, watch by means of a periscope, through which, raised about a yard above the parapet, the white line of upturned chalk can be seen over the tops of the meadow grass and flowers some two or three hundred yards away. We are about four miles up the line from Reims, about a mile out in the plain from the *route nationale* where the kitchens are. In front of us is the Fort de Brimont. We have a fine unobstructed side view of the cathedral. The chimneys of the city are smoking. This sector is really too quiet, it is a place for territorials. I do not believe we shall be here long.

June 26.—On *poste d'ecoute* last night from 8 to 12. Great celebration among the Germans opposite, drunken songs and uproar. Today came the news of the Russian evacuation of Lemberg. That was the reason then. This success of the German armies is of an importance that all the depreciation of the Allied press cannot serve to blind one to. It looks as if munitions were seriously lacking in Russia. I seem to see now the reason for Hindenburg's raid into Courland and the capture of Libau. In conjunction with the present advance in Galicia, this makes a more and more dangerous salient of the Russian central front in Poland.

I believe that the Germans will cut in now from north and south and that Warsaw will be theirs within a month. If they will not then have utterly destroyed the Russian armies, they will at least have so far paralyzed them that they will be incapable of any serious offensive for many months to come. Entrenching therefore on a line that they will be at liberty to choose, the Germans will leave on the eastern front just sufficient troops to cope with the demoralized enemy and transport the bulk of their mighty offensive power, flushed with victory, either to the Italian or more likely to the French front.

It would seem as though now, if ever, were the moment for our great offensive here, for the trenches opposite are probably denuded more than they will ever be at any time to come. But the battle around

Arras has been raging now for a month or more and yet we seem unable to make any serious progress. Optimism does not run very high among us these days and it is not encouraged by the singing and noisy confidence of the enemy opposite.

Merfy, June 29.—Rumour has it that we are not to be here long, but will make another change of sectors even before our next trip to the trenches. Another winter campaign that we have all been dreading has now become a certainty, and the English papers are not hesitating to talk about the postponement of the Allied offensive until next spring. The *Kaiser*, however, has made a speech in Berlin, saying that the war would be over before winter.

To His Mother

July 3, 1915.

We have been spending six days in a pleasant little village here behind the lines. Life has resumed much of its normal aspect. Every evening there is *salut* in the old church and on Sundays mass. The nave is always crowded with soldiers, even though there be few real believers among them. But these services, where the voices of the soldiers mingle in the responses with those of the women and little children of the village, are always peculiarly moving to me. The Catholic religion, idealising, as it does, the spirit of sacrifice, has an almost universal appeal these days.

Things don't seem to be going very well for the Allies of late. More discouraging to me than the Russian defeats in Galicia is the check of our offensive around Arras, which without doubt was not a local action intended only to gain a strategic position, but was an attempt to break the German lines, deliver Lille, and deter mine a German retreat from the north of France. In this larger end we seem to have failed. The first regiment of the *Légion Etrangère* led this attack very gallantly and were almost annihilated. I have friends who were wounded in this affair and I envy them, for we are still condemned to the same old inaction. . . .

Had I the choice I would be nowhere else in the world than where I am. Even had I the chance to be liberated, I would not take it. Do not be sorrowful then. It is the shirkers and slackers alone in this war who are to be lamented. The tears for those who take part in it and who do not return should be sweetened by the sense that their death was the death which beyond all others they would have chosen for themselves, that they went to it smiling and without regret, feeling

201

that whatever value their continued presence in the world might be to humanity, it could not be greater than the example and inspiration they were to it in so departing. We to whom the idea of death is familiar, walking always among the little mounds and crosses of the men "*mort au champ d'honneur*" know what this means. If I thought that you could feel about me as I feel about them, the single self-reproach I have, that of causing you possible unhappiness, would be mitigated.

I do not say this because I do not expect, eight chances out of ten, to come back safe and sound, but because it is always well to fortify oneself against the undesired event, for by so doing you will make that, if it happens, easier to bear and also you will make the desired, if it occurs, doubly sweet.

The article about Rupert Brooke, in which my name was mentioned (owing to the fact that the editor of this department of the *Literary Digest* is an old friend of mine), gave me rather more pain than pleasure, for it rubbed in the matter which most rankles in my heart, that I never could get my book of poems published before the war. . . . . But there is no use crying over spilt milk. I have no doubt the MS. is safe in Bruges, buried as it is; safer, indeed, than it would be, subject to the risks of transportation now. I have good friends who will charge themselves with it if I should be prevented from doing so myself.

We have finished our eighth month on the firing-line. Rumours are still going round of an imminent return to the rear for reorganisation. I think they may really be true this time. I will try to locate parcels, but do not send any more till I do. . . .

DIARY

La Neuvillette, July 8.—Our last six days in the trenches were broken by the most memorable, extraordinary, and happy event since we enlisted. On the evening of July 3rd, the sergeant came quite unexpectedly to get the names of all Americans wanting permission of 48 hours in Paris! We could hardly believe such good fortune possible. But it seems the American journalists in Paris had made up a petition to get us a Fourth of July holiday, and the Minister of War had accorded it. We fairly danced for joy. To see Paris again after almost a year's absence!

We were to leave immediately. So, packing our sacks we walked down the *boyau* about night fall to the *poste du commandement*, where we left all our equipment and got our individual per missions. Then to Merfy, where we spent the night. Next day after breakfast in the village we marched—thirty-two of us in all—to the railway station of Moulin-de-Courmont, on the; line from Fismes to Reims, where we got on the train at two o clock and left. Arrived at Noisy-le-Sec at nine and continued to the Gare de 1'Est on another train. Joy to walk in the streets of Paris again.

Notable absence of men in Paris; many women in mourning. A great many wounded soldiers on *congé de convalescence*, almost all wearing the old dark blue capote and red trousers. A little *malaise* and discouragement among the Parisians, probably at the absence of good news from Arras, the certain prospect of another winter's campaign, and the great weariness of the war, which it is difficult for them to realise so far from the front.

The visit did me good, on the whole, for with all its bringing home the greatness of the sacrifice I am making, it showed me clearly that I was doing the right thing, and that I would not really be so happy anywhere else than where I am. The universal admiration for the soldier from the front was more than any pleasure. It was a matter of pride, too, to salute the officers in the street, especially the wounded, and feel the fellowship with those who are doing the noblest and most heroic thing that it is given to men to do. . . .

Back to the first line trenches again. Then came down here to second line, where we are *cantonne* in a big glass factory just at the point where the Aisne canal crosses the *route nationale*. Factory knocked to pieces by bombardment. Very near Reims, where I hope to get permission to go for a day before we leave. The specialty of this place is beer, which the soldiers bring out from Reims every day at three o clock.

Rumours of great changes in the regiment which have been going about for a long time, seem now to be coming to a head. The Russians, it seems, are to be sent to the Russian army or allowed to join a French regiment. The same with the Belgians. What is left of us after this drain will be joined with what is left of the *1er Etranger* after their charge at Arras, and formed into a single *régiment de marche*. To put through this reorganisation will probably mean our going to the rear for a certain time. Juvisy is the place the rumour has it we are going and the date of our departure July 12. *Vamos à ver!*

July 11.—*Section de garde* yesterday. Put in eight hours under the bridge where the national road crosses the canal. Today a comrade and I were to go to Reims, for the captain had promised us permission. I was very anxious to see the state of the city and of the cathedral. But no such luck. We had only come back from the *poste de police* a few hours when "*tout le mande en tenue, faites vos sacs*" ran down the line from section to section. At first, we thought it was an *alerte*, but a few minutes later the real explanation came. All Belgians and Russians to leave for the rear immediately! This long-heralded change at last arrived.

Great delight among those affected. Great *cafard* among those not, for it meant that we who were left would have to go back immediately to the trenches, after only two days in second line, to replace the men lost from Battalion F. This we did about midnight and, while half the regiment was noisily commencing its journey back to Orléans, the rest came up through the *boyaux* to their old emplacements, where after a night on guard we now are. For how long ? The departure of the Russians and Belgians will take almost two-thirds of the strength of the regiment. Will it be possible to reorganise here on the front, or will it mean going back for a while to a point behind the lines? We all hope so. But all is veiled in secrecy at present.

Courcelles (near Reims), July 12.—Stayed in the trenches only twenty-four hours. At midnight we were relieved by the 75th Territorials. Marched back down the *boyaux* to the glass works at La Neuvillette, and then continued on down the dark towpath of the canal to Courcelles, on the outskirts of Reims, where we were comfortably *cantonnés* for the night. Have been working hard all the morning on *corvée* with the *génie*. We made three trips to Merfy in a big motor lorry, which we had three times to load and unload with planks and logs. Waiting here with sacks made, expecting momentarily to move. Was accosted this morning by a corporal in the *75e* Territorial, who remembered seeing me in Lavenue's at Paris, and recognised me, in spite of moustaches and short hair. I remembered him, too.

Couthenans (Haute-Saône), July 15.—Spent a quiet night and day in Courcelles. Then yesterday morning before daybreak, *réveil, sac au dos, et départ.* We marched to Muizon, and there the battalion entrained for the first time since the trip to Mailly in October. Cattle cars with benches, one section per wagon, very crowded. An exciting journey, for no one had any idea where we were going. The first general supposition was Orléans, *via* Noisy-le-Sec, for we knew at least that the chief reason for our going to the rear was reorganisation, after the serious thinning of our ranks occasioned by the loss of the Belgian and

Russian volunteers, and probable amalgamation with what was left of the *1er Etranger* that was cut up at Arras.

This hypothesis was shaken, however, at a junction near Fère-en-Tardenois, when we turned southward on a branch line to Château-Thierry. We still cherished hopes of going to Orléans by a round about way, even as far as Châlons, and watched eagerly every junction where a line turned to the right. When at Châlons we forked to the left, the last ray of hope was extinguished and every one was sure that we were headed directly for the terrible sectors of the Argonne and the Meuse. But this discouragement was relieved when, after passing Vitry-le-François (where there was a cemetery filled with crosses for the men who fell in the big battle here in September) we did not branch up to Bar-le-Duc, but turned south to Saint-Dizier. The impression then began to grow that we were going down to Lyon, the depot of the *1er Etranger*, and thence to the Dardanelles.

Next morning, however, after one of those frightful nights in troop trains, where, packed together, one cannot stretch out in spite of sleepiness, we woke up at Vesoul. Alsace then seemed to be a certainty to everyone. I for my part was glad, for it is of all places the one which I would choose to fight in and, if need be, to fall. At Belfort, we learned our true destination Montbéliard. Arrived here we expected to go immediately into some *caserne*. No such luck. In spite of lack of sleep and the fatigue of the journey, we had to put *sac au dos* and start off in a pouring rain on a ten kilometre "hike" to Couthenans.

In the villages on the way were cantoned the Algerian *tirailleurs* who had taken part in the Arras actions. Splendid-looking troops in their new khaki uniforms. Here had been cantoned the remains of the *1er Etranger*, but they moved them elsewhere, for there was some idea against the two regiments coming in contact. So now we are back again with the old Moroccan division, the *troupes d'élite*. We shall be here probably several weeks and then go immediately into some important action. It looks as if the Germans will make an attempt to regain the ground we have taken from them across the Vosges; there are even reports that Hindenburg is coming into Alsace.

I expect that we shall go into something very exciting shortly. Meanwhile we are to be reorganised and put through exercises such as we had in Toulouse and Mailly. The country here is very pretty and the inhabitants *gentils*.

Plancher-Bas (Haute-Saône), July 17.—All previsions were reversed last night, when the order came to hold ourselves in preparation for immediate departure. This morning *réveil* at 4 o clock and *sac au dos*. Marched here about 18 or 20 kilometres, through a pleasant hilly country, covered with deep woods and rich meadows, the heavy verdure and vegetation of a land of frequent showers. Beyond Chagey passed a monument to the local soldiers of 1870 and presented arms as we marched by. Had a good breakfast at the little inn on arriving; then went out with the squad on 24 hours guard. The whole *Légion Etrangère* is marching with us and every one expects that we are going into action. I have had the pleasure of meeting Victor Chapman, who is in the *mitrailleuse* section of a *régiment de marche* of the *1er*. It will be pleasant to be together in the big events that we are undoubtedly soon to take part in.

July 19.—I guess we are to be here some time. It is a delightful cantonment. In the little inn, "*Le Cheval Blanc*," right opposite the house where we are billeted, one can dine very well and linger over coffee and *petite verres*. It is the *arrière* in every sense. Once or twice I have fancied that I caught the distant voice of the cannon in Alsace, but in general one feels far removed from the theatre of war. It is the first country we have been in near the front that the Germans have not passed through, and all the civils are here pursuing their ordinary occupations. The race seems to be strong here, the peasant women buxom and often really pretty. We are right at the foot of the Vosges and the scenery is charming.

This morning everyone was full of good will and good spirits, and we really enjoyed the drill and exercises in a big meadow near the town, under a blue sky washed clear by the last few days rains. We shall probably put in a good deal of time in field exercises from now on, which we are really in need of after a winter in the trenches. They will stand us in good stead if we are to attack in Alsace, as I hope. King returns today after two months' permission, and reports that the French are concentrating here in the East, in view of big operations to come. Wagon-trains of the Moroccan division pass through here continually, conducted by swarthy *indigènes* in khaki and red *fez*. They will be good men to fight beside.

Today comes the report that the Germans have crossed to the northern front in Poland, and are therefore seriously threatening the Warsaw-Petrograd Railway. The military situation on the Russian front is very interesting. The Grand Duke will be forced to risk a decisive battle around Warsaw or else abandon it. The first is dangerous for him, the latter a terrible loss. Indeed, it is doubtful if he will now have the time or the means to withdraw his centre in Poland. If the Russian centre is surrounded and forced to capitulate it will be the *débâcle* so far as our Ally is concerned, and the transfer of immense forces from the eastern to the western front will make our task doubly hard.

July 27.—Pleasant days here in the rear. Morning and afternoon, we generally have exercises, *marches militaires*, and reviews. But there is always plenty of time on each side of the morning and evening meal to rest, read, or loaf. This we do—King and I usually—in the *cafés* of the village. There is the *"Cheval Blanc"* across the street, but pleasantest of all is the Café de la Gare, on account of the pretty *gosse* that serves one there. I am reading Treitschke's "Lectures on Politics," that Chapman lent me, and the daily papers, where the news from the Russian front these days is very *passionnant*. The country people here are interesting and agreeable.

Next door I sometimes speak with the old man whom one usually finds walking up and down in his yard alone after dark. His son disappeared in the forest of Apremont in October, and has never been heard of since. It was his only son; the daughter showed me one day the photograph of her brother, a fine-looking young fellow, a corporal in one of the Belfort regiments that marched into Alsace at the beginning of the war. It is one of the thousands of similar tragedies with which France is filled these days.

Of the initial offensive in Alsace and the disastrous adventure at Mulhouse the people here will tell you much, showing the utter foolhardiness and unpreparedness of the enterprise, notwithstanding its gallantry. Bands of *permissionaires* pass through the village daily, for they have begun to give eight days' permissions to the men on the front, and it may be in the course of a few months that I shall be able to see Paris again. Meanwhile our plans are completely unknown to us and to the *commandement*, too, probably. There is a rumour that we shall be here till the 10th of August. *Quién sabe?*

July 30.—Passed a splendid review the day before yesterday at Chaux-la-Chapelle. Got up at daybreak and were off before half-past three. Marched the nine or so kilometres over to the review grounds, each battalion behind its *clairons*. The rainclouds had passed over, the sun was up in a glorious sky. The whole Legion was there, and we drew up in a large rectangular field, the woods on one side and a beautiful view of the near mountains at the end. Here we were joined by the rest of the division, two regiments of *Tirailleurs Algériens*. They filed in behind their music—the famous *nouba*—whose effect was most novel and *émotionnant*, an alternation of *clairons* and a number of curious woodwind instruments, supported by bass and treble drums.

Their brilliant ancient uniform has been replaced by the ordinary light blue *capote*, baggy khaki trousers and red *fez*. While waiting for the arrival of the general, we intermingled and fraternized one with another. In the *4ème Tirailleurs* Boubaccer found his younger brother, whom he had not seen for ten years. He is *sous-lieutenant* now. It was this regiment that was in the action at the Ferme d Alger that I described earlier. It seems the explosion of the mine killed about a half section of the *Tirailleurs*. The rest, after their counter-attack had chased out the assaulting party, threw dead, wounded, and prisoners into the hole and started burying them alive. "*Khouya, khouya!*" (Brother, brother) cried the unfortunates. "*Mais nous avons répondu 'Je connais bas khouya'*" the *tirailleur* continued, and they were all buried up. . . .

Suddenly the *clairons* sound the *sonnerie* of the general, and we all rush to the *faisceaux*. *Baïonnette au canon!* As he rides by, whom should we recognise but the famous Lyautey himself, only recently arrived in France. He rides along the ranks and raises his hat as he passes the *porte-drapeau* of the *Tirailleurs*, who dips the flag at the same time. He visits the detachments of cavalry and artillery, also, whose trumpets sound their own *sonnerie* for the occasion. Then he dismounts in the centre of the field with his staff, receives all the officers and the *sous-officiers* whom he had known in Morocco, and decorates several officers and soldiers, to whom he gives the accolade. After this the *nouba* takes position opposite him and the whole division files by to its curiously exciting music. Return to Plancher-Bas, where we arrive about 2.30 p.m.

July 31.—Walked up to Plancher-les-Mines with Victor Chapman; there met Farnsworth, who is in the *1er Etranger*, and we all had dinner together. A dozen *sous-officiers*—old *légionnaires*—were in the room, drinking and making good cheer. These were men who had been at Arras, and the *camaraderie* of soldiers whose bond is that of great exploits achieved in common was of a sort which does not exist among us, and which I envied.

Today comes the news I have been expecting, that the Russians are to evacuate Warsaw. The Germans then will enter probably on the anniversary of the declaration of war, and a wave of enthusiasm will pass over the country, which will drown all memory of past reverses and all discontent at the unlooked-for prolongation of the conflict. The great question now is whether the Russians started their retirement in time, and whether they will be able to extricate their central army from the difficult position in which it is placed. If they do not, it will mean disaster.

Perhaps historic fatality has decreed that Germany shall come out of this struggle triumphant and that the German people shall dominate in the twentieth century as French, English, Spanish, and Italian have in preceding centuries. To me the matter of supreme importance is not to be on the winning side, but on the side where my sympathies lie. Feeling no greater dignity possible for a man than that of one who makes himself the instrument of Destiny in these tremendous moments, I naturally ranged myself on the side to which I owed the greatest obligation. But let it always be understood that I never took arms out of any hatred against Germany or the Germans, but purely out of love for France.

The German contribution to civilization is too large, and German ideals too generally in accord with my own, to allow me to join in the chorus of hate against a people whom I frankly admire. It was only that the France, and especially the Paris, that I love should not cease to be the glory and the beauty that they are that I engaged. For that cause I am willing to stick to the end. But I am ready to accept the verdict of History in this case as I do, and everyone does, in the old cases between Athens and Sparta, or between Greece and Rome. Might is right and you cannot get away from it however the *ephemeridae* buzz. "*Victrix causa diis placuit, sed victa Catoni*" It may have to be the epitaph on my tomb. I can see it on some green slope of the Vosges, looking toward the East.

August 7.—Coming into the Cheval Blanc this morning I found cloth labels lying out to dry on a table, addressed in indelible pencil to the son of the house, who was made prisoner at Lassigny in the first weeks of the war, and who is now in a concentration camp at Cassel, in Germany. They send him bundles of bread and good things to eat every week through the *Croix Rouge* of Genève, and these *envois* seem to arrive regularly. I remarked to the good woman that her son was really happier as a prisoner than he would be in the trenches, and that she especially ought to consider herself happier than so many other mothers, who must worry all the time and remain in continual uncertainty, but her eyes showed that she had been crying, and she was unable to speak.

It is in these villages behind the lines that one gets an idea how the country is suffering. There is more than one young man back here without a leg or an arm. There is the case of the old man next door that I have already mentioned. But the most tragic seems to me that of a mother whose only son appeared early in the list of missing. After months of uncertainty she read his name one day in a list of prisoners in Germany. Full of joy she wrote him and began sending packages. But one day, after several weeks had passed, she received a letter from the soldier she had written to, saying that he had received the letters and packages, that his name was indeed identical with that of the person to whom she addressed them, but that he came from quite a different locality, and was not the son that she sought! And she has never heard anything more.

Today comes the news of the evacuation of Warsaw!

To His Mother

August 8, 1915.

I may have been a little careless about writing lately. It is because still being in repose far from the firing line the sense of being out of danger had the effect of lessening the importance I attached to keeping you assured that I was getting along all right. . . .

You must not delude yourself about any revolutions in Germany or an early termination of the war. Look upon my being here just as I do, that is, as its being a part of my career. I am not influenced by the foolish American ideas of "success," which regard only the superficial and accidental meanings of the word—advancement, recognition, power, etc. The essence of success is in rigorously obeying one's best impulses and following those paths which conscience absolutely approves, and than which imagination can conceive none more desirable. Given my nature, I could not have done otherwise than I have done.

Anything conceivable that I might have done had I not enlisted would have been less than what I am doing now, and anything that I may do after the war is over, if I survive, will be less too. I have always had the passion to play the biggest part within my reach and it is really in a sense a supreme success to be allowed to play this. If I do not come out, I will share the good fortune of those who disappear at the pinnacle of their careers. Come to love France and understand the almost unexampled nobility of the effort this admirable people is making, for that will be the surest way of your finding comfort for anything that I am ready to suffer in their cause.

9: August 10–September 24, 1915

August 10.—Yesterday the whole brigade marched up to the top of the Ballon de Servance, our regiment from Plancher-Bas and the *1er* from Plancher-les-Mines. For us it was about a thirty-eight kilometre "hike," *sac au dos, tenue de campagne complète*. It was one of the finest and most memorable walks I have ever taken. This was largely due to the weather. After weeks of rain (it is raining now again this morning) it was our luck to hit on a day of unbroken sunshine, not a cloud in the sky of almost tropic blue. After leaving Plancher-les-Mines the road was extremely pretty up the deep, wooded valley of the Rahin. Then came the long climb up the military road.

The summit of the mountain is cleared and covered with grass. Here, favoured by the fine weather of one day in a hundred, the most wonderful view spread out before us. Southward, 236 kilometres away, Mont-Blanc rose in isolated grandeur above the chain of the Jura. Further east stretched the whole snowy line of the Alps the Jungfrau, the Wetterhorn, the beautiful mountains that I first saw at Berne a little over a year ago with André—even more romantic and more enchanting now for their great distance.

After lunch I strolled away alone and found just the right point of view, where the grassy summit sheered off precipitously into the deep valley-head, dark with pine forests and full of the murmur of the stream. A sunny haze covered the plains of upper Alsace. Two captive balloons were all the signs of war that were visible. They hung there, little specks in the distance, a good deal lower than my perch on the mountain top. I sat about an hour absorbed in the beauty of that far view of the Alps that filled me with nostalgia and love of the loveliness of Earth. Strange that the last time I looked on the Jungfrau was in the company of Count von Liebermann, lieutenant in the 5th Regiment of the Prussian Guard. This was on the Thunnensee in Switzerland. I wonder where he is now. . . .

At midday, we started home behind our *clairons*. It happened that three men, who had formed a little kind of German band with three old brass instruments that they found in the village, had brought these along. When the *clairons* had finished, they hit up one of the *chansons de route* from the ranks, much to the general surprise and amusement, and every one joined in with good will. The men were in fine spirits and we came back singing all the way.

August 16.—Another good walk today, this time to the summit of the Ballon d Alsace, the regiment marching without sack. Left at four o clock in the morning. Marched up through Plancher-les-Mines and followed the same road up the pretty valley of the Rahin to the point where the Servance road turns off. Here we kept straight on and then walked up through fine pine woods by steep and stony paths to the summit. Not a bad day but no such fine weather as last week. Sky full of clouds, whose lower edges cut the view from the horizons.

There is a beautiful point of view on the summit, where there is a sharp descent to a deep valley, with green pastures, ponds, a winding road and a little river that flows down through pretty hamlets toward Massevaux, and out into the hazy plains of Alsace. Forty kilometres away could be seen indistinctly the factory chimneys and church spires of Mulhouse. We saw also the Hartmannsweilerkopf, where such fierce fighting has taken place this last winter. Saluted silently distant Alsace, that will probably be the scene of our coming battles. Returned in the afternoon under the same circumstances as last time.

August 19.—We are to leave tomorrow, probably for the Front!

Vitrigne (near Belfort), August 20.—We were ordered to be in readiness at any moment. Late in the afternoon it seemed as if there would be a delay; it was not until ten o clock at night, when most of us were asleep, that the news came definitely that we were to leave today. We were roused, consequently, about two o clock this morning to make sacks. Got off shortly after four. Marched to Auxelles-Bas, where, branching to the right, all prospect of going toward Thann and the theatre of fighting near Munster was dissipated. A beautiful morning as we crossed the continental divide, which separates the waters that flow into the Rhône and the Mediterranean from those that fall into the Rhine and the grey North Sea.

Eastward into the sunrise stretched away the fair plains of Alsace.

Moments of memorable emotion as we marched singing down the winding road that led us off to this glorious goal. Passed through La Chapelle-sous-Chaux and Sermamagny, where I drank during a *pose* with a brown *Algérien* of the *Tirailleurs* who had been at Arras. Then came around through the outskirts of Belfort to this village, where we are billeted for 24 hours.

I am sitting now under a giant pear tree on a green slope outside the town, enjoying the most beautiful landscape as it fades away gradually in the dying daylight. Wide lowlands stretch away—fields of richest green, cultivated acres, hamlets, groves—bounded toward the southeast by the "many-folded mountains" of Switzerland that rise, crest after crest, each one more faint, toward the far clouds pink in the sunset. The boom of the cannon can be heard, more distant now, in Alsace.

Two captive balloons are up along the line of the front. An aeroplane returns toward Belfort from a reconnaissance beyond the lines. A *convoi* of motor lorries raises the dust along the white road eastward. Automobiles dash back and forth. Exquisite peaceful summer evening. The green on forest and field has not begun to be browned yet, but already in the evenings the chill of Autumn is beginning to be felt. Moments of peace, sweet melancholy, resignation, self-content. In the village, a chorus of soldiers singing the *Brabançonne*. Anniversary of the German entrance into Brussels. A year ago I left Bruges for Paris to enlist.

Mortzwiller (Alsace), August 21.—In Alsace at last. Left Vétrigne at five o clock this morning. Followed the Cernay road through Rappe and La Chapelle. Crossed the old frontier line without demonstration. German road posts. Immediate change in architecture; picturesque houses with white plaster walls and inset beams. The people all speak German and very bad French. Many German signs about.

August 24.—Likelihood of an offensive in Alsace is not so good now. The reason we came here was to put in six days' work on the second line defences, each regiment in the division doing its turn. This done, we return, they say, to Plancher-Bas! We have already done two days' hard labour renovating a second line trench. Today, the third, I am sick and am staying at home. Fine weather. There is considerable cannonading about here. Right near the place where we work there is a battery of at least six heavy guns that, directed by a captive balloon not far off, fire terrific volleys, to which the Germans reply weakly or not at all.

News of the fall of Kovno makes these times very grave. This means the breaking up of the last Russian line of defence and the beginning of an indefinite retreat into the interior. How much of this army will be destroyed or fall into the hands of the Germans, as a result of this latest manoeuvre, remains to be seen. Things look badly for the Allies. The only hope of ultimate victory that I can see is the Balkan States marching with us. Today is the anniversary of my enlistment.

Plancher-Bas, August 28, 1915.—Back in Plancher-Bas again! Our march into Alsace, round which I wove so much romance, was only for the prosaic purpose of working on second line de fences, the same kind of work we used to do at Blancs-Sablons. We worked five days and then marched back by the same route, spending the night at Vé-trigne. On the way, we passed the whole *1er Etranger* going out to do their turn. A tough-looking crowd. There is nothing doing and nothing apparently under way in the Upper Alsace sectors, which are held by territorials. Putting one and two together, it seems to me that the General Staff are at present bringing behind the lines as far as possible, as in our case, the best troops and manning the trenches with second-line formations and territorials.

They are recreating a whole *arméee active*, who are not to be put into the trenches, but will be thrown immediately into the next great offensive. A friend who has been at Giromagny, which is now the headquarters of the division, says that the charge of the *1er* at Arras gave the Legion a wonderful reputation, and that we are ranked now with the best. No trenches, then, but alternation between periods of work and periods of repos and exercises until the great day comes.

I have pleasant memories of Alsace, where it is not improbable that we shall return in another week to do another five or six days of work. In the evenings, we would gather in the *Wirtschaft,* drink deep, sing and soon recover our spirits after the hard day's labour. The people are quite German in all outward aspects. The young men are serving in the German army; their little brothers and sisters are learning the "*Marseillaise*" in the village school. I overheard one of these classes a day when I was sick and went up in the afternoon to the *infirmerie* which was situated in the *mairie.* After each *strophe,* the teacher would correct faults of pronunciation, and the chorus of childish voices would repeat after him in con cert, "*abreuve,*" "*marchons*" etc. Outside the door in the corridor were a dozen pairs of diminutive *sabots.*

215

September 1.—Great and unexpected news this morning at report. All American volunteers in the Legion are to be given the privilege of entering a French regiment. I have always been loyal to the Legion, notwithstanding the many obvious drawbacks, feeling that the origin of most of the friction within the regiment was in the fact that we had never been in action, and had consequently never established the bond of common dangers shared, common sufferings borne, common glories achieved, which knits men together in real comradeship. It was a great mistake, it seems to me, not to have put the regiment into action immediately when we came on the front last year, when the regiment was strong and the morale good, instead of keeping us in the trenches in comparatively quiet sectors and in a state of inactivity, which was just the condition for all kinds of discontent to fester in.

Of course discontent is the natural state of mind of the soldier, and I, who am accustomed to look beneath the surface, always have realised this, but it must be admitted that here discontent has more than the usual to feed upon, where a majority of men who engaged voluntarily were thrown in a regiment made up almost entirely of the dregs of society, refugees from justice and roughs, commanded by *sous-officiers* who treated us all without distinction in the same manner that they were habituated to treat their unruly brood in Africa.

I put up with this for a year without complaint, swallowing my pride many a time and thinking only of the day of trial, shutting my eyes to the disadvantages I was under because I thought that on that day the regiment, which I have always believed to be of good fighting stock, would do well and cover us all with glory.

Our chance, now that we are in with the Moroccan division, of seeing great things is better than ever. This has almost induced me, in fact, to turn down the offer and stay where I am, since perhaps the greatest glory will be here, and it is for glory alone that I engaged.

But, on the other hand, after a year of what I have been through, I feel more and more the need of being among Frenchmen, where the patriotic and military tradition is strong, where my good will may have some recognition, and where the demands of a sentimental and romantic nature like my own may be gratified. I think there is no doubt that I will be happier and find experience more remunerative in a French regiment, without necessarily forfeiting the chance for great action which is so good here now. Among the regiments of the 7th Army, from which we were allowed to choose, are three of the active, who it seems are in the Meuse in exciting sectors. I have chosen the *133e de ligne*, whose *dépôt* is at Belley, and will leave the rest to Fate.

September 13.—Another splendid review this morning at La Chapelle-sous-Chaux, before the *Président de la République* and Millerand and several generals. Perfect weather. Thrilled to the magnificent spectacle of the *défilade*, the "*Marseillaise*," the disturbing music of the *Tirailleurs*. The whole division was there. Flags were given to the *1er* and *2me Etranger*. And now on returning comes the news of our definite departure tomorrow. I have reasons to be sorry to leave Plancher-Bas. Have had happy moments here.

Suippes, September 16.—Left Plancher-Bas for good, day before yesterday evening. The fine weather which had lasted without a break for several weeks came to an end, and the grey skies corresponded with the melancholy that many of us felt at breaking forever with associations that had grown so dear to us. Marched away after dark in the rain, our rifles decorated with bouquets and our *musettes* filled with presents from the good townspeople. The *Tirailleurs* and *Zouaves*, coming from the direction of Giromagny, preceded us. We entrained at Champagney, about 45 men in a car. Terrible discomfort. Impossible to stretch legs or lie out flat. Several fights; had a fight myself with the corporal.

Found ourselves next morning at Vesoul and from there followed the same route as on coming, that is, up through Langres, Chaumont, Vitry-le-François, to Châlons. We had been hearing for some time of the big concentration of troops at the Camp de Châlons and were not surprised when we turned north and stopped at the way station of St.-Hilaire. Everything bore testimony of the big offensive in preparation, troops cantoned in the villages, the rail road lines congested with trains of cannon and material, but most sinister and significant, the newly constructed evacuation sheds for the wounded, each one labelled "*blessés assis*" or "*blessés couchés*." Violent cannonade as we disembarked.

Marched seven or eight kilometres up a national road and then made a *grande halte* at sun down for soup. Pleasant country that we marched through, the *Champagne pouilleuse* with its broad plains and vast distances. The good weather had come back and the waxing moon hung in the south. After the *grande halte* we resumed the march at ten o clock. Everyone in good spirits and full of excitement at the prospect of the big action in preparation that everything bore evidence of. Heavy cannonading continued during the entire march and the northern skies were lit up continually with the German *fusées*. During our last *pose*, just before entering Suippes, several heavy German shells fell into the town with terrific explosions. The flashes of the cannon lit up all the sky like summer lightning. Marched into the dark, silent town about two o clock in the morning. The civils apparently have all been evacuated. Marched on and bivouacked in an open field beyond the town. Slept well on the ground.

This morning we moved up here into a big grove and pitched tents, the first time we have done this on the front. Do not know whether we are to go up to the trenches or wait here until we go into action. The *2me Etranger* ought certainly to be first. It is going to be a *grandiose* affair and the cannonade will doubt less be a thing beyond imagination. The attack this time will probably be along a broad front. Our immediate object ought to be Vouziers and the line of the Aisne, but it is probably the object of the *etat-major* to expel the Germans from Northern France entirely. They are fortunate who have lasted to see this, and I thrill at the certain prospect of being in the thick of it.

September 18.—Took pick and shovel yesterday evening and marched up to the front—the whole regiment—where we worked all night. Our road lay again through dark and silent Suippes, where the moonlight, less covered tonight, revealed the heaps of ruins—rent walls, shells of burnt-out buildings, and a whole quarter completely razed by the fire the Germans must have started before evacuating the town a year ago. Took the Vouziers road northward toward the trenches, where the sky was lit continually with the *fusées éclairantes* and the flash of the cannon. At one time during our first *pose* there must have been an attack of some sort, for the German rockets began popping up like "flower pots" of our Fourth of Julys, and the cannon flashes redoubled, but we could hear no fusillade for the continual rumble of traffic on the highroad beside us.

Turned off a side road after a while in the direction of Perthes-les-Hurlus. Climbed a long, gradual ascent. Our batteries fired occasionally close at hand. During last *pose* a half dozen heavy German shells—probably 210s—fell near a battery emplacement near us with the most terrific explosion, the singing shell-fragments falling among us. Walked through the pine groves at the summit of the crest and then came out through a deep-cut *boyau* to a magnificent spectacle. The position here is a valuable one that must once have been fiercely disputed, for it dominates all the low rolling country to the north. Here, illumined by the German *fusées* that shot up continually from their trenches a mile or so off, lay the vast battlefield that in a few days is to see one of the most tremendous actions ever fought.

The clouds had blown off, the stars were all out, the night was a glorious one. We formed a long file, one man with a pick and one with a shovel at five yard intervals down the open northern slope and started digging an immense *boyau* to rush troops up through for the attack. Worked all night, then marched back and arrived at bivouac at dawn. A fatiguing night but can sleep late and rest all day.

September 19.—Went up and worked again last night. Beautiful starry night; bright moonlight. A pleasure walking up, but the work was tiring and the road long. A violent artillery duel. Our advanced batteries of heavy guns fired continually. The Germans replied less frequently, but when their heavy shells fell by twos and fours the explosions were terrific beyond anything I have heard before on the front. They covered the lines with smoke, through which the *fusées* glimmered, blurred and reddened. The smell of powder was heavy in the air. It was daybreak when we returned. . . .

Today at *rapport* the captain read the order from Joffre announcing to the troops the great general attack. The company drew close around him, and he spoke to us of our reasons for confidence in success and a victory that would drive the enemy definitely out of France. The German positions are to be overwhelmed with a hurricane of artillery fire and then great assaults will be delivered all along the line. The chances for success are good. It will be a battle without precedent in history.

September 21.—About twenty heavy shells fell yesterday evening around the Suippes station, which is right near the park where we are bivouacking. Went out to watch them burst; no serious damage. Went up to work after supper. The dead and wounded were being carried in litters through the streets of Suippes, which had been bombarded, too. The fine weather is continuing, and it was a beautiful moonlit night, but frosty. Hard work until two o clock digging communication ditches. Officers went down to the trenches to reconnoitre the *terrain*. The captain spoke to us again at *rapport* today, and gave us his impressions of this visit. The Colonials apparently are to lead the attack; we ought to come in the third or fourth wave. Our objective is the Ferme de Navarin, about 3½ kilometres behind the German lines. Here we will halt to reform, while the entire 8th Corps, including numerous cavalry, will pass through the breach we have made. These will be sublime moments; there are good chances of success and even of success without serious losses.

September 22.—The day ought to be near at hand. The artillery is becoming more and more violent and tonight as I write here by candle light in our tent the cannonade is extremely violent down the line toward Reims. The Germans continue to bombard Suippes and the Suippes station. Luckily they have not discovered our bivouac, for the French keep continual patrols in the air and no German aeroplane dares to come over here. Should they bombard us here the execution of these terrific 210 shells would be appalling.

Today several fell in the park, not more than fifty yards from the tent. I thought they were going to bother us, but these were really bad shots at the station that had gone astray. Spend a hard night at work yesterday, leaving here at 6 p. m. and not getting back till 6 this morning. This afternoon walked to Somme-Suippe to try and buy something, but there is nothing to be had. The fine weather continues. We have received steel casques in place of the *képis*.

September 23.—Bombardment of the station resumed this morning. Went out to the gate to watch the shells burst. The men of the *génie* "beat it" as usual into the fields nearby, but a few nervy ones remained to take the little Décauville engines and a trainload of shells out of danger. When the bombardment seemed over I noticed them all running back and commencing digging. Went over and joined them and helped disinter three men who had been buried alive. They had taken refuge in a deep trench that had been dug for the purpose. But a big shell had fallen right beside this trench and covered the unfortunate men with dirt. We dug and dug and finally came upon a piece of cloth. With difficulty we uncovered one after another and pulled them out, but it was too late. They had been smothered to death. . . . Wild rumours are reaching us of victories on other parts of the line. It is said the French have taken the plateau of Craonne and that the English are at Lille.

September 24.—We are to attack tomorrow morning. Gave in our blankets this morning; they are to be carried on the wagons. Also made bundles, in order to lighten the sack of all un necessary articles, including the second pair of shoes. We are admirably equipped, and if we do not succeed it will not be the fault of those responsible for supplying us. A terrific cannonade has been going on all night and is continuing. It will grow in violence until the attack is launched, when we ought to find at least the first enemy line completely demolished. What have they got up their sleeves for us? Where shall we find the strongest resistance ? I am very confident and sanguine about the result and expect to march right up to the Aisne, borne on in an irresistible *élan*. I have been waiting for this moment for more than a year. It will be the greatest moment in my life. I shall take good care to live up to it.

Note.—The diary ends here, with the following notation: "This diary continued in another that I will carry in the pocket of my capote." All efforts to find this have been in vain.

10: October 4, 1915–April 13, 1916

October 4, 1915.

Am writing you in bivouac in a moment of *repos* between two battles to tell you that I am well and in good spirits. The regiment has been in the big action in Ch—— from the beginning our brigade was the second to leave the trenches. Have been eight days under terrific shell fire. Have taken many prisoners. Am sending S—— as souvenir some German letters picked up in the trenches we carried.

To His Mother

October 25, 1915.

The regiment is back in *repos* after the battle in Champagne, in which we took part from the beginning, the morning of the memorable 25th September. We are billeted in a pleasant little village not far from Compiègne, quite out of hearing of the cannon. It seems that absurd rumours were current about the fate of Americans in the Legion, so I hasten to let you know that I am all right. Quite a few Americans were wounded, but none killed, to my knowledge.

The part we played in the battle is briefly as follows. We broke camp about 11 o clock the night of the 24th, and marched up through ruined Souain to our place in one of the numerous *boyaux* where the *troupes d'attaque* were massed. The cannonade was pretty violent all that night, as it had been for several days previous, but toward dawn it reached an intensity unimaginable to anyone who has not seen a modern battle. A little before 9.15 the fire lessened suddenly and the crackle of the fusillade between the reports of the cannon told us that the first wave of as sault had left and the attack begun.

At the same time, we received the order to advance. The German artillery had now begun to open upon us in earnest. Amid the most infernal roar of every kind of fire-arms and through an atmosphere heavy with dust and smoke, we marched up through the *boyaux* to the *tranchées de départ*. At shallow places and over breaches that shells had made in the bank we caught momentary glimpses of the blue lines sweeping up the hill side or silhouetted on the crest where they poured into the German trenches. When the last wave of the Colonial brigade had left, we followed. *Baïonnette au canon*, in lines of *tirailleurs*, we crossed the open space between the lines, over the barbed wire, where not so many of our men were lying as I had feared (thanks to the efficacy of the bombardment) and over the German trench, knocked to pieces and filled with their dead.

In some places, they still resisted in isolated groups. Opposite us, all was over, and the herds of prisoners were being already led down as we went up. We cheered, more in triumph than in hate, but the poor devils, terror-stricken, held up their hands, begged for their lives, cried "*Kamerad*," "*Bon Français*," even "*Vive la France*." We advanced and lay down in columns by two behind the second crest. Meanwhile, bridges had been thrown across trenches and *boyaux*, and the artillery, leaving the emplacements where they had been anchored a whole year, came across and took position in the open, a magnificent spectacle. Squadrons of cavalry came up.

Suddenly the long, unpicturesque *guerre de tranchées* was at an end and the field really presented the aspect of the familiar battle pictures—the battalions in manoeuvre, the officers, superbly indifferent to danger, galloping about on their chargers. But now the German guns, moved back, began to get our range and the shells to burst over and around batteries and troops, many with admirable precision. Here my best comrade was struck down by shrapnel at my side—painfully but not mortally wounded.

I often envied him after that. For now, our advanced troops were in contact with the German second-line defences, and these proved to be of a character so formidable that all further advance without a preliminary artillery preparation was out of the question. And our role, that of troops in reserve, was to lie passive in an open field under a shell fire that every hour became more terrific, while aeroplanes and captive balloons, to which we were entirely exposed, regulated the fire.

That night we spent in the rain. With portable picks and shovels each man dug himself in as well as possible. The next day our concentrated artillery again began the bombardment, and again the fusillade announced the entrance of the infantry into action. But this time only the wounded appeared coming back, no prisoners. I went out and gave water to one of these, eager to get news. It was a young soldier, wounded in the hand. His face and voice bespoke the emotion of the experience he had been through in a way that I will never forget.

"*Ah, les salauds!*" he cried, "They let us come right up to the barbed wire without firing. Then a hail of grenades and balls. My comrade fell, shot through the leg, got up, and the next moment had his head taken off by a grenade before my eyes."

"And the barbed wire, wasn't it cut down by the bombardment?"

"Not at all in front of us."

I congratulated him on having a *blessure heureuse* and being well out of the affair. But he thought only of his comrade and went on down the road toward Souain, nursing his mangled hand, with the stream of wounded seeking their *postes de secours*.

The afternoon of the 28th should have been our turn. We had spent four days under an almost continual bombardment. The regiment had been decimated, though many of us had not fired a shot. After four such days as I hope never to repeat, under the strain of sitting inactive, listening to the slow whistle of 210-millimetre shells as they arrived and burst more or less in one's proximity, it was a real relief to put *sac au dos* and go forward. We marched along in columns by two, behind a crest, then over and across an exposed space under the fire of their 77's, that cost us some men, and took formation to attack on the border of a wood, somewhere behind which they were entrenched.

And here we had a piece of luck. For our colonel, a soldier of the old school, stronger for honour than expediency, had been wounded in the first days of the action. Had he been in command, we all think that we should have been sent into the wood (and we would have gone with *élan*) not withstanding that the *1er Etranger* had just attacked gallantly but unsuccessfully and had been badly cut up. The *commandant* of our battalion, who had succeeded him in command, when he heard, after a reconnaissance, that the wire had not been sufficiently cut, refused to risk his regiment. So you have him to thank.

The last days of the week we went up into first line to relieve the tired *troupes d'attaque*. It was an abandoned German artillery position, full of souvenirs of the recent occupants and of testimony to their hasty departure. They did not counterattack on this sector and we finished this first period in comparative tranquillity.

Then two days' *repos* in the rear and we came back to the battle field. The attack of the 6th October netted us some substantial gains but not enough to call into action the *troupes de poursuite* among which we were numbered. It became more and more evident that the German second line of defence presented obstacles too serious to attempt overcoming for the moment, and we began going up at night to work at consolidating our advanced trenches and turning them into a new permanent line. We spent two weeks on the front this time. But as luck would have it, the bombardment that thundered continually during this period did not fall very heavily on the wood where we were sheltered and we did not suffer seriously in comparison with the first days.

And now we are back in the far rear again, the battle is over, and in the peace of our little village we can sum up the results of the big offensive in which we took part. No one denies that they are disappointing. For we know, who heard and cheered the order of Joffre to the army before the battle, that it was not merely a fight for a position, but a supreme effort to pierce the German line and liberate the invaded country; we know the immense preparation for the attack, what confidence our officers had in its success, and what enthusiasm ourselves. True, we broke their first line along a wide front, advanced on an average of three or four kilometres, took numerous prisoners and cannon.

It was a satisfaction at last to get out of the trenches, to meet the enemy face to face, and to see German arrogance turned into suppliance. We knew many splendid moments, worth having endured many trials for. But in our larger aim, of piercing their line, of breaking the long deadlock, of entering Vouziers in triumph, of course we failed.

This check, in conjunction with the serious turn that affairs have taken in the Balkans, makes the present hour a rather grave one for us. Yet it cannot be said to be worse than certain moments that arrived even much later in the course of our Civil War, when things looked just as critical for the North, though in the end of a similar *guerre d'usure* they pulled out victorious.

But perhaps you will understand me when I say that the matter of being on the winning side has never weighed with me in comparison with that of being on the side where my sympathies lie. This affair only deepened my admiration for, my loyalty to, the French. If we did not entirely succeed, it was not the fault of the French soldier. He is a better man, man for man, than the German. Anyone who had seen the charge of the Marsouins at Souain would acknowledge it. Never was anything more magnificent.

I remember a captain, badly wounded in the leg, as he passed us, borne back on a litter by four German prisoners. He asked us what regiment we were, and when we told him, he cried "*Vive la Légion*," and kept repeating "*Nous les avons eus. Nous les avons eus.*" He was suffering, but oblivious of his wound, was still fired with the enthusiasm of the assault and all radiant with victory. What a contrast with the German wounded, on whose faces was nothing but terror and despair. What is the stimulus in their slogans of "*Gott mit uns*" and "*für König und Vaterland*" beside that of men really fighting in defence of their country? Whatever be the force in international conflicts of having justice and all the principles of personal morality on one's side, it at least gives the French soldier a strength that's like the strength of ten against an adversary whose weapon is only brute violence.

It is inconceivable that a Frenchman, forced to yield, could behave as I saw German prisoners behave, trembling, on their knees, for all the world like criminals at length overpowered and brought to justice. Such men have to be driven to the assault, or intoxicated. But the French man who goes up is possessed with a passion be side which any of the other forms of experience that are reckoned to make life worthwhile seem pale in comparison. The modern prototype of those whom history has handed down to the admiration of all who love liberty and heroism in its defence, it is a privilege to march at his side so much so that nothing the world could give could make me wish myself anywhere else than where I am.

Most of the other Americans have taken advantage of the permission to pass into a regular French regiment. There is much to be said for their decision, but I have remained true to the Legion, where I am content and have good comrades. I have a pride particularly in the Moroccan division, whereof we are the first brigade. Those who march with the *Zouaves* and the Algerian *tirailleurs* are sure to be where there is most honour. We are *troupes d'attaque* now, and so will assist at all the big *coups*, but be spared the monotony of long periods of inactive guard in the trenches, such as we passed last winter.

I am glad to hear that Thwing has joined the English. I used to know him at Harvard. He refused to be content, no doubt, with lesser emotions while there are hours to be lived such as are being lived now by young men in Flanders and Champagne. It is all to his credit. There should really be no neutrals in a conflict like this, where there is not a people whose interests are not involved. To neutrals who have stomached what America has consented to stomach from Germany—whose ideals are so opposite to hers—who in the event of a German victory would be so inevitably embroiled, the question he put to himself and so resolutely answered will become more and more pertinent.

ARMY POSTCARD

October 27, 1915.

We are in repos now, far in the rear, so do not worry. We passed a magnificent review yesterday before King George, President Poincaré, Joffre, and Kitchener—our glorious Moroccan division and I do not know how many others of Colonials—myriads of troops all returned from the battlefield in Champagne.

ARMY POSTCARD

(Written upon hearing that he had been reported in the American newspapers as missing or killed in the Battle of Champagne.)

October 30, 1915.

I am *navré* to think of your having suffered so. I had just as soon aim my rifle at the fool who played that trick as at any German. But you know what American journalists are. . . . Very soon a week's permission in Paris. I shall be interested to see my poem in print. But I found a glaring grammatical error after sending it. I am usually more careful. Blame it to the trenches. I am writing you in a little *café* amid the best of comrades. You must take heart thinking of me as always content and really happy as I have never been before and as perhaps I will never be after.

TO HIS MOTHER

November 9, 1915.

I should have arranged to cable after the attack had I known that any such absurd rumours had been started. Here one has a wholesome notion of the unimportance of the individual. It needs an effort of imagination to conceive of its making any particular difference to anyone or anything if one goes under. So many better men have gone and yet the world rolls on just the same. . . . Your letter naturally made me unhappy, for it is only in thinking of you that any possible doubts can rise in my mind about having done well in coming here. Philosophy, I know, cannot modify the natural sentiments of the heart, so I will refrain from commenting on your letter. I can only say that I am perfectly content here and happier than I possibly could be anywhere else. I was a spectator, now I am an actor. I was in a shallow, now I am moving in the full current. It is better in every respect, and since it was inevitable, there is no use lamenting. . . .

To His Mother

November 30, 1915.

The prospects are that we are to be here in the rear all winter. The entire division is in repos now and will probably remain so until next spring. We are *troupes d'attaque* and are only to participate in the big actions. In the meantime, rest and keeping in condition.

This is a great piece of luck. I cannot congratulate myself enough on my foresight in choosing to stay with the Legion instead of going into the *170me* with the other Americans. I have letters from them occasionally, and it seems they are still on the front in Champagne, in the same desolate sector hard work at night, guard at the outposts, bombardment, grenade fights three wounded already and evacuated. Whereas here we are quite tranquil, in a big town where everything can be had, barely within hearing of the cannon, and next week I go to Paris for eight days permission. *C'est la bonne vie.* I can go into the *8me* Zouaves if I want, but am not decided yet. Am quite content here. The two regiments form one now (as you see by the address) of three battalions. Our old flag has gone to the Invalides and we march now under the flag of the *1er*, decorated with the *Croix de Guerre avec Palme*, for the citation after the Arras affair last May.

To His Mother

December 19, 1915.

I am just back from a week's permission in Paris. Had a very good time. The sums in bank, which I have drawn on, have often filled with pleasure moments that otherwise would have been empty and discouraging. And naturally they have made me able also to give pleasure to comrades who have nothing at all.

The division is not going to Serbia, so you need not have any inquietudes on that subject. We probably shall not see action again before spring. Then there will doubtless be another *foudroyant* attempt to drive the Germans out of their positions, for which I hope more success than the previous ones.

Meanwhile the conflagration spreads and there is not the smallest glimpse of hope of seeing it finish inside of years and years. This is a little disheartening. But as in times of peace there is nothing better than love and art, so in times of war there is nothing better than fighting and one must make the best of it, finding the recompense in feeling one's heart pulse in concert with those of the elite who are doing the most admirable thing, rather than with those of the multitude who are concerned with second-best things.

It must be some time now since I wrote. But you must not worry about lapses like this, for we are not on the front now and will only take part in the big actions, after which I will see that you are notified by telegraph. There is no news here. Life is uneventful.

To His Mother

December 27, 1915.

I received the two boxes of guava jelly in perfect condition—as if they had come from Paris instead of Cuba. . . . We changed cantonment a short time ago and marched over here to a little village about 10 kilometres south of the Aisne. We are here in reserve in case of a German offensive during the flood season, such as they made last year, where our positions north of the river are a little precarious. We face the enemy here at the point where they are nearest Paris. You can understand my satisfaction that our division is among those assigned to the most responsible posts now. Personally I don't think that the Germans are going to attack and I don t expect to see action again until next spring.

The Ford party is certainly amusing. But you make a mistake in thinking that the U. S. are hated here or even to any marked extent ridiculed. Wilson's notes are laughed at much more than Ford's excursion, for example, which is at least action, though misguided action. His supposedly generous motives are generously recognised. And the ridicule that the obvious futility of the manoeuvre might excite is tempered by the immense secret longing for peace that is the universal undercurrent in Europe now. Only all the nations have waded so deep in blood now that they think it less costly to go right over than to return where they started from, to which a premature peace would be equivalent. So it must go on till it is decided by arms. . . .

February 1, 1916.

I am in hospital for the first time, not for a wound unfortunately, but for sickness. Funny I should be ill this winter when we are in the rear, whereas I passed the last from October to July in the trenches without missing a day. I usually have an attack of grippe every year in midwinter, but this time it took hold of me more seriously than ever before and the fever ran so high that I had to be evacuated. They call it "*bronchite.*" I have been here two weeks and the fever still comes round regularly every evening, but diminishing now. The old trouble of not being able to breathe deep. I am getting well now but am weak. Until further notice do not address letters to regiment but to F. L. & T. Co. The reason is that after leaving here I shall have a *congé de convalescence*, after which I shall probably go to the depot at Lyon instead of directly back to the regiment, according to custom. Then I shall return to the regiment with the next detachment of reinforcements, but will not be assigned to the same battalion or company. This means very likely that I shall not return to the regiment for quite a while to come.

Seeing the division is not on the front, this does not displease me at all. The life in the rear in time of war has lots of drawbacks. What it gains in security it gains also in *ennui*. It is excessively hard, consisting of daily drills and, three or four times a week, all day battalion or regiment manoeuvres, combined with long marches and all kinds of devices to keep the troops in shape. This is all right in good weather, but good weather in France is rare in winter.

The divisions of the colonial corps which are to do big work in the spring are being put through the hardest kind of training, for modern warfare has proved such a novelty that organisation and instruction has practically had to be begun anew. But all this is chiefly important for the officers and *sous-officiers*. I know my business well enough now to be able to dispense with it very easily. I shall get rest and a change of air, liberty and solitude and even the chance to write a little.

As for my book of poems, it is better not to talk about that. It is the great disappointment of my life. . . . When I was in Paris I met the whole Embassy, from the Ambassador down, and they have taken the matter in hand and may surreptitiously be able to extradite the MS. If it is lost it will be a terrible blow to me.

You are right in making the most of past moments of happiness. There is a common *bourgeois* notion which, associated with the common bourgeois ideal of a man finally making enough money to be able to retire and live on his income, pictures the happy life as a kind of steady progression through a series of ups and downs toward a kind of plateau, the summit of which once attained, he can thereafter march along tranquilly on a level of unbroken and indestructible wellbeing.

It is perfectly clear that such a notion is entirely illusory, in the multiple accidents to which life is susceptible, for even supposing that he has attained such a level by the realisation of every other earthly ambition, he is always walking on the unstable brink of the love that he has created for himself and upon which he is dependent, the crumbling of which beneath his feet by death or abandonment would immediately plunge him into the blackest of abysses, where everything else that he had realised would mean nothing.

As for myself, I look upon life as a series of ups and downs, right up (or down) to the very end. The idea of being any higher at. the end than at the beginning was never part of my reveries. I never conceived the advent of a moment when turbulence and strife could be thought of as put definitely behind one. But I clung passionately to, and drank deep of, such moments of happiness as circumstances set before me the importance to me was the moment that joy rescued from oblivion and for me the measure of a happy life was simply the proportion in which the sum-total of these moments of happiness, scattered indiscriminately through it, outbalanced the sum-total of the unhappy ones.

I may not be back with the regiment until spring, but I shall march with it to the big attack. This summer will see the decisive campaign of the war. If we can break through, carry trenches and fortins, get them on the run, advance north, north, through nights red with the flame of burning villages, enter the big conquered cities and deliver a population for two years captive and oppressed, it would be the experience of a thousand years, an emotion that would more than compensate all the sacrifices I have made, something really worth risking your life for. If we don t do it this time, it will be about proven that it can't be done. . . .

TO A FRIEND

February 26, 1916.

Your letter finds me here in the hospital, where I have been for a month now for a "*bronchite*" or "*congestion pulmonaire*" or whatever they call it. . . . I shall soon get out and then will have a month's *congé de convalescence*, which will mean two months' rest and freedom and comfort behind the lines out of a winter of the worst kind of weather. Then rejoining the regiment I shall be just in time for the big offensive, which is the only thing that really matters.

Your letters always have a double interest for me, not only, relatively, as coming from yourself, but also, absolutely, as emanating from a very unusual personality. Old man Yeats (whom, by the way, you ought to know if he is still at the old stand, *quatre cent et quelque* West 29th St., ——*chez* Miles. Petitpas) used to define Culture as the understanding and the employ of intellect as an instrument of pleasure. You seem to have this understanding to a remarkable degree. Remarkable particularly because among women, who are *ipso facto* denied the numerous occupations that men have to choose from to make life seem worthwhile, it is pre-eminently sensibility that is developed far beyond and to the expense of all the other faculties, like the rose that gardeners make exquisite by cutting off all the other buds on the stalk. And remarkable again because the emotional life is not closed to you, as it is to the vast majority of "intellectual" women, whose intellectuality is only a recourse to cover a bald spot, but yours when you choose to yield yourself to it.

Of all the formulas that claimed my early youth, one to which I can still adhere is that of the three categories, the lust for power, the lust for feeling and the lust for knowledge, to one or the other of which I can assign all those who, in their passion to live fully, are the supermen, the *élite* of humanity. Take as respective types Napoleon, Byron, Pico della Mirandola. All superior minds attach themselves more or less re motely to one of these three ideals. I make no distinction between them; those who attain eminence through either one may, in their way, be equally admirable. It is through knowledge that you seek revelation; I seek it through feeling. But I understand the paths that you have chosen, because, as a matter of fact, I started out on them myself.

As you may remember, in the years when I was at college, I was a devotee of Learning for Learning's sake. My life during those years was intellectual to the exclusion of almost everything else. The events of that life were positive ad ventures to me. Few, I am sure, have known more than I did then the employ of intellect as an instrument of pleasure. I shut myself off completely from the life of the University, so full, nevertheless, of pleasures. I scoffed at these pleasures that were no more to me than froth. I felt no need of comradeship. I led the life of an anchorite. At an age when the social instincts are usually most lively I came to understand the pleasures of solitude. My books were my friends. The opening to me of the shelves of the college library, a rare privilege, was like opening the gates of an earthly paradise.

In those dark alleys I would spend afternoons entire, browsing among old folios, following lines of research that often had no connection with my courses, following them simply for the plea sure of the explorer discovering new countries. I never regret those years. They made their contribution. Their pleasures were tranquil and pure. Their desires were simple and all the means of satisfying them were at hand.

I need not describe to you my apostasy from learning, because you can find it described perfectly by Balzac. Take the case of Eugene de Rastignac in Pere Goriot or more particularly of Raphael de Valentin in the Peau de Chagrin. Young men, absorbed, like myself, in their studies, accepting cheerfully solitude and poverty in the pursuit of their one interest, they were suddenly *éblouis* by the vision of the world and the more glittering forms of pleasure to be had through the instrument of Sense. Straightway the charm was broken.

From that moment, they were haunted by an image that destroyed irremediably the peace of mind, the singleness of purpose, the power of concentration, so essential to the intellectual life. Their poverty became irksome, their isolation intolerable. Obsessed by the burning vision of Happiness, they left the quiet groves of the Academy and went down into the city in search of it.

It has been the history of many young men, no doubt. But my hedonism, if such it may be called, was not superficial like that of so many, to whom the emotional means only the sexual. I was sublimely consistent. For seeing, in the macrocosm, all Nature revolve about the twin poles of Love and Strife, of attraction and repulsion, so no less in the microcosm of my individual being I saw the emotional life equally divided between these two cardinal principles. The dedication to Love alone, as Ovid prettily confesses his own in more than one elegy, is good as far as it goes, but it only goes halfway, and my aspiration was to go all the gamut, to "drink life to the lees."

My interest in life was passion, my object to experience it in all rare and refined, in all intense and violent forms. The war having broken out, then, it was natural that I should have staked my life on learning what it alone could teach me. How could I have let millions of other men know an emotion that I remained ignorant of ? Could not the least of them, then, talk about the thing that interested me most with more authority than I? You see, the course I have taken was inevitable. It is the less reason to lament if it leads me to destruction. The things one poignantly regrets are those which seem to us unnecessary, which, we think, might have been different.

This is not my case. My being here is not an accident. It is the inevitable consequence, as you see, of a direction deliberately chosen.

I often wonder if you will ever experience a revolution of sentiment similar to that which I have described and play truant to the idols to which you have hitherto been faithful, absorbed by a new passion which you will find suddenly become all your life and all your thought and all your desire. . . . You have doubtless learned a great many things this year. To what you already know let me, in closing this letter, add one piece of advice. Do not allow Age alone authority in giving counsel. There is that authority also which he alone possesses who, having stood at the very gates of Death, not knowing at what moment his call might come, has, looking back ward, surveyed life in the perspective that can be had from this angle alone. I have seen my life all unrolled, in such moments. And I can assure you that in that panorama everything else faded away, obscured in the haze of oblivion, through which only gleamed clear and distinct, like green, sunlit islands, the hours when we have loved and been beloved.

Therefore hear this my advice. If ever you find yourself suddenly devoured by the divine passion, consult only your heart. Yield to your instincts. Possessed by the force which holds the stars in their orbits, you cannot err. For it is Nature that is asserting itself in you, and in Nature alone is Truth. What though your abandonment to it bring deception and unhappiness. You have yet enriched your life with some particle of a beauty that can never fade. . . . For love is the sun of life. The soul that draws near to it is beautiful as Venus, whose rays, so close it is, are never seen but mingled with the sun's own. The lives that deny it are like Nep tune or those dead planets still farther off, if such there be, wandering around in the cold, outer spheres, without greenness, without warmth, without joy. . . .

TO HIS MOTHER

Argizagita, Biarritz, Basses-Pyrénées.
March 7, 1916.

I hope you got my letters from the hospital soon enough to be reassured about my not being at Verdun. This ought to have been a comfort to you. Of course, to me it is a matter of great regret and I take it as a piece of hard luck. I know the division left early for the scene of action, a kind of fourth alarm, like in a fire, that brought it all the way from the Camp de Crèvecoeur in the Oise. But I have been unable as yet to find whether they have been engaged or to what extent. All my letters to this effect remain unanswered.

The French seem to have done very well in this battle and I am quite satisfied with the result so far. If the Germans find themselves unable to advance on this front, as it looks at present, this affair may mark the turning point in the war, and is sure in any case to have a very important effect on it.

Was it not good of Madame de Bonand to invite me here for my convalescence? It is a most beautiful place; I don't believe there is a finer site in Biarritz. The house too is the very ideal of comfort and luxury. Fancy me after a year and a half of sleeping with my clothes on in trenches and haylofts, sleeping now in a most voluptuously soft bed in a pink and white room, with a tiled bathroom adjoining.

A little reading lamp is by my pillow at night; in the morning around ten o clock I press a button and a maid comes, opens my shutters and brings me *café au lait* and toast and jam. The view from my window is superb: to the right a little corner of sea that looks for all the world like the pictures of the bay of Naples, with a mountain, like Vesuvius, behind. Then all around the rest of the horizon the long line of the Pyrenees, covered with snow now, right to the foot. The air, of course, is, fine and I ought soon to be in the best of shape again.

I am sorry to hear that you could not stay in Havana. . . . All climates are alike to me, but the best now are those that smell of powder in the day and are lit by the *fusées éclairantes* at night. Well, *bon courage*, and lots of love. . . .

Paris, April 13, 1916.

I have been negligent about writing, but seeing that I have not been in danger, I did not feel the same need to keep you informed. . . . I have greatly enjoyed this vacation, which, with the time I was in the hospital, will have given me three months and a half out of the army. I have had the less cause to regret it because neither the regiment nor any units of our *corps d'armée* have been in action, but have still remained in reserve, engaged only on strengthening the back lines of defence tiresome work. When I go back the first of May, I shall probably be just in time for the big spring attacks.

Did I write you that the Embassy have managed to get my MS. from Bruges? It was very interesting to reread this work which I had entirely forgotten. I found much that was good in it, but much that was juvenile too, and am not so anxious now to publish it as it stands, but will probably make extracts from it and join with what I have done since.

I shall go back the first of May without regrets. These visits to the rear confirm me in my conviction that the work up there on the front is so far the most interesting work that a man can be doing at this moment, that nothing else counts in comparison. . . .

11: May 12–June 28, 1916

To A Friend

May 12, 1916.

After spending a very happy month in Paris, I came back to the front the first of this month. I took my fill of all the pleasures that Paris can give (and it was Paris at its most beautiful). I lived as though I were saying goodbye to life, and now I am quite content to return. It means no more to me than going to the country for the summer; I have the feeling of being in an immensely magnified boys camp, where work is play, war a sport, and everyone is joyous and light-hearted.

This bright impression is due partly to Spring, partly to the beauty of our surroundings, and to the tranquillity of the sector. We are in the depths of the spring forest; violets and lilies of the valley bloom in the beechen shade; cuckoos and wood-pigeons croon in the heavy foliage. Our trenches are at one side of a little open valley, and the enemy on the other. But neither side bothers the other very seriously; you seldom hear a rifle-shot, and even the artillery is not very active.

We are not here to fight, but simply to replace troops that have gone to Verdun, and, incidentally, to put in a lot of hard work strengthening our lines. There have been days when the *réveil* was at 3.30, *rassemblement* at 4, work till 10, soup and *repos* till 11.30, and then work again till 5. Hours like this would mean a strike in time of peace when men earn ten *francs* a day for day labour; here where they earn five sous, no one murmurs.

Our position here is a very dominating one, and from the artillery observation posts or through holes in the foliage you can look way back into the *pays envahi*. It is a most beautiful landscape forests, orchards, the red-tiled roofs of little villages that the French artillery has carefully spared. There is something fascinating to me about these deep northern horizons. This north of France has become a kind of enchanted land to my imagination, so inaccessible it seems, so mysterious, so isolated from the outside world. To think that these thin lines of turned red earth in front of us, these *réseaux* of barbed wire, and an utterly invisible enemy behind them, prevent us from going forward and liberating it! I have sat long musing on these beautiful *vistas* and wondering what is going on in those lost cities and villages of the north, where three and a half million French have been living for almost two years now, completely cut off from the rest of their countrymen.

They tell me that Easter morning the artillerymen through a telescope saw the civilians going to church along a country road seven or eight kilometres behind the lines. A patrol that approached very near a village situated right on the German lines reports having heard a woman's laugh in the night. All I have heard here is the eternal "*Français kaput!*" that the Germans shout over at sunrise all along the front.

I had expected to return just in time for a big offensive, but as yet one sees no sign of it. Perhaps the Verdun affair has really retarded our plans, as the Germans no doubt intended in making it. Our general of division is reported to have been very anxious to go to the Meuse, but was told to be patient, that a much greater honour was being reserved for us later. Our whole *corps d'armée* has been unaffected by the battle at Verdun. I hope that there are enough others like it to enable us to resume the offensive in the near future with as good chances as we had in Champagne last Fall, when somebody blundered and we fell just short of success. Cambrai, St. Quentin, Laon, Vouziers—what an emotion to march into them behind our flags unfurled and *musique en tête!* It will be hard, but I cannot think that it is impossible. . . .

To His Marraine, Mrs. Weeks

May 13, 1916.

I presume you received my letter of a few days since. This is the third day of our period in repos. It has been raining all day, which is rather welcome, because it has meant no work—even in *repos*, you know, we are supposed to work, just to be kept occupied and out of the mischief that Satan is supposed to find for idle hands. The *château*, in the grounds of which we are barracked, has a most beautiful name—Bellinglise. Isn't it pretty? I think I shall have to write a sonnet to enclose it, as a ring is made express for a jewel. It is a wonderful old seventeenth century manor, surrounded by a lordly estate. What is that exquisite *stanza* in *Maud*, about "in the evening through the lilacs (or laurel) of the old manorial home?" Look it up and send it to me.

Or send me a little copy of *Maud* complete. But that would be too hard to find.

To A Friend

May 19, 1916.

After a delightful month in Biarritz and another in Paris, I came back here the first of the month. I had really had such a good time, as I say, that I returned quite light-hearted. . . , The sector was the quietest I had seen and onE of great beauty, in the depths of the spring for est. Life here, in spite of the hard work, seemed no more than camping out and war only another way of spending the summer agreeably. These bright impressions, however, received a terrible shock yesterday and as I am still under the emotion of it, I will describe it to you.

With the warm weather, we had left the underground bombproofs and pitched little shelter tents under the trees, where we slept or rested between the hours of guard. The dugouts were too hot and dirty and the sector seemed so calm that there was no danger. There were daily artillery duels, but battery sought battery and we were never troubled. Yesterday morning, however, a German aeroplane came over our lines. The cannonade was violent all day, but no one pays any attention to that and most of us were lying down under our *toiles de tente,* when suddenly *"whizz-bang!" "whizz-bang!" "whizz-bang!"* a terrific *rafale* of shrapnel began bursting right in our midst. Rush for the *abris.*

But that there were victims was inevitable. Moans from outside. Cries to lend a hand. A sergeant and seven men had been touched. The most serious case was Corporal Colette, a splendid fellow whom everyone liked. They took him away on a litter, but he died before reaching the ambulance. Havoc in our little camp that had been so peaceful. Air full of dust and smell of pow der, ground littered with leaves and branches, tents, clothes, equipment, riddled with holes, ground splashed and trailed with blood. Naturally since then we have had to come back into the bombproofs, where deep underground, we live in holes like those that I remember pictured in our old natural histories, that show a gopher, an owl and a snake all living happily together in the same burrow. Here it is men, rats, and vermin.

This is a typical episode in our life here on the front. It happens quickly and is quickly forgotten. Life is so cheap here. The soldier's life has its hard moments, but the bright side is not lacking either—good health and good comradeship, the allurement of danger, joys of the open air, the march, and the celebrations when we go back to the rear.

I am writing you this from the first line trenches. A French aeroplane is circling overhead and being bombarded by the Boches. It is the close of a beautiful spring day. With night fall we will go to the outposts to resume the guard. We do not take this sector very seriously, for we all know that big things are in preparation, wherein our division expects to win new laurels. This is simply an interim. . . .

To His Marraine

May 23, 1916.

The week in the trenches was a week of the most beautiful weather. . . . These days were saddened by the death of poor Colette in the bombardment and by the suffering of his brother who has now returned after the burial. They were marked on the other hand by two afternoons of rather memorable emotion. Exasperated by the inactivity of the sector here and tempted by danger, I stole off twice after guard and made a patrol all by myself through the wood paths and trails between the lines. In the first of these, at a crossing of paths not far from one of our posts, I found a burnt rocket-stick planted in the ground and a scrap of paper stuck in the top, placed there by the Boches to guide their little mischief-making parties when they come to visit us in the night. The scrap of paper was nothing else than a bit of the *Berliner Tageblatt*.

This seemed so interesting to me that I reported it to the captain, though my going out alone this way is a thing strictly forbidden. He was very decent about it though, and seemed really interested in the information. Yesterday afternoon I repeated this exploit, following another trail, and I went so far that I came clear up to the German barbed wire, where I left a card with my name. It was very thrilling work, "courting destruction with taunts, with invitations," as Whitman would say. I have never been in a sector like this, where patrols could be made in daylight. Here the deep forest permits it.

It also greatly facilitates ambushes, for one must keep to the paths, owing to the underbrush. I and a few others are going to try to get permission to go out on *patrouilles d'embuscade* and bring in some live prisoners. It would be quite an extraordinary feat if we could pull it off. In our present existence it is the only way I can think of to get the *Croix de Guerre*. And to be worthy of my *marraine* I think that I ought to have the *Croix de Guerre*.

Here are two sonnets I composed to while away the long hours of guard. . . . I will send you back again the Tennyson after having refreshed myself with it, for one must lighten the sack as much as possible. Found all the old beauties and discovered new ones. Read the last paragraphs of Maud and see if you do not think they have a striking bearing on the present situation.

Bellinglise
1
Deep in the sloping forest that surrounds
The head of a green valley that I know,
Spread the fair gardens and ancestral grounds
Of Bellinglise, the beautiful château.
Through shady groves and fields of unknown grass,
It was my joy to come at dusk and see,
Filling a little pond's untroubled glass,
Its antique towers and mouldering masonry.
Oh, should I fall, tomorrow, lay me here,
That o er my tomb, with each reviving year,
Wood-flowers may blossom and the wood-doves croon;
And lovers by that unrecorded place,
Passing, may pause, and cling a little space,
Close-bosomed, at theorising of the moon.
2
Here where in happier times the huntsman's horn
Echoing from far made sweet midsummer eves,
Now serried cannon thunder night and morn,
Tearing with iron the greenwood's tender leaves.
Yet has sweet Spring no particle withdrawn
Of her old bounty; still the song-birds hail,
Even through our fusillade, delightful Dawn;
Even in our wire bloom lilies of the vale.
You who love flowers take these; their fragile bells
Have trembled with the shock of volleyed shells,
And in black nights when stealthy foes advance
They have been lit by the pale rockets glow
That o'er scarred fields and ancient towns laid low
Trace in white fire the brave frontiers of France.
May 22, 1916.

TO HIS MOTHER

May 23, 1916.
We are just back after six days in first line. We are lodged in a big

240

quarry in the woods. It is rather cold and damp inside, but extremely picturesque—immense subterranean galleries, foursquare, cut in the solid rock, pitch black inside with here and there little points of light where the men stick their candles.

The week in first line was very pleasant. The weather was superb and I was never bored an instant, neither in the beautiful days when the unclouded sunlight came filtering through the branches of the forest, nor in the starry nights that at this time of year fade even before two o clock into the wonder of the spring dawn. Nothing more adorable in Nature than this daybreak in the northeast in May and June. One hears the cockcrows in the villages of that mysterious land behind the German lines. Then the cuckoos begin to call in the green valleys and all at once, almost simultaneously, all the birds of the forest begin to sing. The cannon may roar, and the rifles crackle, but Nature's program goes on just the same.

The likelihood of a big action in the near future is vanishing more and more. The general opinion is that Verdun has not only *mangé beaucoup de monde* but what is more important, *beaucoup de munitions*. As the French seem in counterattacks to be making serious efforts and even on a large scale to regain some of the lost ground, I do not expect anything on other parts of the front for some time to come, unless it be the English. If it turn out that we have actually retaken Douaumont, it will be a magnificent achievement. I shall ask permission to go out and leave the newspapers on the German barbed wire. I have already made several patrols here and know the ground.

Goodbye; *bon courage*.

To His Marraine

June 1, 1916.

What a bitter disappointment! After having worked feverishly on my poem and finished it, in spite of work and other duty, in the space of two days, behold the 29th comes and the 30th, and no permission arrives. It would have been such an honour and pleasure to have read my verses there in Paris; I counted on seeing you and getting a moment's respite from the hard life here. To have raised my hopes and then left me in the lurch like that was certainly cruel. I am awaiting an explanation. I sent my ode yesterday to those who asked me for it, to show that I at least had done my part. They may be able to publish it in the *New York Herald*, but not having graced the occasion for which it was written it is as good as still-born and shorn of all effect.

Meanwhile we have come back to *première ligne* and are again in the little camp where Colette was killed. Strange how quickly one forgets here on the front. For a few days after that disaster the men kept to the *abris*, but now we are again careless as before and are living outside in the fine weather, though the same thing may happen again at any moment. I have a charming little house, made by bending down saplings and tying them overhead into a leafy roof. In this I have made a bed out of four logs, fastened into a rectangle about three feet by seven, between which chicken wire is strung, and then spread with new straw; *voilà* a most clean and comfortable couch. All around are sylvan scents and sounds and the morning sun shine slanting through the heavy foliage.

What have I to thank you for since my last letter? The *briquet*, I think, and the aluminum flask, both of which were exactly the right thing. You cannot imagine what pleasure it is to receive these parcels. You see now we are living entirely in the woods, and never go back to the village cantonments, so that it is extremely difficult to get little luxuries of any kind. The quart and a half of wine (quarter of a litre, understood) that the government gives must suffice and the coarse army bread must be eaten dry, and the meal finished without dessert. That is why *colis* are so welcome and the pleasure of receiving them comparable to nothing except that of a child opening his Christmas stocking. Is it not pathetic to be in a state where a man's utmost possibilities of *volupté* are confined to the vulgar sense of taste, the lowest of all?

The noticeable young man you describe as having seen at Lavenue's was probably myself, for it was my pleasure in those days to be noticeable just as now it is exactly the opposite. Where once it was my object to be individual, it is now an even greater satisfaction to merge into the whole, and feeling myself the smallest cog in the mighty machinery that is grinding out the future of the world, whatever that is to be. . . .

TO HIS MOTHER

June 4, 1916.

We are back again from another six days in the trenches,—back, I say, but not very far,—about 500 metres from first line perhaps, in the big quarry that I think I have already described to you. The six days went off fairly peacefully, though the Germans became aggressive at times and approaching our posts under cover of the forest in broad daylight took pot shots at our sentinels, without however doing any damage. This sector has one exciting feature which I have not found in others: the deep woods allow patrols to circulate between the lines in daylight. There are frequent encounters and ambuscades. This is very good sport.

I hardly think that we are to be here much longer. The enemy are so pushing the game along all the fronts that our reserves will soon have to be thrown in. There is this comfort, that when we go, it will not be to sit in a ditch, wait, and be deluged with shells, but we will go directly into action, magnificently, unexpectedly, and probably victoriously, in some dashing charge, even if it be only of local importance. In that moment, trust, as I do, in the great god, Chance, that brings us in We, not only our misfortunes, but our greatest bits of happiness, too. Think of so many who are ingloriously stricken by accident in time of peace. War is another kind of life insurance; whereas the ordinary kind assures a man that his death will mean money to someone, this assures him that it will mean honour to himself, which from a certain point of view is much more satisfactory.

I was asked by a committee in Paris to write an ode in memory of American volunteers fallen for France and to be read on Decoration Day at a little ceremony before the statue of Washington in Paris. They were to get me a permission of 48 hours for that purpose. I had only two days to work in, days full of *boyau*-diggiug with pick and shovel, but by making an effort I managed to compose the poem in time. And then, after all, the permission never arrived. Imagine if I was not disappointed.

We are having the most beautiful weather and I am in excellent health. I sleep outdoors as much as possible. Of course we would be out all the time if it were not for the shelling, which makes it often advisable to keep to the *abris*. These are formidable affairs now,—tunnelled dugouts, thirty feet or so underground. Inside beds of stretched chicken wire are made in tiers like berths in a ship. . . .

To His Marraine

June 4, 1916.

. . . I hardly think we shall be here much longer. I have a presentiment that we are soon going into action. The last rumour is that we are soon to go to Verdun to relieve the 2nd Moroccan division. That would be magnificent, wouldn't it?—the long journey drawing nearer and nearer to that furnace, the distant cannonade, the approach through the congested rear of the battle-line full of dramatic scenes, the salutations of troops that have already fought, "*Bon courage, les gars!*" and then our own *début* in some dashing affair. *Verdun nous manque.* I should really like to go there, for after the war I imagine Frenchmen will be divided into those who were at Verdun and those who were not. . . .

To His Mother

June 15, 1916.

I have been back in a little village in the rear for ten days, part of a detachment sent to learn the working of a new arm, which will be used for the first time in the coming attacks. These have been ten days of comparative comfort and pleasure, for one can sleep peacefully at night, take shoes off for a change, and in the days after soup there are little inns where one can sit before a table once more and enjoy coffee and bread and jam and wine, between 5 and 8 in the evenings. The new arm, which I am not at liberty to describe, is an excellent weapon and ought to give good results. I am glad to have charge of one, for it is a more or less responsible position, and one where there is a chance for personal initiative.

The hour of our being relieved here seems more and more near now. We shall probably go back for a short *repos* before the big attacks which should not be far off now. I am not going to write you any more at length before these big events come off. Words are perfectly futile at such a time and serve no earthly purpose. I have already said all I have to say,—how I am glad to be here, have no regrets, and would wish to be nowhere else in the world than where I am. We both have to be brave, and you, even, one thing more,—patient.

When we go into action, you will know it, for the French *communiqué* will be brilliant that day for the first time since we helped make it so last Fall in Champagne. As I say, we shall probably not leave the trenches in first wave, but will be *troupes de poursuite*. If we do as well as the Russians are doing in Galicia, we ought to have some wonderful moments. If wounded, will telegraph immediately. . . .

To His Marraine

June 18, 1916.

Back again on the front. But by a lucky chance our return fell just the morning after the company had come back to the *barraquements* in the park of the *château* for a week's *repos* after five weeks in the trenches. So, this has prolonged a little the *bonne vie* of the *arrière*. No

village to buy things and have after-dinner coffee in, but very beautiful surroundings, quiet walks to muse in, peace, and for material com
forts milk and eggs can be bought at the *château* now. I sleep no longer
in the *barraquements* but have spread my bed out in the woods, and
although I have not been able to find any straw yet, I sleep very well
on the ground. . . .

Do not worry about the length of your letters or the pleasure it
gives me to receive them. Cicero, asked which of Demosthenes ora-
tions he liked best, replied: "The longest." It is the same thing.

The prospects of an early *relève*, of a change of scenery and par-
ticipating in a big action, make these days very exciting. Will let you
know about all our movements.

June 21, 1916.

Left our quiet sector in the centre this morning, relieved by a
territorial regiment. Have marched here to a little village in the rear.
Tomorrow take the train for an unknown destination. Fine hot summer weather. The big attacks will come soon now. Wish us good success. It is very exciting to be on the move at last, and I am happy and
contented. I return you the Tennyson, to lighten my sack. . . . I am
twenty-eight years old tomorrow.

★★★★★★

The letter above enclosed his last poem:

Clouds rosy-tinted in the setting sun,
Depths of the azure eastern sky between,
Plains where the poplar-bordered highways run.
Patched with a hundred tints of brown and green,—
Beauty of Earth, when in thy harmonies
The cannon's note has ceased to be a part,
I shall return once more and bring to these
The worship of an undivided heart.
Of those sweet potentialities that wait
For my heart's deep desire to fecundate
I shall resume the search, if Fortune grants;
And the great cities of the world shall yet
Be golden frames for me in which to set
New masterpieces of more rare romance.

★★★★★★

To His Marraine

June 24, 1916.

. . . We had a hard journey coming here. After an early morning's march of about ten kilometres, we took the train and made a trip of four or five hours. Then we started off in the heat of the day on what was without exception the hardest march I have ever made. There were 20 kilometres to do through the blazing sun and in a cloud of dust. Something around 30 kilos on the back. About 50 *per cent* dropped by the way. By making a supreme effort I managed to get in at the finish with the fifteen men that were all that was left of the section. The men were out of training after so long in the trenches without practise. The battlefield has no terrors after trials like these that demand just as much grit and often more suffering.

I shall probably write nothing but post-cards henceforth. In moments like these, words are futile. Think of me when you read the first big *communiqué*, which we shall have had a brilliant share in making.

To A Friend

June 28, 1916.

We go up to the attack tomorrow. This will probably be the biggest thing yet. We are to have the honour of marching in the first wave. No sacks, but two musettes, *toile de tente* slung over shoulder, plenty of cartridges, grenades, and *baïonnette au canon*.

I will write you soon if I get through all right. If not, my only earthly care is for my poems. Add the ode I sent you and the three sonnets to my last volume and you will have *opera omnia quae existant*.

I am glad to be going in first wave. If you are in this thing at all it is best to be in to the limit. And this is the supreme experience.

12: Conclusion

The happenings of the next few days, the last that Alan Seeger passed on earth, have been told by his comrade and friend, Rif Baer, an Egyptian, in these words:

During the night of June 30-July 1 we left Bayonvillers to move nearer the firing line. We went to Proyart as reserves. At 8 o clock on the morning of July 1st there was roll call for the day's orders and we were told that the general offensive would begin at 9 without us, as we were in reserve, and that we should be notified of the day and hour that we were to go into action. When this report was finished we were ordered to shell fatigue, unloading 8 inch shells from automobile trucks which brought them up to our position.

All was hustle and bustle. The Colonial regiments had carried the first German lines and thousands and thousands of prisoners kept arriving and leaving. Ambulances filed along the roads continuously. As news began to arrive we left our work to seek more details; everything we could learn seemed to augur well.

About 4 p. m. we left Proyart for Fontaine-les-Cappy and in the first line. Alan was beaming with joy and full of impatience for the order to join the action. Everywhere delirious joy reigned at having driven the enemy back without loss for us. We believed that no further resistance would be met and that our shock attack would finish the Germans. After passing the night at Fontaine-les-Cappy we moved in the morning toward what had been the German first lines. I passed almost all the day with Alan. He was perfectly happy.

"My dream is coming true," he said to me, "and perhaps tomorrow we shall attack. I am more than satisfied, but it's too bad about our July 4th leave. I cannot hope to see Paris again now before the 6th or 7th, but if this leave is not granted me, '*Maktoob, maktoob*,'" he finished with a smile.

The field of battle was relatively calm, a few shells fell, fired by the enemy in retreat, and our troops were advancing on all sides. The Colonials had taken Assevillers and the next day we were to take their place in first line. On July 3rd about noon we moved toward Assevillers to relieve the Colonials at nightfall. Alan and I visited Assevillers, the next morning, picking up souvenirs, postcards, letters, soldiers' notebooks, and chatting all the time, when suddenly a voice called out: "The company will fall in to go to the first line."

About 4 o clock the order came to get ready for the attack. None could help thinking of what the next few hours would bring. One minute's anguish and then, once in the ranks, faces became calm and serene, a kind of gravity falling upon them, while on each could be read the determination and expectation of victory. Two battalions were to attack Belloy-en-Santerre, our company being the reserve of battalion. The companies forming the first wave were deployed on the plain. Bayonets glittered in the air above the corn, already quite tall.

The first section (Alan's section) formed the right and vanguard of the company and mine formed the left wing. After the first bound forward, we lay flat on the ground, and I saw the first section advancing beyond us and making toward the extreme right of the village of Belloy-en-Santerre. I caught sight of Seeger and called to him, making a sign with my hand.

He answered with a smile. How pale he was! His tall silhouette stood out on the green of the cornfield. He was the tallest man in his section. His head erect, and pride in his eye, I saw him running forward, with bayonet fixed. Soon he disappeared and that was the last time I saw my friend. . . .

★★★★★★

Another participant in the attack upon Belloy- en-Santerre wrote for *La Liberté* of Paris the stirring account, of which this is a translation:

Six o clock at night.

The Legion attacks Belloy-en-Santerre. The 3rd battalion is to carry the southern part of the village. With a rush, it starts, its two leading companies pressing straight forward, beneath the crash of bursting shells, across a chaos of detonations. . . . *En avant!*

The men hurry on, clutching tightly their arms; some set their teeth, others shout.

Three hundred metres yet to cross and they will reach the enemy. . . . *En avant!*

130 — BELLOY-EN-SANTERRE (Somme) – Ruines dans le Village — Ruins into the village.

BELLOY-EN-SANTERRE, WHERE ALAN SEEGER WAS KILLED

But suddenly, hands relax their grasp, arms open, bodies stagger and fall, as the clatter of the German *mitrailleuses* spreads death over the plain where, but a moment before, men were passing.

Hidden in the road from Estrées to Belloy, they have taken our men in flank, cutting to pieces the 11th company.

Cries of anguish come from the tall grass, then the calls of the unhurt for their chiefs. But all, officers and subalterns, have fallen.

"My captain. . . . My lieutenant. . . . Sergeant. . . . ."

No answer.

Suddenly a voice is heard: "No more chiefs left. Come on, all the same, *nom de Dieu!* Come on! Lie flat, boys, he that lifts his head is done for. *En avant!*"

And the legionaries, crawling onward, continue the attack.

The wounded see the second wave pass, then the third. . . . They cheer on their comrades:

"Courage, fellows, death to the Boches! On with you!"

One of them sobs with rage: "To think I can't go too!"

And the high grasses shudder, their roots trodden by the men, their tops fanned by the hail of projectiles.

From the sunken road the German *mitrailleuses* work unceasingly.
. . .

Now, in all the plain, not a movement; the living have passed out of sight. The dead, out stretched, are as if asleep, the wounded are silent; they listen, they listen to the battle with all their ears, this battle so near to them, but in which they have no part. They wait to hear the shout of their comrades in the supreme hour of the great assault. . . . "Where are they now?" they murmur. . . .

Of a sudden, from the distance over there towards Belloy, a great clamour is heard:

"*En avant! Vive la Légion. Ah. . . . Ah. . . . Ah. . . .*"

And the notes of a bugle pierce the air; it is the brave Renard who sounds the charge.

The Legion, in a final bound, reaches the village. . . . The grenades burst, the *mitrailleuses* rattle. . . .

A time which seems to the wounded, lying in the field, to be beyond measure, interminable, a time of anguish, during which one pictures man killing man, face to face, in hand to hand conflict.

The dying look up, the wounded raise themselves, as if all must see how the battle goes.

Then from across the field of combat a cry arises, swells, grows louder, louder: "They are there, it is over, Belloy is taken!"

And the wounded cry: "They have won. Belloy is taken!"

They are magnificent, those men, haggard, bleeding. It is the *Legion fallen* that salutes the glory of the *Legion living*:

"Belloy is ours! *Vive la France! Vive la Légion! Vive la France!*"

Among those who,

> *In that fine onslaught that no fire could halt*
> *Parted impetuous to their first assault,*

one of the first to fall was Alan Seeger. Mortally wounded, it was his fate to see his comrades pass him in their splendid charge and to forego the supreme moment of victory to which he had looked forward through so many months of bitterest hardship and trial. Together with those other generous wounded of the *Légion fallen*, he cheered on the fresh files as they came up to the attack and listened anxiously for the cries of triumph which should tell of their success.

It was no moment for rescue. In that zone of deadly cross-fire there could be but one thought,—to get beyond it alive, if possible. So, it was not until the next day that his body was found and buried, with scores of his comrades, on the battlefield of Belloy-en-Santerre.

> *There, on the outskirts of the little village,*
> *The soldier rests. Now round him undismayed*
> *The cannon thunders, and at night he lies*
> *At peace beneath the eternal fusillade. . .*
>
> *That other generations might possess*
> *From shame and menace free in years to come*
> *A richer heritage of happiness,*
> *He marched to that heroic martyrdom.*

LEONAUR

ALSO FROM LEONAUR

AVAILABLE IN SOFTCOVER OR HARDCOVER WITH DUST JACKET

ESCAPE FROM THE FRENCH by *Edward Boys*—A Young Royal Navy Midshipman's Adventures During the Napoleonic War.

THE VOYAGE OF H.M.S. PANDORA by *Edward Edwards R. N. & George Hamilton, edited by Basil Thomson*—In Pursuit of the Mutineers of the Bounty in the South Seas—1790-1791.

MEDUSA by *J. B. Henry Savigny and Alexander Correard and Charlotte-Adélaïde Dard* —Narrative of a Voyage to Senegal in 1816 & The Sufferings of the Picard Family After the Shipwreck of the Medusa.

THE SEA WAR OF 1812 VOLUME 1 by *A. T. Mahan*—A History of the Maritime Conflict.

THE SEA WAR OF 1812 VOLUME 2 by *A. T. Mahan*—A History of the Maritime Conflict.

WETHERELL OF H. M. S. HUSSAR by *John Wetherell*—The Recollections of an Ordinary Seaman of the Royal Navy During the Napoleonic Wars.

THE NAVAL BRIGADE IN NATAL by *C. R. N. Burne*—With the Guns of H. M. S. Terrible & H. M. S. Tartar during the Boer War 1899-1900.

THE VOYAGE OF H. M. S. BOUNTY by *William Bligh*—The True Story of an 18th Century Voyage of Exploration and Mutiny.

SHIPWRECK! by *William Gilly*—The Royal Navy's Disasters at Sea 1793-1849.

KING'S CUTTERS AND SMUGGLERS: 1700-1855 by *E. Keble Chatterton*—A unique period of maritime history-from the beginning of the eighteenth to the middle of the nineteenth century when British seamen risked all to smuggle valuable goods from wool to tea and spirits from and to the Continent.

CONFEDERATE BLOCKADE RUNNER by *John Wilkinson*—The Personal Recollections of an Officer of the Confederate Navy.

NAVAL BATTLES OF THE NAPOLEONIC WARS by *W. H. Fitchett*—Cape St. Vincent, the Nile, Cadiz, Copenhagen, Trafalgar & Others.

PRISONERS OF THE RED DESERT by *R. S. Gwatkin-Williams*—The Adventures of the Crew of the Tara During the First World War.

U-BOAT WAR 1914-1918 by *James B. Connolly/Karl von Schenk*—Two Contrasting Accounts from Both Sides of the Conflict at Sea D uring the Great War.

www.ingramcontent.com/pod-product-compliance
Lightning Source LLC
Chambersburg PA
CBHW032041080426
42733CB00006B/156